Jarra Freehart has survived and emerged from a life of health issues, emotional trauma, and various negative addictions. He was never going to be normal. His existence evolved into a new version of normal, that only he understood. And that understanding was very limited. Because every time he began to understand what was going on inside his own head, everything changed, and confusion reigned. This state of confusion stayed a constant companion and is still there. Many unfortunate lifestyle decisions were made as a result. But things are much better these days and there is always new hope happening.

The magic café girls performed their magic. And they gradually transformed an old troubled reprobate into a respectful, thoughtful and giving human being.

He not only dedicates this book to them, but his new life as well.

Jarra Freehart

REBIRTH

AUSTIN MACAULEY PUBLISHERS™

LONDON * CAMBRIDGE * NEW YORK * SHARJAH

A CIP catalogue record for this title is available from the British Library.

ISBN 9781035813919 (Paperback)
ISBN 9781035813933 (ePub e-book)
ISBN 9781035813926 (Audiobook)

www.austinmacauley.com

First Published 2024
Austin Macauley Publishers Ltd®
1 Canada Square
Canary Wharf
London
E14 5AA

Julie Olive, for her valued opinions and constant encouragement.

The Gamblers Anonymous compulsives, who also offered valued opinions and encouragement, of a different kind.

And various family members who offered up valued opinions and encouragement, of a completely different kind.

Synopsis

Set in NSW Australia. Suburb of Mayfield.

Covering years up to 2022.

References back as far as 1970s.

Frank had always been troubled, all throughout his life.

After waking up in hospital after being unconscious for three days is visited by a lady who wasn't even there.

She told all him all about his new life. A second chance. Frank was immediately changed from this point, only he didn't know it. And had no idea what the lady was on about.

From there a continual sequence of learning and personal development episodes took place. Until, he finally made it. Well making it was always a confusion to Frank.

But eventually, he did make it. Arguably not all the way. But he did make it.

The main struggle was leaving the old life behind and progressing into the new life. But old habits die hard as they say. And so do old thought processes, programmed in over the decades.

There was much resistance and suspicion from the very beginning. Trust was not in the old programme, you know. And it took ages to get into the new one. But the girls worked their magic. They were full of youthful enthusiasm, kindness, caring, generosity of spirit, understanding and of course, girl power. Yes, the magic café girls were full of girl power. But in a good way.

They taught Frank about himself while having fun along the way. Yes, they educated him, interrupted him, tormented him, tricked him and continually manipulated him. They sure did have a lot of fun with him. But all in a good way.

And when Frank finally did realise how the game was played, he joined in and loved every minute of it. He couldn't get enough fun. Or all the attention that came with it.

Eventually, he learnt about love and respect and honesty. And many other good qualities that were never known about. And also, a secret desire to love all the café girls. But in a good way, of course. In the way that they taught him.

They meant more to him than anything else in the whole new life. But Frank was never going to tell them anything about that. No, that was never going to happen. Never.

But of course, they already knew. Because they knew everything. And that was always a big confusion. But eventually Frank just went with it. There was no use resisting. He could never win anyway. Especially against the most beautiful girl in the world.

He thought he did win in the end, you know. After he realised, he didn't need anyone anymore. Poor deluded old fool.

"Hello, Frank. How are you? Can we have a little talk? Just for a short while. I have something very important to say to you. Now, you must listen closely, Frank. I can't stay long. So, please pay attention to what I have to say."

He'd only been unconscious for a few days this time. But something weird was going on. There was a voice happening. He knew straight away that whatever it was wasn't normal. Not that having a good grip on anything was ever normal. But whatever was going on now wasn't any kind of normal. Could have been dreaming, you know. Or hallucinating. Or having another one of the absent moments. Lots of absent moments happened, during the life. But this was no normal, absent moment. This voice was the reason for waking up. He saw where this voice was coming from. Standing beside the bed.

"Now Frank, you must listen very carefully. To what I'm about to say. Because I'm here to tell you about your new life."

Laying there like a stunned mullet, with the mouth half open. Staring in the direction of where this voice was coming from. Trying to focus. Speaking couldn't happen. So, what else was there to do but listen? She'd bent down and whispered that into the left ear. Sent a shock wave of warm energy, all through the half-dead, wrinkled-up old body. That was certainly the main reason why nothing could be said.

"Oh, you're awake, Frank! How are you feeling! Ok?"

Snapping out of this semi-euphoric condition wasn't easy, you know. But nurses have this way of getting the attention. Wanted an answer, alright. And she was right next to his bed now. But the voice wasn't the same voice. Tell that easy enough.

"Well, Frank! How are you feeling?"

"There was this lady! She was talking to me! She told me about my new life!"

There was excitement building in the head, alright. There was never excitement about anything anymore. But there was now. Wasn't sure why exactly, but there was. The nurse didn't quite know what to say. Just looked down, smiled and put into practice the calming down routine.

"It's ok, Frank! You were probably just dreaming? You've been unconscious for a few days. Just try and relax. You'll be ok. Don't worry about it?"

But the worry was building. Gradually taking over. Along with the confusion, wonder, and the shock of it all. But that feeling of warm invasion was still in there. And that made the response easier. Although, not completely convincing.

"But she was here! I know she was? She was talking to me? Just like you're talking to me right now? I know she was here! I know she was here? She was here! Right where you're standing? She was here!"

Well, what was this nurse supposed to do anyway? The agitation was building in her now as well. She decided to have one more go at it.

"There's no one else here, Frank! Only you and me! That's all!"

"But she was here! She was here!"

This nurse had just about had enough already.

"Whatever you say, Frank. You're tired, that's all! Rest is what you need right now! You never know! She might come back again later! Are you hungry Frank? How about a cup of tea!"

"I wouldn't mind a few beers and a smoke!"

"Well, there's no chance of that happening!"

Yeah. Was really hanging out for a drink. Three days without a drink. Or a smoke. Or a joint. Yeah. Still smoking pot, you know. In his early sixties and still smoking pot. What a hopeless case. Grew the stuff in the backyard. Over the back fence and over a side fence next to the creek, that ran along that side of the property. Yeah, this sad lonely old guy owned a house. Two of them, actually.

"You're a real spoil sport, you are! Ok then, I'll settle for a cup of coffee! Very strong coffee!"

There was still a mixture of tiredness, confusion and worry now. Almost shut down the system again. But there was no rest. Not until this strange lady was dealt with and out of the head. Or the vision of her at least. Knew all about visions. There'd been plenty of them, during the wasted, un-developing years. That's for sure. Something was needed, alright. To help work it all out. And if coffee was all that was available. Then that would have to do the trick. Knew all about coffee. Didn't really know why, but just knew.

It only took a few minutes for the nurse to return with the coffee. Still had that smile on her face.

"Here you go Frank! I hope it's strong enough for you?"

She placed the cup on the little table beside the bed. With some biscuits. Even opened the packet for him.

"Now sit up a bit and I'll adjust the bed? We don't want you spilling hot coffee all over yourself, do we? You really should be having something to eat, Frank! I bought you a few biscuits. If you get hungry? Let me know and I'll arrange something. Ok!"

Didn't hear a word the nurse said. All that could be heard was that lady and her softly spoken, gentle words. All about something about some new life. Could still see her pleasant looking, smiling face as well. And her clear, light blue eyes. There was something unusual about her eyes. They were shining eyes. But not bright shining eyes. They kind of looked familiar as well. But not familiar enough. Got the attention straight away.

Then this feeling of invasion got stronger and stronger. Some kind of energy burst had filled the head and emptied the head, at the same time. That's the only way of describing what just happened. If it had to be described at all. And even if it did. There was no way of putting it into words. Already tried that, with the nurse. Yeah, explaining what just really happened was impossible. Because there was no description available, about what the hell just happened. If something just happened at all, that is. But it happened, alright.

"Well Frank! You have been through quite an ordeal, haven't you?"

She was back. So yes, it must have happened. And the way she spoke was exactly the same. Instant relaxation. Completely fixated by the sight of her again and just laid there. Absorbing, every word.

Hypnotised by some lady who maybe was there or maybe wasn't even there. But she was there, because there she was. Standing right there beside the bed. Exactly where she was before. Couldn't take much more, you know. The head was just about to explode. Especially after this next bit.

"You need to start looking after yourself, Frank! You must start looking after yourself! Let go of those bad habits, Frank! The drinking! The cigarettes! And those drugs, Frank! You need to stop all that! Start eating properly! Start exercising! You're new life! It's beginning right now, Frank! Make the most of it! Not everyone gets a second chance you know! I know you can do it! I have great confidence in you, Frank! We all have great confidence in you!"

"What the! A second chance! What a load of shit! What on earth does that mean, anyway? A new life? A second chance? I must be dreaming? You're not even real! You're not even there!"

Yeah. Wide awake now.

"No, Frank! It's not what you just said it was! Not at all! This is your second chance, Frank! Your second chance at life! And no, Frank! You're no dreaming!"

The fuses started blowing, alright. Listening to some sweet, smiling lady who wasn't even there. But could have been there. Wasn't going to listen to any more of her crap. That's for sure. I mean, there was a lifetime of dumbness involved here, you know. That's for sure. But not enough, to believe any of this new life stuff.

"I'm not interested in any of this new life shit! Just fuck off, and leave me alone!"

"Well really! There's no need for that kind of talk! But that's enough for now, Frank! I know how tired you must be feeling! I'll come back later! When you're feeling better! Goodbye for now, Frank!"

Then the lady, who wasn't there, really wasn't there anymore. Just simply vanished. Right before the eyes. And thank Christ for that. A new life. What a load of shit.

The old coot had already given up on life, you know. More than ready to call it quits. Just hanging around now. Waiting for the inevitable, last breath. Couldn't come quick enough. Nothing to live for anyway. Except indulging in all the things that were needed and relied upon.

Everything to ease the burden of just existing. Drinking, smoking cigarettes and pot. And wasting copious amounts of money, gambling. Addicted to poker machines, you know. Just loved playing them poker machines. They'd taken over the whole life. The only life ever known about anyway. Yes, only lived to play poker machines. If anyone could do with a new life, it was this bloke. That's for sure. Or no life at all. Which is what there was now.

Even a cup of strong coffee and a few biscuits couldn't help the working out. This idea of a new life. What a load of crap. It must be all crap. There was no use, thinking about it anymore. But that lady was there and what she said was still in there. Or, maybe she wasn't there. And maybe it was all just imagined. Which would be no surprise, you know. Not after all the drugs and booze that'd been absorbed over the decades. So, anything was possible. Anything at all.

Anyway, the thinking was starting to rattle what was left of the brain. She was either there, or she wasn't there. Trying to pretend it didn't happen, didn't work. Attempting to block it all out, didn't work. Nothing worked. So, it was decided that it did happen. That was the easiest thing to do. But maybe it didn't happen. Maybe nothing happened at all. Fucking hell. Then the weariness was just too much. Going, going. Gone.

"The lady. The lady. She told me to, to, to—

"I swear to you Frank! There was no lady here!"

But too late. Gone now. Sound asleep again. Like a little baby. The nurse took a big sigh of relief. Tucked the old fella in properly. Then left the ward, with another little smile on her face. Several hours passed.

"Ah Frank? You're awake! How are you feeling now?"

"Good! I'm feeling good!"

If a pounding headache and mass confusion in the brain could be called feeling good, then the feeling was good.

"Are you hungry, Frank? I can arrange a meal if you like?

"Yes, I'm hungry!"

This was Frank talking, alright. But poor old Frank. He didn't feel like Frank at all. Not the Frank he thought he was anyway? Not the Frank he'd always been. Whoever that really was. Something weird was still happening. That energy beam was still flowing through the whole tired, battered, wrinkled up old body. Yes, complete invasion. From the head to the toes. But mostly in the head.

Still had no idea what was happening. But something was happening, alright. That lady would have known. Took a good look around. But she was gone. Frank, never saw that lady. Ever again. After a meal and a few more coffees, the feeling good thing was there and the bladder was ready for a drain out.

"Excuse me, nurse! I need to go for a piss!"

Knew straight away, he shouldn't have said the piss word.

"I mean, I need to go to the toilet!"

What a great nurse. She pretended not to even hear the piss word.

"Sure, Frank! Just be careful getting to your feet! You might be a bit unsteady?"

Unsteady, alright. The head started spinning around as soon as the feet hit the floor.

"Here, let me help you! Maybe I should get you a bottle?"

"Well. Yes, I could do with a bottle! Or maybe two! Thanks nurse!"

"Ha, ha, ha! Very funny Frank! But I'm talking about a bed bottle!"

"A what?"

"A bed bottle, Frank! Then you can pee in bed! Without wetting the sheets! Or you can stand beside the bed and do it that way. It's up to you!"

The nurse thought all that was pretty funny and had an even bigger smile on her face. But there was no bed bottle getting used. And there was no mood for any more, funny stuff either. There was only one kind of bottle in the thinking and it wasn't a bed bottle. That's for sure.

"No! No! I'll be right! And I'm not using any damn bed bottle! And I don't need any help either!"

Such a stubborn old bugger, you know. But this nurse was so smart and experienced. She watched the struggle for a little while. The wobbling around. The swaying backwards and forwards. Smiling that patient, knowing nurses smile, the whole time. Then she reached out an arm. Grabbing hold was the only option and just in time. Total submission. Only because there was no choice. But Frank insisted upon dragging the IV pole trolley along. That's when another strange feeling started happening, while walking slowly along. Maybe this walk had been done before. Several times. That's because it had.

Anyway, it was the longest pee that could ever be remembered. Well, after all. The new life had only just begun. So, this was the first pee that could ever be remembered. Only there was no way of knowing that. Wasn't in any state to know anything. Could only remember back to that lady who wasn't there, but who was there.

Because she was there, beside the bed. Talking about a new life. Could still hear her. Even though she wasn't even there. But she was there. Getting so tired now, you know. The thinking was getting all confused again. All that was really known was that sleep was required.

But on the way out of the toilet, a big mistake was made. Frank took a quick look in the mirror. There was an old man staring straight back. Bloodshot eyes. Unshaven for several days. Hair a mess. Shoulders slumped. Looking pretty miserable. There was no reaction at all. Just didn't know, who this old man was. Didn't want to know either. Didn't recognise him. A complete stranger. Even after blinking a few times, the stranger was still there. Wasn't going anywhere.

Frank pushed the button, to bring the nurse back.

"How old do you think I am?"

This took the nurse back a bit. But nurses are so kind and understanding, you know.

"Well! I don't know Frank? How old do you think you are?"

This confused the situation even more. After taking another long look in the mirror, slowly turned and looked straight at the nurse.

"I don't know. I don't feel old. But I look really old. So, I must be a lot older than I feel?"

"Well, don't worry about it, Frank! It will all come back to you! Just give it time! Now, let's get you back into bed!"

"Hey, how you doing? You look much better! I'm here to take you home!"

"What! Who, the hell are you? I don't know you!"

Poor old fella. Had no idea what was going on. Just sitting there, beside the bed. All cleaned up. Fully dressed and ready to go. Been there for a while now, staring at the floor. From getting back into bed and now sitting beside the bed. All dressed and ready to go home was a complete shock. Couldn't remember a thing about how all that happened. Frank slowly got up and walked over to the ward counter.

"Thank you, nurse! I'm going home now!"

And it wasn't even the same nurse, either. But that didn't matter anyway. There was no eye contact. Because there can't be any eye contact when someone's staring at the floor.

Before this nurse even had time to answer, there was a stranger walking out of the ward, with a bewildered looking old man, following along behind. Like an obedient child who just did as it was told. Once they were in the car and moving off, the stranger gave this old obedient child a quick sideways look.

"Are you hungry, Frank? How about we stop for lunch somewhere?"

No answer. Just staring straight ahead. Still so confused. Never seen this bloke before and didn't know where they were going. Stopped at a small café. Once inside, after checking out the menu, this stranger asked the wrong question.

"How about a steak sandwich, Frank?"

There was an instant, thunderous reaction. A real mind blower.

"No! No! No! I can't have steak! I don't want steak! I won't eat steak! I won't eat steak! I don't want steak!"

The word steak is what caused the explosion. The old child had a vision. Just a flash of a vision. But as clear as a bell, ringing in the head. Of a large animal.

A cow. Hanging up, with a steel hook under its jaw bone and its guts spilling out onto the concrete floor.

The protest was yelled out so loud, about the idea of eating a steak sandwich. That it got everyone's attention and the vibrant little café suddenly went dead quiet. Like someone just turned off a radio. Stopped whatever it was they were doing and looked over to where the sudden outburst had come from. The long-lost brother looked a bit shocked and embarrassed. And who could blame him. Yes, the stranger. He was this old child's older brother.

How could he have known anything like this was about to happen. And the old child just stood there. Staring straight ahead. Didn't even understand why steak couldn't be eaten. Just knew it couldn't be. And it wouldn't be. That's all.

"Ok, well! How about a chicken sandwich then?"

The same thing happened again. Another vision. Of little, yellow fluffy chicks, being sucked down through some kind of steel grid. Didn't know where that vision came from either. So, the long-lost brother checked the menu, one more time.

"What about a bacon and egg roll?

"No! No! No! I won't eat bacon? I can't eat bacon! I won't eat any bacon!"

Yes, another vision. This time of pigs squealing their heads off as they were lowered into a vat of boiling water. The old child had forgotten all about the days, back in the old life. Working in the abattoirs. Seen too much killing of animals and all the blood and guts everywhere. Became a vegetarian. But didn't even realise that. Not until this very moment.

And things were even going to get worse, you know. Because eventually. Slowly but surely. Turning into a vegan, is what happened. No dairy. No eggs. Just loved eggs. But no eggs anymore. No animal products of any kind. Not even butter and honey. But that's a fair bit down the track. Before the no dairy comes into it. And when the old child was a few years older.

By this stage, the long-lost brother started wondering. Whether this old man standing beside him who was years younger than him was completely off his rocker. One's things for sure: they may have been brothers, but he didn't know him from a bar of soap. But he had to do something and quick. The lady behind the counter had a look on her face, that didn't need explaining. She was a big lady covered in tattoos and wasn't about to take any more of this nonsense.

The young fella at the coffee machine thought it was all a great joke. Couldn't get the smile off his face.

"Right, let's try somewhere else!"

They got settled in another café. Not so far away. The brother wasn't about to make the same mistakes as before.

"So, what would you like, Frank?"

"A salad sandwich and a coffee! Please!"

The old child was getting a bit pissed off by now, you know. Didn't even know why it had to be a salad sandwich. Just knew that's what it had to be. Wanted a salad sandwich. Nothing else. When that nurse brought the meal, there were vegetables and mashed potato and two sausages on the plate. The vegetables and potato disappeared quick enough. But not the sausages. Already knew about coffee. The brother went to the counter to order their lunch. The old child was just staring at him. Checking this stranger out. And after he sat back down, just had to know.

"So, who are you anyway? Maybe I should know you from somewhere?"

"I'm Mick! Your brother! Remember?"

Well, that got the old child by surprise. Looked straight at this stranger's face. Blinked slowly a few times. Rubbed the chin around a bit, with the left hand. Squinted the eyes and then suddenly opened them as wide as they would go. Lifted up the right hand and pointed the index finger at Mick.

"You joined the Navy!"

"That's right Frank! Now you've got it!"

This recognition started off a long, jilted conversation. From early childhood memories to when Mick found his brother rolling around on the bed. Moaning and groaning and yelling out various obscenities and all kinds of other muddled words, that Mick couldn't understand. But he knew one thing. His brother was swearing his head off and growling like a wild dog. That's for sure.

When they were talking about childhood memories, it was Mick who did most of the talking. The old child was just pretending to remember. But whether Mick actually knew that or not, didn't seem to matter one bit. Because Mick liked to talk. Could tell that easy enough.

"You talk kind of funny, you know?"

"I've been living in the UK for about 20 years now, Frank!"

"The what?"

"The UK, Frank! England!"

"Oh! Right! England!"

This attempt at showing interest, didn't last long at all. Turns out, Mick had done well. Real well. Worked for a major bank and was raking in hundreds of thousands of pounds a year. Been married to an English lady and had two daughters. But divorce had happened. Mick got retrenched and had returned home. Yeah. Looked sad and broken-hearted, alright. Used some big words, the old child had never heard before.

"You were rather inebriated when I found you, Frank! Swearing like a trooper! I knew something wasn't right! The back door was open, so I came in. You were rolling around on your bed! You put up a rather good struggle! I have to say! But I eventually got you under control. Enough to get you into the car. And take you to the nearest hospital. As soon as they got you into a bed, you were gone! For three days, Frank! You were unconscious for three days!

You sure did give them hell, Frank! It took two wardsmen and a few nurses, to get you into the bed!"

"Yeah well. I was probably in a bad mood. Drink too much, eh. But I'm off the grog now, you know! And I've given up the smokes! And, no more weed either! Have to start looking after myself, you know! That's what the, er, the errrr…"

There was an excited old child there now. But not for long. The talking just suddenly stopped. As quickly as it started. Wasn't going to tell anyone else about that lady who wasn't there. But she was there. Because she was there. Was pretty sure about that now. But that nurse didn't believe him and Mick wouldn't believe him either. Just knew it. So, the talking just had to stop. And it did.

Another reason why the old child was in such a state when Mick found him was because there'd been another massive bender. For days. Forgot to take the epilepsy medication again as well. This happened every now and then. Usually after a rare win on the pokies.

Mick couldn't help smiling. But it was a warm, knowing smile. He knew it was only a few days since Frank was completely blotto.

"That's good to hear Frank!"

Mick took a long look at Frank then. This brother he hadn't seen for over 20 years and he didn't quite know what to make of him. This pathetic old man. This hopeless alcoholic, sitting there in front of him. Munching away on his salad sandwich, like he hadn't eaten for weeks. The hospital meal had already been forgotten about.

From there, Mick dropped Frank off at his house. But when he got out of the car, he just stood in the middle of the footpath. So, Mick got out and walked him to the front door. That's when the old child snapped back out of wherever he was. Dug the keys out of the pocket and opened the front door. Suddenly an adult again. Yeah. The old child had disappeared.

Mick couldn't help smiling at him again. Then let out a bit of a sad look and a few words of advice. Before leaving him there, standing in the front doorway.

"Good to see you, Frank! Look after yourself! I'll call around in a few days if you like and see how you're going!"

"Yes, ok. That'll be fine! That'll be fine! Yes! See, you later!"

So, what else could Mick do, besides turn around and be on his way? He figured that Frank just wanted him gone and he was right.

Good to see you, Frank. That's pretty much what everyone said, whenever they saw this old goat wandering around and knew the name. That was more of a conversation than was ever wanted anyway. Still didn't like people and avoided them as much as possible. And then it suddenly dawned. This brother Mick. Dumb as a post, when he was a kid. So maybe he's not really a brother after all. Started thinking really hard about this brother situation, when an interruption came flying in from somewhere.

"Now Frank, you need to start cleaning up your house! Your bedroom would be a good place to start!"

What the fuck. That was that lady in the hospital. Yeah. It was that lady again. Well, not really the lady. Just her voice. She was there again. Stopped him, dead in his tracks. The confusion was starting all over again. But Frank went for a wander through the house anyway. Looked in every room. Behind every door. In every wardrobe. Under every bed. Under the kitchen table. In the cupboards and even opened the fridge. But there was no one in there. The only things in the fridge were cans of beer.

If she was anywhere in the house, he'd find her. You could bet on that. After being convinced there was no one else in the house, wandered back into the bedroom and took a casual look around. The room was a mess, alright. What happened next was a big surprise. Not at the time. But a few hours later, when the memory of doing it, came floating through the head.

There was no one else in the house. So, it had to be him that did it. Unless it was Mick. Could have been him, you know. No. If it was him, he would have said so. But maybe he did it and just didn't say anything. That could have happened as well. Anyway, it didn't matter.

Yeah. Picked up the empty cans, empty cigarette packets and dirty clothes off the floor. Put it all on the bed. The old frying pan used as an ashtray was full. Took that outside and emptied it onto the grass. Which hadn't been mowed in many, many months. It was a jungle out there, rather than a backyard. But Frank liked it that way. Grew the pot plants all around the yard. That's why. Where the grass was the highest.

Sometimes, losing track of where they all were was a bit of a bother. But it didn't matter. If anyone ever found out about the pot plants in the yard, he could just say he didn't know anything about it. Just play dumb. Cunning old dog, alright. And besides, he looked about as dumb as anyone could be.

"I knew you could do it, Frank! I'm so proud of you! We're all so proud of you, Frank!"

Did somebody just say something? Yeah. Knew it was her, alright. But kind of wasn't sure either. Maybe if she was ignored, she might just go away and leave him alone. Never know your luck, eh.

Noticed the whiz bins, sitting in the long grass. They hadn't been moved for months. All the rubbish was left in the house. On the floor, under the bed and all over the kitchen sink, which was stainless steel. But looked like it was painted black. With some kind of tar. And it was so greasy. There were dead flies and cockroaches stuck everywhere. The whiz bins were full in no time. But it took several weeks to clear the house out completely.

Yeah, that was that lady again. Heard her, alright. But she wasn't so smart, was she? She didn't know about the plants. Frank gave up trying to find her. Just had to get used to listening to her. There was no getting away from her now. She was there whenever she wanted to be there, and there was nothing to be done about it. Knew that already, eh. Wasn't completely stupid.

Mick turned up again a few days later. Just like he said he would. They went for a coffee. Had a chat about stuff in general. After about an hour, they'd both had enough of each other's company. It was the longest conversation Frank had ever had with anyone, for a very long time and he was exhausted. Mick was aware enough to know that. So, he ended the coffee session and dropped Frank back home again.

"I'll drop back in again in a few weeks. If that's ok with you? We can go for coffee again!"

"Sure, why not! See you later!"

Meanwhile, the cleaning and rubbish removal continued. It was a gradual process at first. But Frank was an all or nothing type bloke, you know. Full speed ahead, or dead stop. 100% effort, or don't bother. The thoughts of; if it's worth doing, then it's worth doing right. And; you're as good as any and better than most were in the head. How they got in there is anyone's guess. But they were in there, alright. Was probably that lady who put them there. She was putting everything else in there. So, it must have been her, eh.

Bang. Bang. Bang.

Oh fuck no. There's someone at the door. Frank decided not to answer it. Didn't like visitors. Usually wanted something. Probable them fucking Jehovah's Witnesses again. Told them to fuck off last time.

Bang. Bang. Bang.

Better not be them fucking Jehovah's Witnesses again. Told them to fuck off last time. Yeah. The emotions started playing up quick enough. Really didn't want to answer the door, you know.

Bang! Bang! Bang!

Fucking hell. Them bastards never give up. So, the door got opened.

"Hello, there Frank! We knew you were home! Thought you may have been asleep! These two beautiful young ladies are my daughters! Your nieces! They arrived yesterday, from the UK! They wanted to meet you!"

Yeah. Just standing in the doorway, dumbfounded. Staring at these two young girls. They were beautiful, alright. With big smiles on their faces. And wide-open sparkling eyes. The oldest one did the talking.

"Hi Uncle Frank! We are so pleased to meet you! Daddy has told us so much about you!"

There was a reluctance to answer at all. But a little mumbling did manage to escape.

"You're well. I hope it was all good?"

Took a quick look at Mick, who had this sheepish look on his face. But then remembered the state of the house and what an untidy, stinking mess it still was. And what an untidy, stinking mess was standing there in the doorway. Staring at these unwanted visitors. Brother or not. Nieces or not. Beautiful or not. Just didn't want any visitors. But they couldn't be told to just fuck off either. After all, they weren't Jehovah's Witnesses, were they?

Still hadn't cleaned the kitchen sink. Never had any visitors and sure didn't want any now. Said it, before even thinking about it.

"How about we go somewhere for lunch? Just give me a minute!"

Disappeared into the house. Dug around in a pile of clothes in a corner of the bedroom. Found a crumpled-up shirt and a new pair of shorts, that'd been forgotten about. The shirt was at least clean and covered the filthy dirty, stinking singlet. The shorts were a perfect fit. The thongs weren't a matching pair, but weren't all that old. So, he almost looked tidy. Except for the messed-up hair and dirty feet. A quick trip to the bathroom took care of that. So, all ready to go and out he went.

"Lunch is exactly what we had in mind, Frank! Where would you like to go?"

But Mick knew exactly where they were going for lunch and so did the girls. They had everything planned already. Frank was so relieved when Mick insisted on paying. Frank was flat broke. Frank was always flat broke. As you already know, all the available money went on beer, pot, smokes and gambling. Not on the races either. Just on lotto and poker machines. Yeah. Those diabolical machines had hold of the psychological balls, alright.

There was always a pile up of unpaid bills. The only time an attempt was ever made to pay a bill was after a big win on the poker machines. Managing to get home with any of the winnings left was the big problem there. If the car needed petrol, which it usually did. It was filled up. Always stopped at a supermarket. Loaded up a trolley with food. Mainly canned fruit and vegetables. Long life milk and frozen stuff. But nothing that went rotten in the fridge. Because anything in the fridge was usually forgotten about. Except for the cans of beer. I mean, once you put fruit and veggies in the crisper, you can't see them, can you?

And there was never any meat in the fridge either. Or the freezer. And of course, a stop in a drive through bottle o was essential. Load up with cartons of beer and bottles of the good stuff. Jim Beam. Vodka. Southern Comfort. Ouzo and a few other favourites.

Once all the essentials were taken care of. A few bills were sometimes paid. Especially, if there were any nasty letters about late payments. And sometimes there were messages sent by email on the computer and text messages on the phone. But they were usually deleted. The bills got paid, when the bills got paid. Simple as that.

The thinking always was who the fuck do they think they are, anyway. Liked being in control, you know. Always in control. Yeah. If there was any such thing as being in control, of what wasn't in control, then everything was under control.

Whenever money was left over from the previous day, it was down to the bank. To pay off the credit card. Which was always maxed out, or close to it. Then sometimes a compromise got made. Depending on how much was left. And one or two really overdue bills might have got paid. But there always had to be plenty left over. To feed the poker machines. Till there was nothing left. Sometimes it took hours to go broke. Sometimes it took days and sometimes it took a few weeks. If a few lucky streaks happened, it could take several months. But they didn't happen very often. That's for sure.

Yeah, always in a pub or a club, playing poker machines. Whenever there was money in the wallet, you could bet it wouldn't be there long. Knew every poker machine there was and had lots of favourite ones. The internal cursing started, every time the wallet was empty. Fucking hell. You idiot. You've done it again. You fucking dick head. Knew there was a big problem, alright.

The interesting thing was that when the machines were getting played, nothing else existed. No smoking. No drinking. No getting stoned. No eating. No nothing. Just sitting there, mesmerised by the machines. Pushing the play again button and watching the reels spin around. Like a fucking zombie.

Eventually, a wallet full of Gamblers Anonymous cards had been collected. There was a little plastic box at the end of a row of machines. Started taking one of these cards, every time the figuring started up. About maybe not playing the machines anymore. Just had to stop playing these fucking things. Stop the madness. Yeah. The madness had to stop. Knew that, alright.

Especially after going broke again. When the internal cursing began. When the realisation hit home. That a big win on the poker machines, rarely ever happened. Even when it did happen, it was only a matter of time, before all the money went back in. Fucking hell. Let me out of here. But there was no getting out. Not yet anyway. But he kind of liked it in there too, you know. And kind of didn't like it either.

And so, the vicious cycle would start all over again. Just so far gone now, you know. Completely controlled by the diabolical poker machine addiction. Needed help, alright. But just wouldn't take that necessary first step. Couldn't do it. Could beat it by himself. Without any help from anyone. Stupid, stubborn old bastard.

"Oh Frank! Look what you're doing to yourself! You're so much better than this! You really are! You must start believing in yourself, Frank! I have great confidence in you! We all have great confidence in you! We really do! There's still time, Frank! We'll never give up on you, Frank! Never!"

There was no use trying to listen to the lady after going broke. Too busy with the cursing. And too pissed off. And why was she always there with the bothering, when sleep was the only thing that was needed. But sleep was impossible, you know. After a solid hit out on the poker machines. Win or lose. Because the brain, or what was left of it was burning up. There were bells ringing in there as well and lights and music and five reels spinning around. Right in front and behind the eye balls. Closing the eyes didn't help either. Just got worse if the eyes were closed. Putting a pillow over the head, didn't help either.

Frank had become nothing more than a biological poker machine. This fucking madness had to stop. But knowing that was the easy part. Doing something about it was the complicated bit. Very complicated. Especially for an old fool, who'd been fucking things up in one way or another, his whole life. Yeah, the time was fast approaching, when the help finally arrived.

"You need help, Frank! You need help, Frank! You need help, Frank!"

Yeah. Someone was trying to get the message through. That's for sure. Even the biggest fool that ever lived, will accept help sooner or later. Even this one.

It's amazing how all the little schemes, failed to stop the compulsion, to always return to poker machines. If Frank started with $200 and got $500 in front. Which meant there was $700. And that was enough to cash in and head for the exit. But more often than not, the exit was never reached. Well, there's a vacant machine. There was just no walking past a vacant machine on the way out, without trying the luck.

The thought process was: We'll just put a fifty in this one. Even if we lose that, we'll still be $450 in front. But when that fifty disappeared, in went another one and another one and another one.

Yeah, it was always a case of just one more, until there were no fifties left. Then it was back to the teller machine, to get more money. Until the teller machine said, no more funds available. It really pissed Frank off, whenever that happened. So, the head went down, the same cursing routine began, the swearing and home he went. Broke again. You fucking idiot. You've done it again. You fucking dick head.

When on one of the real lucky streaks and couldn't lose. No matter what machine it was. And the wallet was packed full of notes. Frank became another Frank. It was like some kind of creature sprang out of the dark shadows, and took control of the situation. No worries. Super Frank was here. Beer and cigarettes were rediscovered. And this Super Frank was friendly and generous. All warm and tingly inside. Yapping his fucking head off. Talking to anyone who got near enough. Buying beers for anyone. Offering a smoke here and there. Yeah, everyone was his friend, alright.

One establishment after another was invaded. We'll try our luck here. We'll try our luck there. We'll try our luck everywhere. We can't lose. Fucking idiot. He knew where all the pubs and clubs were and he knew every machine in every one of them. There was always an exceptional memory available, when it came to poker machines, you know. Fucking idiot.

The favourite thing to do, during one of these rare lucky streaks was to open the wallet just enough and repeatedly count the notes. Knowing how much was there was so very important. But the thrill of counting the notes was the real reason. Fifty, one hundred. Fifty, two hundred. Fifty, three hundred. Just loved doing that. Was the best feeling ever. To be several hundred in front and sometimes several thousand.

Trouble was it was never enough. No amount of winnings was ever enough. To make up for all the losses over the years. Frank knew that but didn't want to know that. So, always decided not to know it. And super Frank couldn't give a fuck. Because he soon vanished, when the wallet was empty again.

"Oh Frank! You're such a rascal, aren't you! But we'll never give up on you! You know that, don't you Frank! We'll never give up on you!"

Yeah, he knew it, alright. Knew that damn lady was never going to leave him alone as well. So, that's why the GA number got rung didn't it. Just had to get her off his back. And that's the only reason. Gamblers Anonymous, here we come. Fucking hell.

"Oh, we're all so proud of you Frank! We knew you could do it! We're all so proud of you! You know that, don't you Frank!"

Yeah, yeah, yeah. Right. So, you're all so proud of him. Big deal. The thing was if the lady kept butting into this new life, then facing up to reality was likely to end up happening. And that was the scariest thing. Didn't like the thought of that at all. Enough to frighten the shit out of anyone. Just didn't want to do it. But knew that's what had to be done. Facing up to reality. Didn't really want to.

But did want to. There was the need for it, alright. But no, fuck reality. Oh, fucking hell. Didn't know what the hell to do.

Anyway, it was all the lady's fault. She's the one who started all this new life bullshit in the first place. Should have told her to just fuck off. Straight away. Then none of this shit would be happening. Being all spaced out when she first appeared, didn't help. In a bad place. The thinking wasn't right. She took advantage, alright. Poor bastard had no say in the matter. No say at all. And he did tell her to fuck off in the first place, you know. But she just didn't listen.

Certain events drove the sucker back to poker machines a few times, you know. Well, more than a few times actually. But he got there in the end. Kind of. What the lady put him through, before getting completely clean, almost finished him.

One night in the most favourite pub, playing the second most favourite machine, one of those rare lucky streaks happened again. Cashed in a number of times. A big thrill it was checking the wallet and counting the notes several times. $1700.00 in hundred-dollar notes. Not fifties. Hundreds. Enough to buy a lawnmower. He'd already decided to mow the back yard, you know. The lady kept whingeing about it. Kept at him, about how long the grass was and how untidy it looked.

Yeah was just sitting there, pushing the button, when all of a sudden it was closing time. Just hated it, when this happened. Especially when on a lucky streak. Winning heaps. Like now. Fucking hell. Closing time. But what choice was there. None.

Next day, after recounting the winnings a few more times, the biggest event was checking out about how much lawn mowers cost. He'd already ruined the two old mowers that were under the house. That's another reason why the grass was so long. He liked the one that was just under $600. So, he figured to keep at least that much and get one later that day.

You see, there was always a problem with making decisions. Had to think about things for a while. Especially, when it came to spending any gambling money. Playing poker machines. That was always the first priority. Well, pretty much the only priority. Everything else depended on what was left after playing the machines.

Somehow, between checking out the lawnmowers and actually returning to buy one, all the money just disappeared didn't it. Fucking idiot. After deciding to go for a swim in the ocean baths, Frank passed through a suburb, where there was a pub. One of the favourite pubs. Never got to the ocean baths, eh. Couldn't even remember parking the car and walking into the pub. But there he was sitting in front of a poker machine. Eyes fixated on the screen, pushing the button.

Several hours later, back on the veranda. Can of beer in one hand. Nice fat joint in the other and flat broke again. Contemplating another failed attempt to hit the big jackpot. Eventually, figured that $1700.00 would have bought two lawnmowers, with about $500 left over. That would have taken care of a few bills, piled up on an old chair in the lounge room that never got used.

So pissed off again, you know. But that was nothing unusual. To have that feeling of being a pathetic failure. At everything you've tried to achieve and to have achieved nothing at all. Ever. A feeling that Frank and others like him could only understand. Yeah, knew the feeling, alright.

Another time, Frank went to cash in and forgot to put the winning poker machine on reserve. Some bastard was playing it, when he came back. And winning. Got the feature and the credits were clicking up. But Frank forgot that he forgot, to put it on reserve. Then this bastard gets the big jackpot, doesn't he? Over $20,000.00. Frank just couldn't believe it. Went right off. Been playing these poker machines for fucking years. Now some arsehole, pinches his machine and hits the big one. Fucking hell.

The young fella, who was playing the machine and a few of his mates, thought it was Christmas. Laughing, yahooing, hand slapping. Yeah. Having a great time.

"That's my machine you're playing! I put it on reserve! It's my jackpot! So just fuck off!"

"There was no one playing it, mate! And it wasn't on reserve! So, you just fuck off!"

"Yeah, fuck off mate! Ya silly old cunt!"

"I put it on reserve! So, you just fuck off! It's my machine! I was playing it! It's my machine! It's my jackpot! I put it on reserve! So, you fuck off mate!"

Things were getting really heated. Some pushing and shoving was happening. These younger blokes were getting really pissed off. Frank was just about to get his lights punched out. That's for sure. But as it happened, one of the poker machine attendants was walking around and came over. Saw the whole thing.

"The machine wasn't on reserve, Frank! I was here when they started playing it. It wasn't on reserve!"

Every attendant in every pub and club that Frank visited, knew who he was. He'd been in arguments before, many times. Always about poker machines and how some low life bastard took his machine. When he went for a piss, or went to cash in. But most of the time it happened, because Frank forgot to reserve the machine or was away too long.

But this was the worst time ever. I mean, to miss out on the big jackpot. Just because of a bad memory. Or maybe not concentrating enough. Not thinking straight. Yeah. That's probably more like what happened.

So, here's Frank back on the veranda, a few hours later. Getting completely smashed and staring off into the night sky. God only knows what time it was. I had that machine on reserve. I know I did. Fucking cunts. Yeah. Still couldn't get it out of the head. Got ripped off. He knew that. That attendant was probably mates with them bastards. He probably got a share of the jackpot. Fucking cunts.

But after a few more joints and a few more cans, this brilliant idea began to slowly formulate. Why not get some of that poison. There were a number of different kinds of poisons in one of the little sheds in the yard. And sprayers and all kinds of other stuff.

The old guy who used to live there must have been some kind of a fanatic or something. The yard was in perfect order when Frank moved in. Like a bowling green. No weeds. Everything in the sheds was in its place, you know. Neatly placed on shelves or on the work benches.

All kinds of tools were hanging on a board, with their shape marked. So, there was no way of hanging one in the wrong place. The old guy had all the right gear. Didn't take Frank long to fuck it all up.

Yeah, kill every blade of grass in the yard. No need for any lawn mowers then, eh. So that's what he did. After waking up, midway through the afternoon. Which afternoon that was. Bit hard to work that out. Could have been one, or maybe two days later.

Should have thought of this, ages ago. Remembering about the precious pot plants was a bit of a surprise. Have to be careful, not to kill them all off. Problem was remembering where they all were. Beer only made him drunk and forced occasional black outs. Smoking pot, always put him into dreamland and he loved being in dreamland. And tripping out on the LSD was even better. The best ever dreamland experience.

But there was always a heavy price to pay. And there wasn't anywhere he knew of, where he could score any LSD tabs anyway. Still missed those trips but.

So, pot and beer would have to do. Tripping out was a luxury he would never experience again. Already knew that. Didn't know how. But just knew. Some things were just known and some things weren't. Simple as that.

So Frank got up and went for a walk around the yard. Ripped out all the plants that were big enough and marked the spots where the rest were.

Of course, drinking the heavy spirits like Southern Comfort, Vodka and any number of others was always an option as well. When the money to buy them was available. The next day was always something Frank tried considering the next day, you know. When the head was booming. But there were always at least a few blank days, after a binge on the good stuff. So, the next day's thinking occasionally had to wait for a while. Maybe another day or two.

"What are you doing, Frank? I thought we agreed that all this nonsense had to stop. You need to stick to the plan, Frank! Get fit and healthy! Change your diet! And Frank! Stop playing those terrible machines. We made a deal! Remember?"

Oh, not now. Please. Not now.

"What fucking deal, anyway? I don't remember making any fucking deal? What are you going on about anyway? It's none of your business what I do. So just fuck off! Leave me alone! I'll do what I bloody well like!"

That should shut her up for a while. But Frank was in real trouble now, you know. Answering the lady back. Told her to fuck off as well. Shouldn't have done that. But the head was just booming out of control right now. So, anything was possible.

"Oh dear! You are in a bad mood! But there's no need to be so obstreperous, Frank! But I'll never give up on you! You know that don't you, Frank!" We'll never give up on you!"

What. What was that. Obstreperous. What the hell does that mean.

When the mind was half functioning again, the word obstreperous got looked up;   disorderly—rowdy—wild—unmanageable—uncontrollable—disobedient—disruptive—attention-seeking—undisciplined—troublemaking—rebellious—mutinous—anarchic—chaotic—lawless—insubordinate—defiant—wayward—wilful—headstrong—irrepressible—unrestrained—difficult—intractable—out   of   hand—refractory—recalcitrant—boisterous—

31

lively—loud—noisy—rollicking—romping—rumbustious—reckless—heedless—contumacious.

Smart bitch, eh. What a load of shit. Anyway, he'd never been attention-seeking. Never in his whole life.

Eventually, the number was rung. Gamblers Anonymous. But it was in a weak moment. Lost all the money again. Was completely smashed. Wasn't quite himself. There was a local meeting in a few days. A few hours after making the call. When the wits were back in alignment. Decided not to go. And that was that.

"I don't need any of that shit!"

Yeah. Frank was talking to himself again.

Mixed up the poison and sprayed the whole back yard. Within a week, there was a sea of dead grass. The yard was completely dead, alright. Except for the plants that weren't pulled out. But they were looking a bit drooped over. After taking a closer look, Frank realised the poison must have spread into the soil and was killing the plants. So, they got pulled out too. They all died.

But they weren't thrown away. Oh no. That was never going to happen. Couldn't bring himself to do it. Rolled up joints out of them and smoked them just like normal. Couldn't tell the difference. And that was a bit of a shame. A new mind-blowing situation was half expected, with all that poison in there. But it never happened did it. Bummer.

There was money in the bank account again. Because the medical retirement pension appeared there like magic, every fortnight. Although Frank was pretty much useless at everything, there was still just enough knowledge there. About using a computer. The years spent in the public service weren't a complete waste of time, you know. Had access to the internet. An on-line banking account. Microsoft word. And a number of other programs that were never used, except for all the card games and Mahjong.

This was another side of Frank that no one else knew about. All people saw was a dirty old man wandering around, who looked like a homeless derelict. And that's exactly how Frank liked it. After all, no one ever bothers homeless derelicts, do they?

There were various other sides to this social misfit as well. The poker machine Frank. The binge drinking, alcoholic Frank. The pot smoking Frank. The book reading Frank. The sneaky Frank. The argumentative Frank. The kind and gentle Frank. The helpful Frank. The knowledgeable Frank. The dreaming

Frank. The suspicious Frank. The cynical Frank. The organised Frank. The unorganised Frank. The paranoid Frank. And maybe a few other Franks, that even Frank didn't know about.

Only a few of the Franks, knew about some of the other Franks. But none of the Franks, knew about all of the other Franks. Frank didn't even know about some of the other Franks. And he was the main Frank. This was often what the Franks were contemplating over, when they were in the right mood. And that was usually when Frank was sitting on the back veranda smoking pot. Slowly getting pissed, or just wandering around the backyard or along the street.

So, if anyone did stop him for a friendly chat. Even Frank didn't know which Frank, they were likely to end up talking to. But you have to give Frank some credit here, you know. Because Frank always kept all the other Franks under control. By not letting any of them say too much. Things could turn ugly very quickly, if one of the wrong Franks managed to spit out a few words, at the wrong time. Or took offence to something that was said to Frank. Frank had become pretty smart over the years. That's for sure.

One day, after the daily swim in the ocean baths, Frank was sitting on a concrete ledge, soaking up some sun. This was the favourite place to sit. Just up from the magic café. That's what he called the café now. The magic café. But he never told the café girls that. This dirty, old stinking drunk walked straight up to him.

"Hey Franky! How ya doin, man? Yeah! How ya doin?"

What the… Here's some fucking dirtbag. Pissed to the eyeballs. Didn't like alcoholics, you know. Couldn't stand the sight of the stinking bastards. The guy was a real mess, alright.

"I remember you, Franky! Yeah, I remember you! Snooker room, mate! Yeah! Snooker room!"

This miserable looking fool had a huge smile on his sagging, sad old face. Bloodshot eyes and long, greasy, multi-coloured hair. Standing there, about half a metre away. Chirping away, like an excited little canary. His eyes were watering up. Was almost crying. You could tell he'd had a hard life. When Frank looked down, he saw a pair of dirty bare feet, with what looked like moss growing between the toes. He wanted this bloke gone. That's for sure. Had about enough sun anyway and was getting hungry.

"Anyway mate, I've got somewhere to go!"

And with that, it was a case of sliding down off the wall and disappearing. Then it was remembered about the wallet and the phone and that fucking face mask. There were restrictions on, you know. Because of the pandemic. Yeah, COVID-19. You had to wear a mask everywhere. Or you couldn't buy takeaway and there was food required. Right now. Because that was the routine. A swim, some sun and then takeaway. Sweet potato chips and coffee. There was no time for talk, especially with some stinking alcoholic.

So, the old drunk was just left standing there. Hadn't moved one inch. Frozen to the spot. Looking lost. There was one more look at the pathetic old coot. And the decision was made. Walked straight past him. Real quick. Took the long way back to the car. Didn't want to be followed. That's for sure. Already had enough of this old loser.

Off the grog now, by the way. Hadn't smoked a joint for months. Been going to Gamblers Anonymous as well. Swimming almost every day. Going to the gym five days a week. Looking pretty fit and healthy. For an old guy. Had a nice tan. Yeah. Looking good. A new man, alright. Just hooting along. In the new life. No time to lose. And no looking back. That was the plan. The, new life plan. It was a good plan. And it was working. Yeah. The first plan that ever really worked.

"You're doing so well, Frank! You look great! You've come such a long way! I'm so proud of you, Frank! We're all so proud of you!"

She was saying that kind of stuff all the time now, you know. Liked hearing it too. Couldn't hear enough of it.

There was usually a line up at the takeaway counter. With the restrictions on, takeaway was all you could buy. After arriving at the front of the line, it was always the same welcome. No matter which girls were on duty.

"Hi Frank! Been for your swim! A coffee and sweet potato chips? Same as usual!"

"Yes please. Same as usual!"

This healthy, fit, sun tanned, swimming, new life individual, ordered the same thing, you know. Every day. Always smiled back at whoever was behind the counter. Just couldn't be helped. Wasn't up to saying too much back to them yet. Was no chirping canary. That's for sure. Not yet anyway. But there were changes happening, alright. Slowly. But they were happening.

Well actually, the café girls were doing the changing. Working their magic, on the old fool. But there was no realisation about that. None at all. But that's what was happening, alright. And only the café girls knew about it too. Just so blind to a whole lot of things, you know. Things that anyone in their mid-sixties should know about. But not this fella. After all, this new life had only just begun. So, what was there to know. And surely excuses were acceptable, for the naive behaviour. At this early stage of the new life development, anyway. But there was still a stupid old fool in there. That's for sure.

Getting takeaway was ok. Because there was always somewhere to sit and watch the surf roll in. And this was an enjoyable thing to be doing. As long as it wasn't raining or too windy. The seagulls had to be watched closely. The bloody things would swoop down and be off with a chip, before they were even seen coming. One of them that was always there, had a fishing hook sticking out the side of its beak.

Poor thing. But trying to catch it, proved too difficult. Seagulls aren't smart enough to know when someone is trying to help them, you know. There're just scavengers, who are wary of people.

So, maybe that makes them more smart than dumb. Or more dumb than smart. That idea was always in the thinking. Because that idea had always been in the thinking. Just not usually about seagulls.

One day, there was a pigeon hopping around on the concrete. There was what looked like cotton, binding its toes and legs together. The thing couldn't even stand up properly. It was a dark checker pied hen bird. Pigeons had always been a part of the old life, for as far back as could be remembered. Since about eight years of age was the closest guess. Knew every type of pigeon there was.

A few bits of chip were dropped down. But the seagulls were too quick for the starving pigeon. So, a few chips were thrown a few metres away. And when the gulls went off squabbling after them, a few small bits were again dropped down. And the pigeon hopped over. Close enough to be grabbed and examined properly.

The tangled mess around its feet and legs was cutting deep into the skin. So, it was taken home. Holding this half dead pigeon in one hand and the steering wheel in the other wasn't all that difficult. Lucky the car was an automatic.

Took about an hour to cut all the cotton away and clean the feet up. There were still some old breeding cabinets in the yard, leaning up against the side of the old pigeon loft. Locked it up in one of those and filled the water container up. And then drove down to the local pet supplies shop and bought a small bag of wheat. Took good care of that bird for a few weeks. Pigeons are tough, hardy things you know. It was looking strong and healthy and just wanted to get out.

So, it was liberated. To use a pigeon racing term. Took off like a rocket. In an Easterly direction. Straight towards the coast.

A few days later, there it was again. Almost in the exact same spot, at the exact same time. Scrounging around, for whatever morsel it could find. Before the seagulls got there first. Only it wasn't hopping as much now. And it got a good feed of chips as well. There was a big smile on the old fella's face for at least a few minutes.

Before the pandemic hit and there were no restrictions, is when this episode shook things up. Sitting in the café, enjoying the lunch and having a read of the paper. Some yelling started going on at the counter. Yeah. Some untidy, scruffy old bloke was abusing one of the girls. Not the old drunk from before. This was another no hoper.

"Well, you can just piss off then!"

There were some other words spat out. Couldn't understand any of that. But there was one thing understood. Frank wasn't going to just sit there and watch a café girl get abused. Not by anyone. So, up to the counter, to sort this moron out. But the moron was aware enough to realise, trouble was coming his way. Quickly headed for the exit and took off. The girl was shaken, alright.

But before anything else could happen, several of the other girls and a few of the chefs from the kitchen were already comforting her. After they went back to what they were doing, there was still a feeling there and the need to say something.

"Well, I bet that doesn't happen very often? But the law of averages says, it's going to happen every now and then. Are you ok?"

That was the most talking ever achieved, since going to the magic café— without feeling self-conscious. This girl just smiled her usual warm, friendly smile. She seemed just fine. But very soon after that, she left the café and went for a walk. In the opposite direction to what the moron took. This girl had previously walked up one day. Frank was just standing there, at the water dispenser. Filling one of the re-usable plastic cups.

"Have you been for your swim?"

Whoa. One of the girls was actually talking to him. And she wasn't even behind the counter. The answer was a short one.

"Yes, I have!"

"I think I'll go for a swim later, myself!"

This answer struggled to come out as well. But at least a few words escaped.

"Yes, I think you should!"

Then this sweet looking little girl got right in Frank's face. Eyes glaring. And in a raised voice said it again. "I think I'll go for a swim later, myself!"

Holy shit. This verbal explosion, more than shocked the internal structure a little bit. That's for sure. Took a step backwards and was kind of trembling. Face was warming up and there was an emotional pressure building up as well. Struggled even more answering this time. But managed to get it out.

"Yes, I think you should! I think you should!"

Then quickly changed the subject. There was a pinkish smear on the inside of the cup.

"Is that lipstick?"

She takes a quick look. "Yes, I think it is!"

She was back to her normal self again now. What a relief that was. Maybe there was a crazy one, working in this place.

"Well, I'll just drink from the other side. It won't kill me!"

Wasn't really talking to the girl when that came out either. More like a communication, with an internal being. Wasn't even looking at her. Then just walked off. Didn't even stop to think about the girl and what she thought. Even though she was a really beautiful looking girl. Not quite as beautiful as the most beautiful girl in the world. But just beautiful.

So, that's what she was called from then on. The beautiful one. But she had a few tattoos and there wasn't a liking for tattoos. Especially on girls. And especially on beautiful girls. The ugly girls could cover themselves in tattoos if they wanted to. Who cares, what the ugly ones do. Anyway, the only thoughts that were ever in this new individual's head now were the new individuals. That's all. No room for anyone else's.

There was a GA meeting that night. Been going to meetings for a few months now, you know. Self-conscious at first. But eventually started sharing. This was when each member had the opportunity to introduce themselves and say what they needed to say. About what was happening in their lives and how their gambling problem was going.

Honesty was always considered crucial during sharing. Some of the stuff that was shared was just shocking. It'd been a charmed life, compared to some of these sad cases and what they'd gone through. And that's not being unkind either. But some of them were just sad cases. Simple as that.

Honesty will come into your life if you let it.

"Hello, I'm whoever and I'm a compulsive gambler."

That's how you started, when it was your turn to share. You didn't have to share if you didn't want to, either. But most of the regulars usually had something to say. Any new problem gamblers, often just sat in for a few meetings, before they opened up. Some just came for one meeting and were never seen again. Some young gamblers were brought in by one or both parents. Some came in with a loved one or a partner. And they weren't all hopeless drop outs either.

There were compulsive gamblers from all levels of society. There were even a few suits sitting there. Spilling the beans about their dirty little gambling secrets. A real eye opener. That's for sure. Eventually looked forward to GA meetings. And there developed some kind of an internal secret pleasure, listening to everyone else's shit. Why this was is still uncertain. But it was there. That's for sure.

"I've been gambling my whole life. I've wasted so much money. We lost the house. I lost my job. My wife left me. My kids won't talk to me. I've hurt so many people. I've got no friends. No one wants to know me. I've lost everything because of gambling."

This was just an example of what could come out, during someone's sharing. There were lots of similar stories and lots of them were just so pathetic. And not being emotionally affected by some of them was just impossible. Even by someone who was an expert at hiding emotions.

Yes, there were emotions hidden in there. And controlling them on a full-time basis, required a full-time effort. Bust outs happened from time to time, you know. And that's why Gamblers Anonymous meetings were so critical.

For many, it was the last line of defence, against going under completely. In terms of financial security, and the loss of personal responsibility. And the loss of everything and everyone, who meant anything to them. And of course, the possibility of self-destruction.

It was all just so tragic. Many of these compulsive gamblers were also alcoholics and drug addicts. So, there was a feeling of relief, right from the very first meeting. Yeah. Frank fitted in, alright. And it didn't take long to realise that most of these other compulsives, knew who each other were. Because quite often, their shares were much the same.

Sometimes, it was like everyone was talking about everyone else in the room. And that was a little disturbing at first. When it's realised, there's plenty of others out there, with exactly the same affliction. And exactly the same thought processes, when it comes to dealing with that affliction.

"Hello. I'm Frank and I'm a compulsive gambler!"

"Hello Frank!"

"Hi Frank!"

"Hello Frank!"

Yeah, everyone said hello or hi or some other greeting or acknowledgement, when anyone introduced themselves. Before they started sharing.

"I haven't played poker machines for another week!"

"Hey, well done!"

"That's great, Frank!"

"I'm doing very well. I haven't been drinking either. Or smoking pot! And I'm still off the smokes as well."

Being off the drinking, pot and smokes was still a week-to-week thing, you know. Just like not playing the machines was.

"I'm going to the gym and swimming and then going for lunch at a really good café. Things couldn't be any better for me right now. One of the café girls even told me, how good I was looking. And she was going to start doing what I was doing. And she's a good looker too. And young. So, yeah! I'm going really well! Anyway. Thanks for letting me share."

"That's good to hear, Frank! Well done!"

That was the controller. Usually said something like that to everyone after sharing. Unless it was bad news that they were sharing. Then something else was said. To make them feel better about themselves, even though they'd stuffed up really bad.

"Yeah, well done, Frank!"

"Good on ya Frank!"

"Be careful with them young girls, mate! They'll get you into all kinds of shit!"

Yeah, well. Never much good at listening to advice, eh.

"I've been around too long, mate! Too smart for them young ones! They wouldn't know shit anyway!"

Everyone started laughing and clapping and saying more nice things. Until the controller took control again.

"Would you like to share anything else, Frank?"

"No, that's all from me this time. Thanks for letting me share!"

That's what you always said after sharing.

"Ok! Thanks Frank! Would, anyone else like to share?"

Then the sharing continued, till everyone shared, who wanted to share. Frank loved sharing now. Sometimes even found it hard to shut up and give someone else a go. And what a surprise that was. Sometimes the sharing got a little out of hand, you know. Until the controller got things back under control. The one who controlled the meetings wasn't called the controller at all. Only Frank called the controller, the controller. But never told the controller that. All the meetings always ended the same way. Everyone stood up.

All together now.

"To the God of our own understanding. God grant me the serenity to accept the things I cannot change. The courage to change the things I can. And the wisdom to know the difference."

After this bit of bullshit was said. And Frank knew it was all bullshit. Everyone held hands with whoever was standing beside them. On both sides.

All together now.

"Thanks for sharing! Thanks for caring! Keep coming back! The meetings make it!"

Meeting over.

And some of the members you had to hold hands with. Fucking hell.

After listening to many sad, real-life stories, from even sadder individual compulsive gamblers, Frank began to realise a few things. About himself. Maybe this was an expected reaction for members, who stuck with the steps of the GA programme. There were twelve steps and Frank was only up to step two. He also began to notice the knowing, understanding look of the controller, who'd been through the mill, alright. The whole gambling experience. Anyone could see that.

The controller, shared as well you know. Whenever the controller felt like sharing. Always mentioned about being clean for over seven years and very proud of it. A real inspiration, alright. That's for sure. And very likeable. For a controller. Yeah, everyone had great respect for the controller.

Driving home one night, after another very interesting meeting, Frank had a fleeting thought back to that stinking drunk, who had the nerve to interrupt him, while he was sunning himself at the ocean baths. Still couldn't remember this old bloke, like he was so sure about remembering Frank. But got to wondering about this hopeless nobody. Maybe he wasn't so different. Just like some of the other members of GA weren't so different from himself either. So, the decision was made. Have a friendly chat to the drunken bum, if he was ever seen again.

After arriving home, a realisation happened. Not even the thought about dropping into any of the favourite haunts, for a quick gamble. Didn't even enter the head. That was real progress, or maybe just a lapse in concentration. There was money in the wallet as well. Even a few fifties. Eventually, it was decided. Significant progress had been achieved and he should be so proud of himself. Could have even been smiling. Just a little bit. Still wasn't much smiling going on in the new life, you know.

"I'm so proud of you Frank! We're all so proud of you!"

Just knew she was going to say that. And there was no arguing with the lady anymore either. Not this time anyway. Feeling the positive energy, alright. That's for sure. Soon, could even be a believer.

"Hi Frank! Good to see you! Having the usual?"

"Yes thanks! Just the usual! It's good to see you too! Gee, it's busy today!"

But there was no time for chit chat. Yes, Frank was chit chatting a bit now. It was just before Christmas. At least a year before the pandemic. People everywhere. The café was crowded. Frank always sat at the same table, if it was vacant. In the furthest corner from the counter. Liked being as far away from other people as possible. Some things never change, you know. Always sat at the table, with the back to the other tables. Staring out the window. Watching the ocean and the waves rolling in and crashing onto the rocks.

And the people walking along the shore line. And kids building sand castles or just digging holes in the sand. Sometimes there were dolphins swimming in the waves and sometimes there were whales, breaching further out. There were always people taking photos of the whales.

And yes, there was that irresistible urge to watch all the trendy, young girls prancing along the promenade. Especially the ones in their G strings. Many with tanned, muscled-up young men walking with them. Talking and laughing away. Like they didn't have a care in the world. And they probably didn't. Just the sight of all these terrific looking young people was kind of annoying, you know. Because watching and reminiscing were the only options available. Brought up the memories about old times. Or what could be remembered about old times anyway. In the old life.

But there were no memories to be found about young girls walking around, with next to nothing on. That's for sure. Might as well have been naked. But there was no harm in looking either. I mean, if they had a problem with an old man watching them walking along, then they should cover themselves up, eh. That's what the thinking was anyway.

Although, the thought also occurred. That some of these young girls should never be allowed out in public in a G string. What a strange world it was now. Not a world for some beaten up old reprobate, to feel comfortable in. Didn't belong here at all. Knew that, alright. And the thought of it kept hounding the head space, you know. That lady had no idea what she'd done. And lots of these young people were covered in tattoos as well.

One day, while swimming along, an old memory did pop up. That maybe only people who ever had tattoos were bikies and criminals. In the old world anyway. Where he came from and still belonged. But now, everyone seemed to have at least one tattoo on their body somewhere. Swimming was a good time to do the thinking, you know. All kinds of old memories went through the head, while swimming. But nothing these young people would know anything about. That's for sure.

Yes, as the fitness and health were improving. So was the remembering. About the old life, and the life he could have had, but never had. The realisation of being robbed of a good life was always there as well now. Pulsating in the brain. Burning even. About the early life. But especially the teenage life. And what a nightmare that life was. A very enjoyable nightmare. But a nightmare just the same.

Watching young people wrapped around each other, in the middle of the baths. Oblivious to everything except each other. Hit a nerve, alright. And all the sun worshippers lying around everywhere. Chatting away and laughing and enjoying their seemingly care free life. A young boy and girl walking along together got the thinking going. About how there were no memories of ever having a girlfriend. Or a proper relationship with a girl. Well, never a relationship at all actually. Not even a friendship, of any kind.

Mind you, there were always plenty of girls around, you know. And lots of stuff happened, with lots of these girls. If you get the idea. And you probably do. Just not with the same girl, for very long. No, not very long at all. And what was the point of getting to know them anyway. That idea, never even entered the head. There was only one thought that was ever in the head, you know. And you probably do know. Well, of course you do.

And all the young kids running around everywhere. Jumping in the water and calling out and pushing each other in and everything else kids do, when there're having fun. No memories of any of that stuff either. And there was a big effort put in, trying to get any such memories out. But they just weren't in there. Simple as that.

But what really affected the internal workings the most was noticing a mother with a very young child. Either playing together in the kid's pool or just walking along, holding hands. Or just giving her little darling kisses and cuddles and whispering gentle words.

Or maybe a father, fooling around with his kids. Dragging them around on some inflatable pool object. Maybe teaching them how to swim. Laughing and having fun. Yeah, a father having fun with his kids. No memories of any of that stuff either. Not anywhere.

And if there was ever a mother noticed, breastfeeding a baby. It set off these strange feelings, you know. Feelings inside, that couldn't be explained. Strong feelings they were too. In the chest and in the head. And it wasn't because a mother was breast feeding her baby in public either. These feelings should just, never have been there. That's what the thinking was anyway. But they were there. And there was no reason for them to be there. Not that could be understood anyway.

Better off not even trying to work it out. And better off, not even noticing any mother breastfeeding in the first place. So that's what eventually happened. Yeah, the eyes always closed and the head took a quick turn, whenever a breastfeeding situation came into view. Problem solved.

No, Frank still didn't know how to understand feelings. Didn't know what they were, or why they were even there at all. But they were always there. Somewhere. And came out. Usually when they weren't even thought about. And what a nightmare that was. Being continually ambushed by feelings.

But one thing was certain. And it may be surprising how many old men are guilty of this age-old social activity. Something they all know is very naughty and very sexist and unacceptable and they shouldn't be doing it. But they still do. Because they can't help themselves, can they. And it's not only dirty old men that do it either. Called perving.

But there's basic perving and an advanced level of perving, you know. And Frank was at the advanced level. Evaluating every girl, or woman, just walking along. Minding their own business. Rating them from one to ten was the preferred method. There were a number of criteria and sometimes things got a bit complicated.

This evaluation process often started with how beautiful or ugly they were. How fat or skinny. How firm the bum cheeks were. How tall they were. How short they were. How smart or dumb they looked. What their feet and toes looked like. The colour of their hair and whether it was natural or died into another colour. There was always this liking for blonds, you know. And whether they were fake or not.

Some of them walked quicker than others. And it was a common thing for some of them, to do a quick half turn. When it wasn't expected. And the watcher did a quick half turn as well. But usually too late. There was no embarrassment about being caught either. It was all about the law of averages, you know. If you keep doing something you maybe shouldn't be doing. For too long. Chances are, you're going to get caught out, every now and then. And that was an understood thing. But it was also a great game to be playing.

Yeah, more than guilty of all these visual assaults, you know. But whose fault was that anyway? Well, maybe it was obvious in the old life, where the fault lay. But you couldn't blame anyone for the same thing in the new life, could you. Except maybe, the lady. It was all her idea in the first place wasn't it. All this mysterious new life business. All this new thinking happening in the head. And with all these young people parading along, like movie stars. With all their private bits hanging out. What else was there to do, but perve on them.

Anyway, how was anyone supposed to just sit there and relax and enjoy their lunch, with all that near nudity. Just there. Right in front of the eyeballs. That never happened in the old life. That's for sure. So, it wasn't really fair, was it?

Reading the newspaper kept things under control. For a while. But the eyes kept wandering around, you know. Like they had a mind of their own. Positioning the chair to face the opposite direction, didn't work either. And trying to just ignore what was happening out there, only a few yards away. That was just impossible. Especially, for a lonely old compulsive deviate. Well, not really a deviate. Just a confused lonely old compulsive. Anyway, what would be the point of admitting to anything at all, when there was no need to.

Worst of all were the tall girls, with skinny legs, knobbly knees and long skinny fingers and toes. Enough to put anyone off their lunch. Or when a girl looked completely stupid, but had a great body. Or when one had a horrid looking body, and was dead ugly. But looked pretty smart. They came in all shapes and sizes. That's for sure.

But trends are trends aren't they. And try telling any young girl, she shouldn't be wearing, what all the other young girls are wearing. Or not wearing. Especially at the beach and the ocean baths. Or telling these young people that covering their bodies with tattoos was a bad idea.

But the thought was always crossing the mind. That old age was a terrible thing and there was no going back. And there was plenty of old age involved here. But who'd want to go back and start all over again. No, there was no going back. Especially to that old life. Which was a complete disaster. So, adapting to the new life seemed like the only option now. Just have to do it.

And another thing that just had to happen. If this new life was going to take off. And that was listening to the lady who wasn't even there in the first place. And not telling her to fuck off or anything.

After being caught out ogling, a few times too many. Or perving. The decision was made. Start reading the newspaper even more. And not just one paper either. All the papers that were available. One after the other. In between mouthfuls of lunch and sips of coffee. Had to change the focus somehow. Take the mind off all the beach beauties and uglies. That nothing could be done with anyway.

So, the mind started thinking along the lines of cardboard cut outs. Yeah. They were all just cardboard cut outs. Or maybe shop dummies. Or mannequins. Drifting along, with a little breeze behind them. And that seemed to ease the pain somewhat. Most of the time anyway.

"Oh, Frank! You've got so much to learn! But don't worry! Your new life has only just begun! So, there's plenty of time. Don't panic or start stressing about it all. The new Frank will emerge. Just give it time! Just give it time! You'll see. Everything will work out! Just be patient, Frank!"

Well, that all made a lot of sense. Yeah, of course it did. You know, she just dropped in. Blurted stuff out and then just dropped out again. She was always doing that. Leaving the poor bastard there more confused than ever. Maybe, she deliberately did that. Wouldn't put it past her.

Although, perving could be considered an acceptable social pastime. For any red-blooded male. Even for males, with no red blood at all. There shouldn't really be any ridicule involved here, you know. Males will be males, after all. Not many old men would admit to being old perverts anyway. Not unless they were forced to.

There was this story in one of the newspapers one day. About when something was in the DNA, it was a natural thing to be doing. And couldn't be helped. So that's what perving must be. Something in the DNA. And that settled all the feelings down, as far as perving was concerned. So, no more thought was put into it. Especially about what DNA was. Not then anyway.

But just imagine an old man, fronting up to some young G-string.

"Hi there! I'm Frank! You look great! So, what's your name darlin'?"

Yeah right. You don't have to think too hard about what'd happen there, eh. And it wouldn't matter how tanned up, or muscled up, or how many teeth were still there either. The reaction would still be the same. Shock, horror. Maybe laughing. Or maybe just, fuck off, you dirty old bastard. And that'd be a good idea. Before the boyfriend or the husband. Or the partner, come over and had his say in the matter. Or, maybe her say in the matter. Or maybe just getting arrested.

There'd been some other reading in the newspapers, you know. About old men. With bucket loads of money. And they somehow had beautiful looking girlfriends and in some cases wives. And these wives and girlfriends, usually had huge boobs. That were propped up and sticking right out. Like footballs. And with make-up, plastered all over their faces. And there were stories on the television sometimes. About rich old men, who could get anything they wanted. With money.

And there were sometimes stories, about these filthy rich men who were getting divorced. And getting cleaned out by their wives or girlfriends. Or at least having to pay them, huge amounts in settlements. Just to get rid of them. For being unfaithful or for any number of other reasons. But quite often, it was the filthy rich men, who were the unfaithful ones. Or at least, that's what the pissed off wives and girlfriends always said. And lots of other unkind things as well.

Sometimes the old wives just got traded in, you know. Like an old motor car. For a new trendy, hot, younger model. With bigger, firmer knockers. And who could wear a G-string in public, without being laughed at. Frank loved reading about all this stuff, you know. Whether it was true or not, didn't matter. Thought it was hilarious. Never going to happen to him but, eh. He'd already been cleaned out. Heaps of times. By them fucking poker machines. So, he knew the feeling, alright. And it was a much worse feeling than just being married. Although, there were never any marriages, you know. And now, there never would be either. Especially after reading about all that shit.

Anyway. Lucky there'd been the prostate cancer. So, that put an end to the idea of a wife or some started up young girlfriend. Was just like a safety barrier. And it wouldn't have mattered how big the boobs were either. Or what shape her arse was in. Couldn't even get the thing up for thirty seconds. Let alone do any shagging. Not like back in the old life. And all the Viagra in the world wouldn't help either. Knew all about Viagra. Could have learnt about it on television. Or maybe read about it in one of the newspapers.

Anyway, bucket loads of the stuff wouldn't help. So, there was no use even thinking about it all. So, a new thinking was developed. About the sexual relations activities. Shagging was only for young people and animals. And that thinking worked. So, that's how the thinking stayed.

"Oh! No! No. No! No! That's a terribly way to think Frank! You need to do better than that! You really do!"

Well, how was he supposed to look at it then.

But there was no money involved here. Not enough anyway. So, what else was there to do, but perve. On all the girls that couldn't be had. Even if they could be had. What a dilemma. Yeah. Painful at times. But it was better that not looking at all. Might as well be dead, eh. If you can't even look. Looking doesn't hurt anyway. No. Can't hurt. So that's what happened. You know the saying. Look but don't touch. So, the old bastard became an expert looker and sometimes, an expert looker and a frustrated non-toucher. At the same time.

But there were these thoughts creeping in, you know. About perving. And then the understanding happened. Maybe it wasn't such a good idea, to be continually staring at young girls. Especially the ones in g-strings. Well, some of them didn't seem to mind at all, you know. Not one bit. They enjoyed being perved on. Tell that easy enough. Even smiled when they caught someone at it.

Then another understanding started taking shape. They were just young girls after all. Enjoying the freedoms of being young girls. And old men were just old men, who couldn't really enjoy much of anything anymore. Except maybe, perving on all the young girls. Not so much the older ones. Who'd want to perv on the older ones.

Although, some of them did still have a bit of shape about them, you know. And some of the older ones, still thought they had it too, you know. That was so funny. Watching them, casually strolling along. Trying to look sexy in their G-string. Yuck. Talk about getting put off the lunch. Easy enough, to give the perving a rest for a while then.

Could hardly remember being young enough, to remember anything, anyway. Not like the young people who lived in this new world. That Frank had just been dropped into. Against his own free will, I might add. And becoming like some kind of a prisoner. No wonder the confusion was out of control. Bet the lady didn't figure on that situation developing, did she? No. She wouldn't have even thought about that. Thinking about calling her a stupid, nosey bitch, you know. But she wasn't stupid. Just nosey. And she probably wasn't a bitch either.

'Oh yes, Frank! You're starting to see things in a new light now! That's wonderful! And don't worry! The confusion will ease over time! It just takes time, Frank! That's all! You're doing so well! I know you'll make it Frank! We all know you'll make it!"

Yeah. Yeah. Yeah. Here we go again. Oh shit. If she knew about the confusion bit; she'd know about the bit about thinking about the bit about calling her a nosey bitch. Well, he did call her nosey, alright. But at least he didn't call her a bitch. Maybe she's a bit deaf or something. Well, you know, she could be deaf. After all, she always did the talking and Frank always did the listening. So maybe she was deaf. Or just plain stupid after all. Yes, that would explain it.

"Or maybe just very caring, Frank! And forgiving! Did you ever think about that?"

Uh. Not really. No. Yeah. The guilt trip was happening again. But there was no telling the lady that was there. She never listened to anything anyway. And you never knew when she was there or not there. And sometimes when she went away, she came back and you didn't even know she was there. Like just then. She was pretty sneaky, alright.

Anyway, while all this thinking was invading the mind, he'd wandered through the café and into the toilet for a pee. By the time he came back out, there were three people sitting at his table. Bugger. So, the girl gave him a number for a table outside. But when he went out to sit down, some pumped-up women was dragging the second allocated table over to where she'd already dragged two other tables.

Looked like there were about twenty people, ready to sit down and share a Christmas lunch together. What else was there to do, but just stand there and watch it all happen. Moving the head from side to side in shock and amazement.

While this skirted, middle-aged maniac, feverishly moved the tables and chairs into position. She was a big fat thing as well. Devastation was eventually the only reaction left. That was two tables in about two minutes. More, than anyone could take.

"They stole my table!"

Blurted that straight out to the girls behind the counter, after rushing back inside. There were about half a dozen of them there now. They all burst out laughing. They'd obviously seen the whole thing.

"Don't worry about it, Frank! We'll give you another table! This kind of thing happens all the time!" Just go out and sit wherever you like! We'll find you!"

They were all still laughing as he walked back out. There was only one other table vacant. And it was covered with other people's leftovers. But it was that or nothing. Anyway, one of the girls came and cleaned it all up. And gave the usual little smile as she turned and walked away. She had really nice eyes, this girl. They were blue and green, at the same time. Sometimes more green than blue and sometimes more blue than green. Called her miss nice eyes. Or just nice eyes.

"Oh, that was funny! That was just so funny!"

Yeah, some old women just appeared out of nowhere. Standing there. Smiling away. Like it was the funniest thing she'd ever seen.

"Well, it's just a table. And it's just as good sitting here as anywhere. They said I could sit anywhere I liked. And they'd find me. And this was the only table left anyway."

Talk about babbling on. He'd outdone himself, alright. The old women didn't say anything else. But she got this weird look on her face. Something between a smirk and a smile. Then she just wandered off. Shortly after that, the meal and coffee arrived.

"There you go, Frank! Just chill! Everything's fine! Just chill out!"

And he got another one of those special, café girl smiles as well. Yes, that nice little wave of warmth, drifted through the whole body again. Twice in a matter of minutes. And the chilling out started immediately. And that's who she always was after that. The chill out girl. Yeah. She was always telling him, to just chill out. And that's what always happened. Another spell was cast. He liked the chill out girl, alright. But she was never going to know anything about that, was she?

But you know. It got a bit difficult after a while. Liking all these café girls so much. And not being able to tell any of them, anything about it. Had to be, just an old man's secret. Better off that way.

The table stealing episode sparked the idea for a new plan. From that day on, Frank always went to the table first. Before ordering. Put the worn-out, dirty old cap down. Along with the cheap sunglasses. And always offered to take the cutlery and a few serviettes, after ordering. With all that stuff on the table, no one was ever going to pinch his favourite table, ever again. That's for sure. Yeah. Getting smarter all the time.

If the most favourite table wasn't available, the next favourite table was claimed. Or the next one. Or the next one. Ended up being lots of favourite tables. But changing tables only happened, if there was no choice. The first favourite table was always the most favourite table.

But this little episode was nothing compared to what happened, with one of the other café girls. Had only been going to the café for a few weeks. After ordering on this particular day, this girl really let go, with the verbals. Really let him have it. What a bitch. There was another girl standing beside her, with a big smile on her face. But it wasn't the usual warm, café girl smile. More like a little smartarse smile. They were obviously working together. The evil little twins, is what they got called. Straight away.

"You're here at the same time every day! You order the same thing every day! You always sit at the same table! Every day! You, never talk to anyone? You never smile! What's wrong with you?"

Fucking hell. Yeah. This was a new life experience, alright. Shook the internals right up. Giving this cheeky little bitch the evil stare was the necessary thing to do. The little smiling mate got a not so friendly look as well. Shock had set right in. No emotion. Just shock.

And if it was known then, what was in store down the track, they both would have been told where to go. And he'd have got the hell out of the place. And never gone back. But the idiot didn't know, did he? And he came back again and again. What an imbecile.

"Creature of habit, mate!"

Didn't even know he was going to say that. Just did and then took off and sat at the table. But after sitting down, the urge was just too overwhelming. Staring at this girl, who just abused the shit out of him. And she was staring back as well. Just as hard. It was a real long-distance stare off, alright. That's for sure. Another thing for sure was that this girl was the most beautiful girl Frank had ever seen and he'd seen a few in his time. In the old life and now in the new life as well.

Yes, she was beautiful, alright. There was no denying that. She frightened the shit out of him as well. No denying that either. That's when the thought first started. About never coming back to this café. Ever again. But it was too late for that now. The flip was hooked and didn't even know it. Not yet anyway. What an imbecile.

There were lots of other cafes around, you know. Where you didn't get the shit blown out of you. For no reason at all. What a fucking bitch. Her and her evil little mate. The evil twins. Although, the little mate, may have been just as evil. But was nowhere near as beautiful. Just average looking. That's for sure.

And that was somehow a known thing, you know. Especially when girls hung out together in groups. There were never two really beautiful girls. It was usually one really beautiful one. One or two not so beautiful ones. A few average looking ones. And one or two really ugly ones, who just felt so privileged to be included.

"What's going on with her anyway? Does she talk to everyone like that, or what?"

"No, not everyone! Enjoy your lunch!"

Then the little evil mate, placed the lunch on the table, turned around and headed back to the counter. Checked her out as she was walking away. Gee these girls looked good in their tight jeans, you know. She might have been an evil little bitch. But she did have a nice arse. That's all that was in the head. Anyway, how could he not notice. Was still alive, after all.

Oh, no. She turned around and headed straight back. Stopped right beside him and looked down. He was going to cop a mouthful, just like before. But he was ready this time. But he got ready for nothing. Because the café girl smile was there. And the eyes were friendly. But what happened next was a big shock to the system. That's for sure.

"Are you married, Frank? Or, do you have a girlfriend?"

"What! Married! Girlfriend! No! You must be joking!"

"So, I take it you're not married or anything!"

"No, I'm not! And not likely to be either!"

There could have even been a little aggravation creeping in here, you know. What a nosey bitch.

"Well, I was just curious! That's all!"

Then she turned around and took off. Straight back to the counter. Then disappeared out the back. She fancied him, alright. But it was never going to happen, was it? Not with her anyway. And how the hell did she know his name anyway.

After only a few mouthfuls, the coffee arrived. The same girl who did the yelling, shoved it down in front of him and just stood there. Her very presence felt like a huge weight sitting on top of his head. Getting heavier and heavier. Looking up was the only option. Their eyes lined up and she gave him the biggest, warmest smile you could ever imagine.

Then some kind of eye lock, energy beam thing happened. Whatever it was filled the head right up. Until this girl suddenly broke off the engagement, slowly turned around and started cleaning up a few of the nearby tables. Looking over to where Frank was and smiling at him, every time he took a quick look at her.

Just couldn't help himself, eh. But it was like she already knew when he was about to look. Caught him at it every time. Frank decided then and there, that this girl was one smart-arse little bitch, alright. A very beautiful smart arse little bitch. But a smart-arse little bitch, just the same. There was no other explanation. Yes. What a fucking bitch. An evil fucking bitch. And maybe a little crazy as well.

Then it hit him. A warm, pulsating, rhythmic wave of inner chest movement. What the fuck. What the hell's happening in there was all that was going on in the head? Frank just sat there, mesmerised. Forgot about the lunch and the coffee. Forgot about the girl. Just forgot about everything.

Yeah, Frank had been transported. To some unknown place. A total, internal freak out situation was happening. There's no telling how long it went on for either. But eventually, the spell was broken. He snapped out of it. Yeah. Back, alright. With a few blinks of the eyes and a rigorous shake of the head.

Fucking hell. What was that all about. There were no ideas coming. None at all. But the poor old heart knew what was happening. Pounding away like mad. It wasn't going to forget about what just happened. That's for sure. And whatever it was that just happened, lasted for days.

"Are you alright?"

The evil little mate was back again. Into him straight away.

Frank wasn't all right at all. Nothing like it.

"Yes, yes! I'm alright! I'm alright!"

Just staring straight ahead. Seeing nothing and talking to nobody. Yeah, he was alright. Like fucking hell. Next minute, the evil one's back again. Hovering over him, like some starving vulture. She bent down and moved her head around. Yes, she was staring straight into his eyes again. With that big, warm friendly smile, stuck on her beautiful face. The energy beam thing was happening again. Boring straight into his already confused brain. The flip, just had to come back and look at her again, didn't he? This girl's completely fucking crazy. Yeah. That was the only conclusion available.

She must have known what the thinking was. Because she suddenly broke off the eye contact. Straightened up, turned around and took off. Frank's head turned automatically as she was walking away. This girl had a few extra little lumps of beef here and there, you know. So maybe she wasn't so young after all. Not as young as the rest of the girls anyway.

After stuffing down the lunch and drinking the cold coffee, it was a case of getting up, going for a pee, and then getting the hell out of there. As quick as possible. Exactly what should have happened in the first place. Getting the hell out of there, that is. Before all this shit started.

"See you later Frank! Have a nice day!"

Didn't know who said that and didn't care. Didn't bother taking a quick look to find out either. Just wanted to be gone. Never going back there, ever again. Wasn't going to cop any of her shit. That's for sure. Driving home, Frank decided she must have been some kind of a fucking witch or something. As well as a bitch. An evil little bitch and a fucking witch. And crazy as well. Fucking hell. Both of them. Her and her little fucking mate. Two of a kind, alright. Both crazy.

"Hello, I'm Frank and I'm a compulsive gambler."

"Hi Frank!"

"Hello Frank!"

"Hello Frank!"

The usual response from all the other members, who were there.

"I busted the other day! But it wasn't my fault! Some girl made me do it. A real little bitch. She got into my head and almost sent me crazy. It was three days, before I had no money left. I lost about three and a half thousand dollars. I've had no sleep and nothing to eat and I'm just about fucked."

The emotion was building up, alright, so the talking just had to stop. Just sat there, staring at the table. Before remembering. There were procedures to be followed at GA meetings, you know.

"Thanks for letting me share."

Every one clapped. They always did, no matter what was said. Then a few of the other members started offering a few comments. Then asking questions. About who this girl was and how did he know her and how come she almost sent him crazy.

"Reminds me of me ex, mate! What a bitch she was eh!"

Yeah, just couldn't help themselves.

"There're all the same, mate! Can't trust none of them!"

A couple of the female members jumped in, with a little bit of their knowledge about men.

"Yes, it's always our fault, isn't it! You slimy pigs, never do anything wrong!"

"Driving men crazy! It's just what we do!"

Well, there were all kinds of advice and comments, coming from everywhere. Everyone was pissing themselves laughing by now. Or at least, trying not to. Frank was just sitting there with the head down, looking miserable. The controller took over. Quietened everyone back down. Yeah. The controller, knew how to take control, alright.

"That's bad news, Frank. But everyone busts. We all have. Talking about why it happened, is the best thing to do. Understanding why it happened. Then not letting it happen again. At least you're back here talking about it."

All the laughing stopped as soon as the controller started talking. The long-term members just sat there listening, with knowing looks on their faces. They all knew where Frank was. As far as feeling the pain and misery, associated with busting. And the emotionally sinking feeling of failure that always came with it. Yes, they'd all been there. Some more than others. But I bet none of them ever had the most beautiful girl in the world, haunting their every thought. Fucking bitch.

Causing them to sink into a nervous depression and sending them back to the poker machines. No, none of them would know anything about that would they. Well maybe they did. Anyway, Frank was just about gone now. The internal emotions were exploding everywhere. But the controller was pretty smart, you know.

"Anyway, Frank! Remember when you first turned up? You looked like something the cat dragged in. You leant in the doorway. Didn't even want to come in. I had to just about drag you in. Remember that, Frank?"

Everyone cracked up laughing again. Frank's head lifted straight up. He remembered, alright. Started laughing as well. That got the controller on a real roll. Just couldn't stop. But also knew when to stop talking. Frank had seen the controller in action before, when a member stuffed up. Knew how to release the emotional pressure out of the compulsives. That's for sure. And now it was his turn.

"You looked a real mess, Frank! Remember! You had those old ugg boots on. With all that electrical tape holding them together. And that old coat. Stiffer that a piece of cardboard. It had so many stains on it, you couldn't even see what colour it was. And you stunk like a polecat, Frank! I almost told you to get lost! You don't know how lucky you were, even getting into this place! You were a total grub!"

By now, there wasn't one member who wasn't pissing themselves laughing. Frank had tears rolling down his cheeks. Tears of joy that is. Yes, going from the deepest level of pain and misery that only a long-term compulsive gambler could understand. To the lofty heights of emotional elation. In just a few short minutes. And this was involuntary emotion, you know. No thinking involved. It just happened.

Yes, the controller was a true psychological genius. That's for sure. And the only qualifications involved was real life experience. That's all. And you can't get real life experience, any other way. Other than having lived it. Everyone had the highest respect for the controller. You could tell that. But Frank didn't like being called a grub, you know. But he never said anything about that.

This meeting finished in the usual way. God give me the serenity and all the rest of that bullshit. Then the little hand holding ceremony.

After the meeting finished, one of the other compulsives approached Frank.

"This girl you're talking about. How do you know her?"

"Well, I don't really know her. She just works at a café I go to, that's all."

"Would that be the café near the ocean baths?"

"Yes, but how do you know that?"

"My wife knows the girls who work there. There're going to have a lot of fun with you!"

Then he just smiled, turned around and walked out.

What the fuck was that supposed to mean anyway. Frank thought about it, while driving home. Was still thinking about it several days later. Just couldn't stop thinking about what this other compulsive said. There're going to have a lot of fun with you. There're going to have a lot of fun with you. There're going to have a lot of fun with you. Over and over again. And over again. What the fuck was that supposed to mean anyway.

"Oh, they are, are they? So that's their game, is it? Well, we'll soon see about that, won't we!"

Yes, Frank started talking to himself more and more. And it was all about the girls in the café and one girl in particular. The idea of hating her was creeping into the head now. After what that other compulsive said. But no hate was really there at all. But the little bitch did get into the head, you know. Didn't know how she did that and it wasn't a good thought to be having in there either. But she put it in there didn't she? What a clever little witch.

How the fucking hell, did she do that anyway? Maybe there was imagination going on, you know. That wasn't an unusual thing at all. But Frank was sure, he was sure there was no imagination happening. No, it was her, alright. She got in there. The bitch. But she wouldn't be doing it again. Nothing could be surer than that.

And that thought of how there're going to have a lot of fun with you was always at the top of the thinking now. Whenever it was time to enter the danger zone.

Yeah! The defensive strategies started formulating, you know. Next visit to the café, there'd be no looking at her. No eye-contact. She was too good at that game, anyway. Just, ignore the bitch. Pretend she wasn't even there. But wait a minute. Never going back there again. Ever. Remember. Yeah. But decided to forget about remembering about that. Didn't take long either.

Maybe just one more time, you know. Give the most beautiful girl in the world, a bit of her own medicine. Wasn't about to let this little popped-up tart get the better of the situation. There was a war going on here now and things were just starting to warm up. And the figuring was there was no way she was going to win. That's for sure.

"Oh dear, Frank! You've let yourself down badly, haven't you? But that's okay! You're going to the right place! I can only talk to you and offer you advice. But these people at Gamblers Anonymous understand you, Frank. They just want to help you. That's all! I know you'll get there, Frank! We all have great confidence in you! By the way Frank! She may be trying to help you, you know!"

"What! Help me! Don't be stupid! She's trying to fucking kill me!"

Right at this moment, the last thing that was needed was the lady in the head. She meant well, alright. Yeah. Just trying to help. Just like everyone else. But no one asked for any help in the first place, did they? Never got help from anyone in the whole life. Of course, that would be the whole old life wouldn't it. Didn't know about any help in the old life. Didn't understand about help.

The dopey old bastard got plenty of help in the old life, you know.

And there was plenty more help on the way in the new life as well. Only, there was no way of knowing that yet. Anyway, there was still a lot of confusion going on. Between the old life and the new life. And there was no instruction manual either.

There're going to have a lot of fun with you.

"I don't feel so well! I think it's food poisoning!"

You should have seen the look on her face, when that one came out. Put the wind right up her. Got rid of her too. Then one of the boys from the old life, just happened to wander into the café. Not the drunken bum either. This guy liked a drink or two, but was no alcoholic. Just an old mate. With a big presence in his younger days. A good street fighter. And a good bloke. Known him for years. The recognition was there straight away.

"Hey Frank! Thought it was you, mate!

"Hey! How you going! Long time, no see!"

He sat straight down, like he was expected or something. The lunch had just been finished and there were only a few sips of coffee left. Would've been gone in five minutes. But was ready for a little catch-up chat, with this old mate. Then that nosey bitch was right there again. Like she had to know, who this other bloke was. Must have been watching all the time. Nosey little, evil fucking bitch.

Anyway, that's when the idea came. About putting the miserable look on the face and rubbing the stomach.

"Oh, the pain is killing me! It must be food poisoning! Has to be!"

The stupid bitch, believed every word of it.

"He's just pulling your chain, love!"

The old mate just blurted that one out. Yeah. The look on the face. Worth gold to the old fella. And who was smiling now. Not her. That's for sure. Stupid bitch. Yeah. Put the horror look on. Goes to say something. But says nothing. Just turns around and storms off. Like a cranky cow. That'll teach her. Get that up ya. Bitch. Couldn't be happier about how this one turned out. Put it up as a win, eh.

"Oh Frank! That's a terrible way to think! The poor girl! You've, hurt her feelings!"

Yeah right. Well, what about this old boy's feelings. She didn't care about those feelings, did she? Too bad, there'd never been any feelings there in the first place. But this was no time to be thinking about feelings. Got the bitch. Fixed her right up.

"Oh dear! This is not good at all!"

"He's making no real progress. We've made a mistake with this one! He's a failure! We should send him back! There's plenty of others to choose from!"

"Yes, we should send him back! Before it's too late! Some of them are just so non-retractable! And this is obviously one of them!"

"I agree! Send him back! We could destroy him altogether, if we continue!"

"No! No! Please! I still believe there's a chance of redemption! Let's give him one more chance! I think he can make it! I really do!"

"Well, he'll be your responsibility then dear!"

"Yes, I agree! He'll be your responsibility!"

"Right! We'll give him one more chance then! Is there anyone against the idea? No! Ok then! One more chance it is! But only one! Is that understood?"

"Yes! That's understood! He'll be my responsibility! I'm sure he can make it! I'm sure he will, eventually!"

Yeah. There'd been lots of help by quite a few people, during the old life. But forgetting about pretty much all of the previous life was too easy. Ever since waking up in hospital the last time, the mind had been filling up with new information, you know. From new experiences. From new people. There was a re-loading process going on. Right from when that lady appeared out of nowhere. Then the most beautiful girl in the world got in there. Causing havoc.

And hearing all the sad stories at the GA meetings. And the rest of the café girls being in there as well. All enough to drive anyone completely crazy. And it almost did. Yes, drowning in new information. And a new kind of craziness. Fucking hell.

There're going to have a lot of fun with you.

And with that in there as well. Head explosion on the way, alright.

But something else that had been completely forgotten about. Was that craziness had always been part of the old life. And when little bits and pieces of these past crazy times, did came to the surface, is when all the trouble really started. Relating to what actually happened and if that stuff really happened at all. But all that stuff must have happened. Otherwise, how did it get into the head in the first place. A real puzzle, alright. And no one else could work it all out. There was only one person who could work it all out and that was the biggest problem.

"That's not right at all, Frank! All the help you need, is available! I'm always here for you! You know that! Where're always here for you, Frank! Always!"

"Yeah! Yeah! Yeah!"

Oh shit. Talking to himself again.

"Well, I'll be going now, Frank! But we'll talk again soon! A little break might do us both the world of good!"

Yeah well, she got that bit right.

One such memory, that leaked out by surprise was all about a boxing match. Yeah, in the ring. Slugging it out with this other bloke. After belting this guy for three 2-minute rounds, Frank was ahead on points. Just before the end of round three, smashed the other guy with a big right hand. Smack in the middle of the face. The poor bastard just stood there in the middle of the ring, swaying around a bit. Eyes blinking slowly. The referee was taking a close look.

"Hit the cunt again! Hit the cunt again!"

That's what the trainer was screaming out. But Frank didn't hit the cunt again. Just stood there, with the right fist clenched tight. Ready to hit the cunt again, but didn't hit him. Didn't want to hit this guy again. Should have but. The bell rang to end the round. Needed the rest, alright. The other guy was just about to fall over. His trainer and corner men helped their boy back to their corner and started working their magic.

"Why didn't you hit him again! Are you deaf or something! That would have finished it! You would have knocked the cunt out! Now go out there and finish him!"

Ding, ding, ding. Round four was under way. The last round. Whatever they did to the other guy and whatever was said, worked, alright. Came out swinging, like a mad man. Complete opposite to the first three rounds. Frank copped a hiding. Managed to get a few good shots in as well, but was gassed right out. Lost the round. Ahead enough on points, to be declared the winner. But only just.

Frank only started boxing, because of getting flattened twice in a club one day. Couldn't remember the circumstances leading up to this episode. Yeah. Still into heavy drinking and drugs, you know. Making all kinds of dumb decisions. And getting sucked into putting the hands up on this occasion was one of the dumbest ever. That's for sure. Wasn't hurt at all, because the head was as hard as a lump of concrete. With nothing much in it, eh?

But the reactions were shot, you know. Couldn't function. Just froze up. Down and back up. Then down and back up again. The other guy was a big lump of a bloke. Knew how to throw a punch. That's for sure. Didn't want to hit this poor bastard again, so just sat back down. After wandering around for a while, the drained out, pathetic, completely obliterated, pissed to the eye balls junkie, wandered out of the club and wandered home.

This unfortunate episode caused another downward spiral into the deep darkness of depression. But downward spirals of depression were nothing unusual. So, there was nothing to worry about. Familiar territory, alright. Just went with it. What was different this time was the discovery of poker machines along the way. While down there in the black world, dabbling here and there with the machines, a new discovery was made.

Drifting into another black world was a great way of forgetting about the other black worlds altogether. But not really forgetting about the other black worlds at all. Just hiding from them. Drifting from one black world into another black world. An even blacker, black world. But there was a liking for the black worlds, you know. Frank had been in all of them. Lots of times.

Yeah. Frank, knew his way around in the black worlds. That's for sure. But the black world of poker machines became the new favourite black world. Right from the start. These were the days when silver coins were dropped into the slot. One at a time and the handle was pulled down. They were called one arm bandits. Added another dimension, alright.

Soon realised, when playing the bandits; as they were called, nowhere land was the end destination. Where nothing mattered. Because no thinking was required in nowhere land. Of course, alcoholics and drug addicts, always lived in nowhere land anyway. Felt relaxed in nowhere land. Yes, always safe in nowhere land. No one ever bothered anyone in nowhere land. Most of the time anyway. So peaceful in there, you know. Never wanted to come out. That's for sure. Blacker than black. And black had always been the favourite colour. When everything's black, no other colour shows up anyway. Made the life so easy. Just so easy.

There was the colour white, I suppose. But the black had this way of absorbing the white. If the white ever did try and show up. Which almost happened, every now and then.

No, there was never any long-lasting light in nowhere land. And no one could see anyone else in nowhere land. Or, at least that's what they thought, when they were in there. If they decided to start thinking about that at all, which was unlikely. But anyone could see who was in nowhere land, just by looking at them. But whoever was in nowhere land, didn't even think about who saw them in there.

Because when there're in there, they don't care about anything else. And they don't hear anything else. They don't want to know about anything else. They don't want to be disturbed. Except by the machines. When they get a big pay. Or hit the feature. Or even the big jackpot. Which almost never happens anyway. And so, the terrible poker machine addiction began.

A few weeks after getting flattened, Frank decided to go to a gym. Where there was a boxing trainer. Wandered in there and started learning about how to fight properly. There was this idea of learning how to fight and then going back to that club and belting the shit out of that bastard, who took advantage of him. When the drugs and the drink had possession of the whole body and what was left functioning in the slopped-up brain.

So pissed and out of it, you know. Couldn't think straight. Couldn't think at all. But that idea just went missing didn't it. What happened was. Well, you already know what happened, eh. And this club episode was forgotten about anyway. Until years later. That happened all the time, you know. Remembering about things that happened, years later.

After the one and only professional fight, Frank decided to retire undefeated. This was shortly after the trainer mentioned a few things.

"You're soft in the middle, son! You haven't got what it takes to make it in boxing! Maybe you should go and get a job! Selling vacuum cleaners or something!"

Everyone in the gym, cracked up laughing. So, this was the easiest decision ever made. Got the message, alright. About never going back there again. And never did.

One thing about that fight that will never be forgotten; was what happened after climbing out of the ring when it was all over. A whole bunch of people came rushing towards them and they were all this other guy's friends. There seemed to be hundreds of them. Frank kind of almost shit himself, when they arrived. But the slaps on the back started coming.

"Good fight, man! Good fight!"

"Yeah, good fight, man!"

There were big smiles everywhere. Even the guy who lost was smiling. They all couldn't be happier. No bad feelings anywhere. What a big surprise this was. Thought they were going to take revenge, for beating their friend. But they just loved the fighting game, you know. It didn't matter who was doing the fighting either. Or who won or lost. They just got off on it. Simple as that. There were a few girls there too. Giving the big smiles everywhere. Could have been in there for sure. Only the trainer came over and ruined everything.

"OK, the party's over!"

There was no time for socialising. The trainer had no more fighters on the card, so no mucking around. Straight out of the club, and straight back up the highway.

There was never any real recovery from this failed attempt, at becoming a somebody. Instead of the nobody that had always been there. Whenever looking in a mirror, this nobody was staring straight back and that didn't help things at all. But there was nothing to be done about it either. Nothing at all.

Although, there was no solid memory of ever looking in a mirror before. The first time was in that hospital toilet. After the first ever pee. After the lady appeared beside the bed, with all the news about a new life. That nothing was known about or understood. Yes, the lady who wasn't there but she was there. Caused all kinds of problems. Right from the start. But knowing she was there and hearing what she said couldn't be denied. Or forgotten about. That's as far back as the memories went, whenever any remembering was attempted.

So, that's where it all must have started. This new life business. Back at the hospital. With the lady who wasn't there. There was no trouble remembering that bit. That's for sure. Although, there were sure to be other memories back there somewhere. Older memories. That were just hiding in the dark shadows. Ready to leap out, for a surprise attack. And that happened lots of times.

When the getting fitter programme was up and running, the backyard is where it all started. Yeah, around and around the yard. Reaching the back-fence the first time, almost stopped it all before it even got started. The lungs was puffed right out. The poor old heart was pounding. Walking back to clothes line was a big effort. The breathing eventually returned to where it should have been. Before this new craziness began.

Took several days before one complete circuit of the yard was achieved, without stopping. Then twice around and then three times. The confidence was building, alright. Started running up and down the street, for a few hundred metres each way. Wasn't long before that developed into several kilometres each morning. Then some jumping around in the backyard. Eventually learnt about calisthenics. So, the jumping around slowly got refined a lot. Till a programme was developed, according to how all the exercises should be done properly.

There was a big self-conscious feeling at first, you know. Imagine an old guy in the mid-sixties. Probably about 40 kilos overweight. Running around the neighbourhood, like a teenager. A heart attack waiting to happen. That's for sure. The dope, didn't take it easy either. Into it, full steam ahead. 100 miles an hour. One extreme to the other. No wonder after a few days, physical movement became a big issue. Couldn't walk. Couldn't even get out of bed. Completely fucked. But kept at it, you know. You have to give the old bastard credit for that, eh.

What an effort it was struggling to get up. Into the bathroom for a pee. Then to the fridge for a few beers. That'd do the trick. Fix things right up. Get some fluid back into the system. Opens the fridge and reaches for a can. Yeah, just busting for a good session on the grog.

"Don't do it Frank! Don't do it! Think about what you're doing, Frank! Please! Think about what you're doing!"

Oh fuck no. Not her again. Not now. But it was the lady, alright. Hadn't heard from her for a while. She said she'd be back and here she was. Knew what was coming now. Didn't want to hear it all again. Always the same shit. But the guilt trip started as soon as she started up. And that was an uneasy feeling.

"You've come such a long way, Frank! Don't ruin it all now! Tip all that beer down the sink, Frank! Go on Frank! You can do it! Tip it down the sink! We know you can do it! Imagine how fit and healthy you will get, without all that beer! And those drugs, Frank? You have to stop smoking those drugs!"

Fucking hell. Here we go again. Another big decision that had to be made. The lady was always calling pot drugs, you know. Thought that was pretty funny. It was only pot for Christ's sake. Not drugs. She didn't even know the difference. Anyway, the cans got opened up, one by one and emptied down the sink, didn't they? This was not an easy thing to be doing either. That's for sure. Pure agony.

"You did it Frank! You did it! This is such a huge step forward for you, Frank! A huge step! I knew you could do it! We all knew you could do it! Well done, Frank! Well done!"

Yeah right. Feeling like shit. But she wouldn't understand anything about that would she. She had to go. Yes, something had to be done about the lady. She was driving him fucking crazy. She'd already got in there and wiped out the old life. Or was trying to. Now she was fucking up the whole new life as well. Yeah. She had to go.

Would have been better off listening to that nurse, when she said there was no lady there at all. When she was there, but wasn't there. But she was there, alright. And she was still there. And she was going nowhere. Anyone could know that. That's when everything started going wrong, you know. As soon as that fucking lady turned up.

But the lady didn't know about the plants, did she? Not the ones that were pulled out. Or the ones that were accidentally poisoned. Or the ones over the side fence, near the creek. But they were still there, you know. So, she wasn't so smart after all, was she? Yeah. Over the fence to get enough pot to roll up a big, fat joint and wander off to some wonderland and stay there. At least for a few hours anyway. That was the latest plan. But that's not what happened.

What a shock it was. Some bastard put a whole bunch of cows in the vacant land and they'd eaten all the grass and weeds and the plants. The fucking things had eaten everything. No leaves lying around or broken off bits and pieces of storks or anything. To scrape together for a joint. Devastation and shock invaded the whole internal structure, alright.

This land next door had been empty for years. Next minute, it's full of fucking cows and there've eaten everything. Now there was no beer and no pot and not even a cigarette. And no food in the house either. Fucking hell. What a nightmare.

Had to settle for a drink of water. Yeah. Been drinking lots of water lately. Exercising. Losing weight and drinking lots of fucking water. Water was for washing in, not for drinking. That was an old memory. Must have plucked it out from somewhere.

Eating in cafes had become the normal thing now. Ever since the continual feeding of those rotten poker machines stopped. The fucking idiot feeling wasn't so strong now either. Always enough money, to be looked after a bit better in the new life. But there was still a long way to go. And yes, busting did happen a few times. Well, more than a few times. But that was always because someone else did the upsetting. Enough to cause an emotional flip out.

Then it was back to GA, to get the head sorted out. Yeah. The GA meetings. An emotional flip out trip within themselves. That's for sure. There were plenty of down sides for compulsive gamblers, you know. At GA meetings, the compulsives told you about all of them. They knew everything about everything. That wasn't good to know anything about. That's for sure.

But they also learnt a lot about themselves in the process. Especially the one where're concentrating on here. What made the head tick and what really pissed it off. This new head. That was still getting stuffed full of new information. Learning about life. Like a new born adult infant. And especially understanding, what sent it back to the machines. And learning about other people as well. Too bad they were all compulsives, eh. That's what they were all called now, you know. Compulsives. And no one was going to teach the big new compulsive baby anything other than a bunch of other compulsives.

The nieces turned out to be good girls, you know. Convincing their wayward uncle to visit the gym for the first time. Had to do the talking around bit first. That was the hardest part. But they were so determined, you know. Got the old fool there in the end. To at least try it out.

"Come on Uncle Frank! Come with us! Just once! See if you like it there! You'll never know, unless you try! Come on! Give it a go!"

Yeah, their persistence paid off. Loved the place straight away. Wasn't long before it was a 5.30 start, every morning. That's the time it opened. Taking it easy for a while would have been the smart thing to do. But that didn't happen. Just like running around. Too much too quick. Ended up stiffer than a plank. Fucking idiot.

A few of the personal trainers tried to get the message through. About taking it easy for a few weeks. Gradually building up to heavier weights. But listening was never a developed attribute, you know. But this time, listening would have been a good idea. That's for sure. The decision was made. Never to go back to the gym. Ever again. The place was killing him. Just another fucking nightmare.

Anyway, those personal trainers, you know. They were always on the lookout for more beginners to personally train. And drain money out of as well. Wasn't falling for that old trick. Yeah. Getting smarter all the time.

"Oh Frank! Stop thinking so negative all the time! This is only the beginning! Keep going! You don't know what you're capable of! Follow your instincts Frank! Just follow your instincts! That's all you need to do! Don't give up Frank!

Don't give up! You've come such a long way! Don't give up now! Just keep going! You can do it, Frank! We all have great confidence in you!"

Fucking hell. Here she goes again. But she was right, as usual. And she probably also knew that if the fridge was full of beer, it would have disappeared. The whole lot of it. In one session. Till it came out of the ears. And if there were any plants anywhere, they wouldn't have lasted long either. Pulled out. Rolled up into nice, fat joints and that wonderful place called nowhere land would have been calling. Or was it wonderland. Anyway, it didn't matter. Either one would have been better than right now. Hadn't been there for so long, you know. Missed the place, alright. Whatever that place was.

The eventual decision was to stay clean. No easy decision either. Sat on the back veranda for hours, thinking about it. Although, getting up from time to time. Double checking the fridge. Looking under the beds. In a few cupboards and anywhere else previously used to keep emergency supplies was a bit of a worry. But there was no luck, or bad luck. In finding anything. Nothing anywhere. This no doubt, assisted in the decision-making process.

There'd been cheating a few times, here and there. With the grog. Managing without the weed was hard at first. The cravings were enormous. Filled the new head completely. But beer was too easy to get hold of, you know. There were bottle shops everywhere and there was one only a few kilometres down the road.

Yeah. Always sneaking down to get a carton. Sneaking down there was necessary. Because if the lady found out. She'd be onto him. What she didn't know wouldn't hurt her but, eh. But she probably knew anyway. Kind of figured that she did. She knew about everything else.

Every session on the grog, forced the guilty feelings to resurface; resulting in another cleaning rampage through the house. Or mowing the back lawn. Yes, there was a lawn mower now. A ride on lawnmower. Almost new. Had it all along. Was in one of the old garden sheds. Hadn't touched the thing for nine years. That's when the house was bought. Hardly ever went into that little shed and forgot the mower was even there.

Got the tyres pumped up. Got some petrol into it. Eventually started it and started mowing. Until the thing just stopped mowing. So, down on the hands and knees. Took a look underneath. Fucking hell. One of the belts had crumbled to pieces and the other two were full of splits. And two of the tyres had gone flat again.

Well, that's fucked that up. Back into the shed it went. A few weeks later, Frank drove past this place that sold ride on lawnmowers. Parked and went in. Explained to the bloke behind the counter what the situation was. The guy listened, alright, with a big smile on the face.

"Mate, we don't carry parts for those old mowers anymore! And they don't make the belts anymore either!"

But luckily, one of the repair guys was there and heard the conversation.

"We might still have some old belts out the back! I'll go check!"

Anyway, turns out there were a few belts and a few other bits and pieces. So, Frank went home and got a neighbour to help load the mower onto the trailer and deliver it to the lawnmower place. Six weeks later, there was a phone call.

"Hello, is that Frank!"

"Yeah, that's me! What do you want?"

Never good with phones, you know.

"Your mowers ready, mate!"

"Oh right! How much was it?"

"We put new belts on! New spark plug! Cleaned out the carbie! Gave it a good tune up! Tightened up the brake!"

"Yeah, sounds good! But how much was it!"

There was no point listening to all that shit. Didn't understand a word of what this guy was on about. All this lawnmower talk. Just caused more confusion, you know. The only thing worth understanding was how much. No point hearing anything else.

"All up! $650."

"Fucking hell!"

The other end of the phone went dead quiet, didn't it.

The neighbour helped pick it up and now there was a lawnmower. A $650 lawnmower. That was there in the shed. The whole time. What a fucking idiot.

So, the backyard was now regularly mowed. Yeah, here's Frank sitting on the veranda. With a strong cup of coffee. Big smile on his face. Yeah, feeling very good about things. Always coffee now, by the way. Nothing else but coffee. And water.

Well and truly on the way to recovery now. The positive feelings were happening, alright. But these positive feelings and the recovery thing had all been there before, you know. Years ago. In the previous life, that could hardly be remembered. Except in bits and pieces. But something always happened that opened up the old wounds. Usually, some bastard upsetting the internal mechanism. Or some smart arse, little bitch. Or even some lady that wasn't even there.

There was still little understanding about what to do, when some arsehole came along and mixed up the thought processes. And that still didn't take much. Not much at all. And it all built up, over a few days, or weeks, or months sometimes. Then the emotional structure slowly lost the balance again. All patience, understanding or thinking, flew out the window. And it was back in there again. Into the black worlds. Yes, getting blotto, smoking pot and playing poker machines were always the only avenues for escape. The only ones that ever worked anyway, especially playing the machines. Reality was just blotted out, whenever in action. That's what they called it in GA. Being in action.

The thought of re-entering reality was only a last resort. And only ever happened, after losing all available money and that was most of the time. On seconds thoughts. This compulsive loser had never been in reality. Not real reality anyway. Living on a personal merry-go-round, might sound like fun. But it was no fun. Especially, if there was only one horse on it. Well, more like a donkey than a horse. And everybody knew who that donkey was. That's for sure.

The backyard was looking good. And going berserk with the cleaning inside the house was happening as well. Cleaned everything properly. First time ever, since moving in. Swept the wooden floors. Vacuumed the carpets. Cleaned the bathroom. What an effort that was. Dead flies and cockroaches everywhere. And yes, even the kitchen sink got scrubbed clean. Took several days to do all this.

"You're doing so well now, Frank! You've accomplished something really worthwhile here! Look what you've done! Just look at how clean and tidy your house is now! You should be so proud of yourself!"

Too bad about being completely fucked, eh. But how would she know anything about that. She never got in and helped, did she? Always good with the orders. Well, not really orders. More like suggestions. That just sounded like orders. From now on, she was going to get put in her place. That was the latest decision. And it had to be done. Survival was at stake here now. Didn't need her hanging around anymore, anyway.

One day, during one of these frenzied cleaning sessions, a look was taken behind a bedroom door. For the first time in nine years. There, right in front of the eyes was a carpet sweeper.

"Well, I'll be fucked!"

The carpets had already been vacuumed, but it was an old vacuum cleaner. There were still bits of fluff and crumbs everywhere. But not after a good run over with the carpet sweeper. Yeah, new discoveries were being made, about what was hidden away in the house. And there were a few more to come as well.

The people who sold the house, left it full of furniture and kitchen items, blankets, sheets, pillow cases and all sorts of other essential household items that had never even been used. The cupboards and wardrobes were full of all kinds of good stuff. Knowing they were full was one thing. But checking to see what was there. That idea never even entered the head. Why would it anyway.

"Hello, I'm Frank and I'm a compulsive gambler."

"Hi Frank!"

"Yeah! Hi Frank!"

"Hello Frank!"

"I've been going well! Still haven't played poker machines!"

"Ah, well done, Frank!"

"Good on ya, mate!"

"Yeah, well done, mate!"

The controller and a few of the regulars were quick to jump in there. Everyone gave the big clap, you know. All these compulsive gamblers, knew just how easy it was to have a bust and slip back into black abyss of pain, misery and self-imposed, psychological torture. That's for sure.

"I'm still off the grog and no weed either. I'm so proud of myself! I've got great confidence in myself now! I've been going to the gym. I've started running! All around the neighbourhood! I'm as fit as a thirty-year-old! I'm just following my instincts, you know! That's all! It's easy! There's, no stopping me now! I'm so glad I came here!"

Everyone was cracking up by this stage.

"That's great news Frank! See, if you work the programme, the programme will work, for you! But be careful! Don't drop your guard! Because the compulsion will always be there, Frank! It will just wait till you're in a weak moment and then it will strike! And all your good work will come undone!"

"Always remember! You are a compulsive gambler! Not you were a compulsive gambler. Not even an ex-compulsive gambler. Today, you are a compulsive gambler. Tomorrow, you will still be a compulsive gambler. And you will die a compulsive gambler. The only decision to make, is whether you will die free from an active life of gambling or not."

Well, all that settled the mood back down again didn't it.

Yeah right. Here we go again. Decisions. Decisions. Decisions. Yeah. Brought everything back down to earth, alright. With a thud. The whole room went dead quiet. Everyone knew the controller was right. Heard enough stories, about how a compulsive can be up there enjoying their life. Free from the strangle hold of the machines or the TAB or the race track or whatever. But then come crashing back down. Because of one thing or another.

Strangely enough, it always seemed to be something related to emotional instability that usually caused the disaster. Didn't take long to figure out what a fragile lot these compulsives could be. And being fragile was something in there, that couldn't be denied. There was no doubt about that now. None whatsoever.

"And I cleaned my whole house out too. I feel like I've accomplished something really worthwhile! Yes, I'm going so well now! I'm so proud of myself! Well, that's it from me! Thanks for letting me share."

Another big round of applause. There was no denying the flush of positive vibes that flowed through the whole emotional structure, when the clapping started. Especially this time.

"Would anyone else like to share?"

There were a few more shares. And listening to some of these other shares was always a sobering experience, you know. Some of the compulsives, repeated the same story, every time. But that didn't matter. What had to be said was said. Simple as that. In that respect, everyone was in the same situation. And that was usually a bad situation. Or, they wouldn't even be there would they. But the same amount of support and good wishes, came from all the other compulsives. No matter who was sharing, or what they were sharing. And of course, there were always the odd words of good advice from the controller. Yeah. Meeting over. Here we go again.

"To the God of our own understanding!"

All together now.

"God, give me the strength to accept the things I cannot change! The courage to change the things I can! And the wisdom to know the difference!"

Can't forget about the stupid fucking hand holding bit, eh.

All together now.

"Thanks for sharing! Thanks for caring! Keep coming back! The meetings make it!"

What a lot of shit. Still couldn't quite get the head around the God bit. Driving home after this particular meeting, lots of thinking started happening. There were usually between six and twenty compulsives at each meeting, you know. But there were several thousand poker machines, scattered throughout society. In every pub and club. And hundreds and thousands of players.

The thinking was that how many of these players were compulsives, like the ones at GA. And how many of them should be at the GA meetings. Getting help to stop being compulsives. And if they weren't compulsives, then how could they play the machines and not become compulsives. But the thinking just wasn't capable enough to work that one out. So, giving up was the only option and that's what happened.

"Hi Frank! Just the usual?

"Yes please, just the usual."

"You look good today, Frank! Are they new clothes?"

"Uh, yes! I thought it was about time I got some nice new clothes!"

Liar. The only new clothes he ever bought were underpants. Even Frank couldn't imagine the idea, of stepping into someone else's used underpants. Some standards were still there, you know.

"Well, you look great, Frank!"

"Yes, you sure do, Frank!"

"Check out Frank's new clothes!"

There were about four or five of them there now. All smiling that warm friendly, café girl smile. Yeah, just loving it. Till the huge embarrassment set in. Warming the face up and making what was in the chest, beat faster. Quickly paid for lunch, turned around and headed for the table. The girls got a good little giggle out of it. Nothing unusual about that.

This ended up the shortest amount of time ever spent in the café. Even shorter than the time, when the first attack happened. By the most beautiful girl in the world. There was some kind of new trouble, happening in the head right now. Nothing that could be explained either. But it was in there, alright. Emotional disturbances were still bubbling away. And they weren't going to stop. Just had to get out of there.

"There you go Frank! Enjoy!"

Lunch and coffee together. Loved it when that happened.

"Oh thanks!"

"Do you let thinks bother you, Frank? When they build up inside you and you can't relax!"

She had no real reason to say that, you know. But she was the knowing girl, this one. Had that look about her. That said it's ok. Everything will be fine. Just relax. What an instant, calming influence she had, with those lovely light blue eyes gazing down upon him.

And there was usually a little conversation as well. Whenever the opportunity was there. But not this time. And what a relief that was. For sure. Because there were more cracks opening up. Let me out of here. Let me out of here. And that thought was getting louder.

She only hesitated for a short time, before heading back to the counter. But the look on her face and the different little smile said it all. She knew, alright. That's why she was the knowing girl.

Yeah. Lunch and coffee. Downed in record time. And out of there. Not even enough time, for a good perve. Didn't even check out the counter. To see if any girls needed saying goodbye to.

Anyway, they didn't have to know, the new clothes came from St Vincent de Pauls, did they? Or St Vinnies as it was called. Or just plain Vinnies. All these new clothes came from there. They were the cheapest clothes anywhere. And there was always some good stuff on the racks. His mother was always at Vinnies. Especially in her later years, which were arguably the best years. Because she did what she liked. When she liked, with no one controlling her life.

Until of course, the time came for the nursing home. The little conversations with the mother during this time, will always be special. That's one thing the new life had already given the understanding of. How something could be special. Nothing had ever been special or meant anything. Ever before. Especially between this mother and son.

That may sound a bit cold. But that's just the way it was. Sad but true. But changes were gradually happening now. Not that were fully understood or anything. But they were happening, alright. Yes, there were lots of changes happening right now.

Just about to get into the car, when it became clear. And took over the mind completely. Driving right now would have been impossible. So, something that had never happened before, happened.

Sitting on the sand, staring out over the ocean. With no glass window and no g-strings on display. And no other disturbances. What caused this change in the normal routine, came flooding in.

She was just sitting there in her chair, resting.

"Oh hello! No one ever comes to see me! You're the only visitor I've had!"

"Hello mum! Well, I'm here now! So, that's one visitor you're getting! Would you like a cup of coffee?"

It was understood that forgetfulness was now the major issue. Dementia and Alzheimer's, you know. Both progressing. Getting worse all the time.

"Yes, I'd love a cup of coffee!"

"OK then! How about we go for a walk around to the visitor's room and we'll have a coffee there?"

So, they get to the visitor's room. All the facilities were there, for making cups of coffee and tea. Biscuits were available as well. It only took a few minutes preparing the coffees, before taking the three steps to where his mother was sitting.

"Oh hello! I never get any visitors!"

"Hi mum! Would you like a cup of coffee?"

"Yes, I'd love a cup of coffee!"

"I thought you would! Here you go! So, how have you been going?"

It was an accepted reality by now, that his mother was sometimes not quite with it. But at other times was fully aware of what was going on. And she could drift from one state to the other, a number of times in the space of a few minutes. Frank knew all about drifting. And now, conversations with his mother were always a hit and miss proposition.

"Poor Dorothy! She didn't know what happened to the rest of us!"

Yeah. Suddenly coming out with random comments was nothing unusual now. Could happen at any time.

Frank already knew about Dorothy. And knew lots of other stuff about his mother's early life as well. She kept mentioning little bits and pieces, during every visit. Like they were little secrets that she'd never told anyone before. And Frank pretended he'd never already knew about any of them. That was the best thing to do. Just let her talk away, like no one else was even there.

Sometimes, she talked for as long as her coffee lasted. Or only for five or ten minutes. And sometimes, not very long at all. Then she would just stop talking and give the blank look and smile. Sometimes she'd start up again and other times she wouldn't. Such a warm, friendly smile. She was the most-gentle person, you know. So kind and generous. To everyone and anyone. But there was often that sad look that crept into her eyes. It wasn't there all the time. Just sometimes. But when it was there, it was something that couldn't be hidden.

There was still a lot Frank didn't know about his mother. And the wondering was always there. His mother had always been a real sometimes kind of person. But now, she was a sometimes kind of person, all the time. That's for sure.

Yes, Frank only started getting to know his mother, when it was almost too late. But that was better than not getting to know her at all. And it's a bit of a weird thing, you know. But she only started letting go of her secret personal knowledge. Little by little. After becoming ill with dementia and Alzheimer's. And being admitted to the aged care facility.

But at least, he was getting to know her. And that was something to be happy enough about. But unhappy enough about, at the same time. Patience and understanding. That was the name of the game, alright. But who knows, where it all came from. It'd never been there ever before.

"There was a big black car there, when we got home from school. Your mother's dead! So, you have to come with us! And then they put us in the car and took us to an orphanage!"

She'd already finished her coffee and the words stopped coming. So, Frank figured it was time to go. Those sad eyes were there again now and that always happened, just before drifting off. Frank had seen her drift off many times. So, he walked her back around to her room. She sat in her chair and smiled up at him. The sadness had gone now.

"OK mum! It's been good talking to you! I'll see you next time!"

"Oh hello! No one ever comes to see me! You're the only visitor I've had!"

One of the nurses came in to check up on things.

"Oh Hello! No one ever comes to see me!"

Yeah, it was time to go, alright. Time to head for the baths. The mother visits, usually created a contemplative mood and this time was no different. And there was more to her dead mother's situation, than she'd let out. The story was well known within family circles. But the details were always a bit sketchy, you know.

According to a newspaper article on Friday, 25 August 1933; the bitter crying of a baby was the warning given to others in the house, of the tragic and sudden death of his mother's mother.

The story of the finding of the dead women, with the crying baby pinned underneath the mother's lifeless body was told at the inquest.

A verdict of death from natural causes was returned.

The Government Medical Officer said that death in his opinion was due to heart failure, caused by dilation and chronic pleurisy.

No one in the family could argue about any of that. But there was confusion about the identity of the baby, trapped under the dead body. The owner of the house, where his mother's mother rented a room; had said there were three children living in there, with their mother.

One was Frank's mother, who was six at the time. One older sister, who was Dorothy and one older brother. So, when it was stated that a baby was trapped under the dead body, several family members believed, there were actually four children living in the room with their mother and not three. Eventually it was discovered that his mother's mother had five children and not three or four. What happened to the fifth child—who ended up being the eldest, came to light, several years later. But that was only by accident.

There was also another sister discovered who was four years younger, than his mother. So, she could have been the baby trapped under the dead body.

Somehow, everything between this sitting on the sand episode and waking up the next morning was blurred right out. What happened in between never came to light. And trying to work it out became too complicated. So, it was never worked out. There was no gym that morning. Plenty of coffee. But no gym.

Anyway, the usual number of laps had been exceeded. The breathing was heavier than usual. Exhaustion had taken over. Swimming usually took 30 minutes and now 45 minutes had passed. The thinking was so intense, you know. Well, there was no actual thinking about anything. But whatever it was, was intense. That's for sure.

The big clock on the wall of the dressing sheds was completely forgotten about. Fucking hell. Running late. Everything done now was according to schedules, you know. Same thing. Same time. Every day. No mucking around. Stick to the schedule and everything's just fine. And don't let anyone or anything fuck the schedule up. That was the new thinking process. And it worked. Except for the last 24 hours or so.

"Hi Frank! You're late today! What going on?"

"Yes, well! I got carried away didn't I! I'm so fit now, you know! I could swim for hours!"

"So, you've been for your swim then?"

"Yes! Did an extra 15 minutes today as well!"

"That's great, Frank! You must be getting very fit by now! How was the water? Having the usual?"

"Oh good! About 18 today! Yes please, just the usual!"

This was the have a little chat girl. She was such a nice girl, you know. She was the have a little chat girl, because she liked having a little chat. To everyone.

Anyway, that was pretty much the longest conversation that had ever happened. Frank never said too much, no matter which girl was taking the order. But considering the old fella didn't even talk to the girls when he first started going to the café, it was a big improvement. The intensity had eased off as well. And that was a noticeable thing and surprising. Maybe a light just got flicked on.

Actually, the poor old fella didn't talk to anyone. Only, didn't even realise that. Putting words together, while on the sauce or high as a kite was one thing. But try doing the same thing after drying out and giving the pot away. Different story altogether.

So, at the favourite table. Staring out the window. Checking things out. Same as usual. Whoa. What the…

"Do you think I'm a good dancer?"

One of the girls was swirling around, right in front of everyone. Arms in the air. Feet going in all directions. She looked fucking ridiculous. Last thing that was needed right at this time was some girl dancing around asking dumb questions. Just couldn't believe someone could bounce around like that in a half-crowded café. And she'd interrupted the thinking as well. The same thinking, that wasn't really thinking at all. But it was interrupted anyway.

"If you've paid for dancing lessons, then I'd get my money back if I was you!"

She just started giggling her stupid head off. Then walked back to the counter. But at least she stopped dancing, or whatever it was she was doing. But it wasn't dancing. Anyone could see that.

This crazy girl did her little dancing act, every now and then. Especially for him. That's what the thinking was anyway. Especially after she said so, a few times. And this was another one of those times. Yeah. Next minute, here she is back again.

"So, do you think I'm a good dancer?"

"I'm bloody well sure I don't!"

Oops. He couldn't believe that just came out the way it did. And the voice got raised a bit as well. There was always this feeling you know. Of being under pressure to behave, whenever in the café. There was just something about the place. The pressure was real too. The pressure to behave. Show the best side of the nature. That's just the way things were. In the magic café.

"Well, you could at least tell me I am! To make me feel better! You're so mean!"

And with that, she quickly turned and walked off. But she gave him a cheeky little smile and a giggle first. What else was there to do but just shake the head and have a little laugh. Yes, a little laugh. Laughing, just didn't happen. But it just happened. So, this girl had to be the crazy dancing girl. Started making comments about her, to the other girls.

"How did she get a job here anyway? She must know someone!'

They all just laughed and kept doing what they were doing. One day, the crazy dancer was at the counter when he walked in.

"Can I take your order, sir? What are you having today?"

What a little smart alec. It was a sweet potato chips day. With vegan aioli. The new favourite. Such an easy order to put in. Only had to push a few buttons. But because she got so smart, Frank decided to order one of the old favourite meals. That'd fix her right up. She had trouble pushing the right buttons the last time. And sure enough, that's what happened again. Had to call over one of the other girls, to show her what to do. Lucky for her, it was the have a little chat girl. Just couldn't help himself, could he?

"How did you get your job here anyway?"

They both just ignored him.

"So, what was it again? Sour dough bread, avocado, mushrooms, spinach, tomato and relish!"

"And vegan butter! And a coffee! In a takeaway!"

"Oh yes, that's right. Nuttelex! And your coffee! Large cap with oat-milk and caramel! In a takeaway!"

"Yes, that's it! You've finally got it!"

It was one thing knowing what the meal was and another thing pushing the right buttons on the cash register.

Frank was a vegan now, you know. It was hilarious watching the crazy dancer, pushing buttons and then cancelling them out and then pushing buttons again. There was a big smile on the face as well. The have a little chat girl was very patient. But she had to show the crazy dancing girl about three or four times, before it finally sunk in. Figured her to be completely stupid, alright.

"Well, that took a while, didn't it!"

Yeah, just loving it.

"That'll be $27.80. Thank you, Sir!"

She spat the sir bit out, like it was an afterthought. But the cheeky little smile was there. She was just loving it as well. The have a little chat girl was cracking up by now. Did well to last as long as she did.

"That's how much it normally is! So, at least you got that bit right! Anyway, you must be getting smarter! You only had to be shown five times, this time!"

She just gave one of her weird, rolled eye looks, then disappeared out the back. And the girl at the coffee machine. She'd turned around with a huge smile. It was the forget her name girl. Didn't call her that yet. Because he didn't know her name yet. So, it hadn't even been forgotten yet. Or maybe he was told her name but just forgot. But he liked this girl. Great smile. And it was a good feeling when any of the girls let out the big smiles.

Things were looking up, alright. This old guy was learning how to communicate with a younger generation. That's for sure. Could feel it happening. And they were mostly young girls and that made it even better. And what great girls they all were. But he was never going to tell them anything like that was he. Or the young fella that worked there either. I mean, fancy telling some young fella what a great young fella he was. No. Don't, think so. Probably think there was a poofter hanging around.

There're going to have a lot of fun with you.

Yes, that statement. Was still fresh in the mind and still very confusing. Maybe these café girls, really did know what they were doing. Or maybe it was all just happening. Because it was all just happening. Working out which was just another new problem to be solved. Even bigger than the constant craving problems.

It'd been months now. But the thoughts of a session on the grog, or a nice fat joint. Or a good crack at the pokies. Were all still there. Lurking in the dark shadows. Could feel them, alright. Like an internal pressure cooker. The obsessions. They never go away, you know. There're always there. Always.

"They care about you Frank! That's another one of your big problems! You have to start letting people care about you! You're worth it, you know! Trusting people, has never been easy for you Frank! We all know that! You certainly do have a trust problem! But you can trust these girls, Frank! Let your guard down! You can do it, Frank! I have great confidence in you! We all have great confidence in you!"

Fucking hell. He couldn't even enjoy sitting at his favourite table. Looking out over the ocean, without her yapping away. He liked watching the surfers get a wave and stay on, without getting dumped. But he liked it even better, when they did. He'd have liked to give the lady a good dumping. I can tell you that. When she finally did shut up, there appeared another memory. A more recent memory, about the smiling gym girl. Maybe she hasn't been remembered yet. But she will be. That's for sure.

In the pool one day, these two girls were out in the middle, having a good old talking session. While swimming straight towards them, the realisation clicked in. One of them was a café girl. Something was almost said, but it wasn't. There was a quick figuring going on. The last thing they wanted was an old man, stopping and disrupting their conversation. So, swimming straight past and ignoring them was the correct decision. No doubt about that.

"There you go, sir! Enjoy!"

"Uh! Oh thanks!

That put an end to that little memory. Lunch had arrived but not the coffee. And it was the dancing girl who gently placed it down on the table. With a sweet little smile. Cheeky bitch.

"Do you do the same things every day, Frank?"

"What! Yes, I do! I have favourite things to do now! I've got a good routine! And if I stick to it, nothing goes wrong! And I don't like interruptions when I'm having lunch either!"

She didn't like that much. I can tell you that. And the smile wasn't quite the same either. The café was busy by then so there was no chance for any more, smart comments. Didn't get a chance anyway. She took off so quick, you know. The thinking wouldn't have been fast enough anyway.

Now, where was it all going. There was sometimes a problem getting back to the thinking, after getting interrupted. And that's what just happened. Again. Yes, it was happening all the time now. Getting interrupted. By one of the café girls. Or that damn lady who wasn't even there. There was something weird going on here. That's for sure. But that's as far as that thinking went.

There're going to have a lot of fun with you.

Yeah. Not long after seeing the girls in the baths, the café girl walked up and just stood beside him. Yeah. Here's Frank at this little table, at the front of the café. Checking in with the mobile phone. You had to check in everywhere you went now, because of the pandemic. This was before you had to wear a mask and before you had to show a double vaccination certificate. What a pain in the arse that was.

Frank didn't really give a stuff about anything too much by now, you know. Getting easily upset wasn't even in the programme. Not so much anyway. There'd been enough hard times already. But this pandemic shit was really starting to boil the nerves up again.

"Why didn't you stop and talk to us?"

"There you go! Sir! Enjoy!"

Oh no. Someone else just jumped into the memory. But it was only that crazy dancing girl again. With the coffee. He wasn't sure it was even her. But it must have been her, because there was the coffee. Sitting right there on the table. But she was nowhere. Anyway, just the way she said, sir. It had to have been her.

Uh, didn't know what to say to that, did he? But something had to be said. So, back to memory land again. That wasn't even a decision by the way. It just happened. Sometimes the memories just pleased themselves. Whenever they wanted to be remembered.

"Well, you guys were talking and I didn't want to interrupt. I didn't think you'd want to talk to some old guy in the middle of the baths!"

"Yeah! You should have stopped!"

"Ok, if I ever see you in there again, I'll stop and say hello!"

"Yeah, well make sure you do!"

Then she disappeared out the back. They were never seen in the baths again, were they?

There're going to have a lot of fun with you.

A few weeks later in the gym, the same two girls walked in. It was about 6am. They looked just great in their gym gear. That's for sure. Frank casually walked straight up to them. "Hey girls, what are you doing here?"

The gym girl did the talking. "Oh, hi Frank! We signed up yesterday!"

Yeah. This conversation happened in the middle of the gym, for Christ's sake. A surge of real excitement, going through the whole body, alright. I mean, talking to two gorgeous young blond girls in the middle of a gym. Then something happened, that could have ruined everything. But it didn't.

An arm was put around the café girl and she was drawn close. Yeah, a little cuddle happened, alright. She didn't seem to mind at all and kind of pressed her head against the cuddler's beating chest. For about half a second. Then dragged herself away, with a big smile on her face. The cuddler's face was hot, alright and the chest was still going ballistic. Embarrassment for both of them. That's for sure. Yeah, there was a high on, for the rest of the day. I can tell you that.

A few days later at the café, is when another episode took place.

"Hi there, gym buddy!"

It was her, alright. Came up from behind. Got him by surprise. Last thing that was expected. Almost scared the shit out of him. But seeing it was the gym girl brought the panicked excitement back to acceptable levels, you know.

"Hey! I haven't seen you at the gym for a while!"

Well, you know, it'd only been a few days. But at least something was said. Instead of nothing being said. What progress that was eh. Talking to a café girl, like there was nothing to worry about. Like there'd always been something to worry about, ever since going there in the first place. And that was because of being so old and they were all so young. Except maybe one of them. But she wasn't there anymore anyway. Or she hadn't been seen for a while at least. And what a relief that was.

"I've been going in the afternoons! It works in better with my shifts! I was getting a bit tired getting up so early!"

"Oh right! That makes sense!"

Yeah. From then on, this girl was always the smiling gym girl. Yeah. She was always smiling and Frank liked her, alright. She was a nice young girl. But she'd never know about that thinking. That's for sure.

"Oh Frank! I'm so proud of you! We're all so proud of you! Look at you now! You've come such a long way! Don't stop now, Frank! Whatever you do! Don't stop now! You're going to make it, Frank! You're going to make it! We all just know you are!"

Yeah, the figuring was already starting to happen along those lines, you know. But getting told all the time wasn't a bad thing either. The lady could say stuff like that as much as she liked. Getting there was happening, alright. Wherever there was. But getting there was much better than getting nowhere. Or being nowhere. And nowhere was always the place that had been there. So, anywhere was better than nowhere.

So, sitting at the favourite table, staring out over the calm, blue ocean. Finished the lunch and was half way through sipping the coffee. Counting the ships anchored out there. Waiting to come in and be filled up with coal. That's what the thoughts decided anyway. Coal ships. They had to be coal ships. One, two, three, four, five, six, seven. Yeah. There were seven coal ships out there. Just loved counting coal ships.

There was a sudden awakening then, you know. About why the gym girl was cuddled. Sometimes in the café, the girls would have these little cuddle sessions. This was always a fascination. I mean, a bunch of young girls, having group cuddles in the middle of the café. Especially, if they hadn't seen each other for a few days. What the hell was going on here?

"Oh hi! I haven't seen you for days! How are you! What have you been doing? Blah, blah, blah!"

"Oh hi!"

"Oh hi!"

Yeah, next minute, there's a whole bunch of them. Chattering away like budgerigars. These little get-togethers only lasted a short while.

"Okay bye! Good to see you!"

"Yeah, you too!"

"See ya!"

"Yeah, see ya!"

"Bye!"

Bloody hell. They didn't even care who was there. Or who was listening or anything. Next time, one of the girls was close enough, the question just popped straight out.

"What's with all the cuddle sessions, anyway? Cuddle session here! Cuddle session there! What is it with you girls?"

"We all love each other, Frank!"

Holy shit. The poor old fella. Straight away, the thought was there. They all must be sleeping with each other. You know. Lesbians. I mean, that'd always been the understanding. About love and sex being the same thing. When you heard about people making love. That just meant they were having sex. Rooting each other. Screwing. Being fucked. Bonking. Or whatever girls do with each other. When they make love or have sex or whatever. Confusion had set right in by now. Just couldn't believe this girl would admit to something like that. In the middle of a busy café, of all places. Fucking hell. Was pounding between the ears.

"We love each other, Frank! That's all!"

Something would have been said back for sure. If something could have been thought of in time. But it wasn't and she'd already disappeared out the back anyway. The only thing that she left behind was that café girl smile.

Maybe she saw the look of shock and horror on the old guy's face or something. This girl seemed to be one of the main girls in the café, you know. And it was only after a few weeks of pondering, before the reality about all the cuddling business hit the thinking. In the positive way. The right way. The new life way, anyway.

Yeah. She was always talking to people and cuddling people. Not only the other girls either. But just people who came in, that she obviously knew. And after watching her cuddle so many people, and not disappearing with any of them out the back for a while, Frank finally began to understand, what she meant by love. He figured it just meant being pleased to see someone and cuddling them. Just to let them know that you loved them. And they cuddled you back. Just to let you know, that they loved you too. Nothing had ever been known about cuddling before. But that must be what it was. So, they weren't all rooting each other after all. And what a relief that was.

Anyway, she was just irrepressible, this girl. And that's who she was from then on. The irrepressible, cuddling girl. There were already secret wishes going on, you know. About how she'd maybe come up and cuddle some old fella. A whole lot. Some old fella, who'd never been cuddled properly in the whole old life. Or even in the new life either. Not yet anyway.

Well, there was that little cuddle in the gym wasn't there. But it wasn't the gym girl who did the cuddling. And that was only an accident anyway. The getting cuddled wishes were very strong wishes too, you know. But the irrepressible cuddling girl was never going to find out about any of that. That's for sure. Driving home that afternoon, the lady got into the head again.

"Oh Frank, you're making such good progress now! Yes! Loving someone, is far more important than just having sex! Hopefully one day, you will be able to appreciate the difference! To actually love someone, Frank! Then you'll know what I'm talking about! It's such a wonderful thing! To love someone and be truly loved in return! Well, you've started thinking about love Frank! And that's such a big step forward! You can still find love Frank! It's never too late!"

There was no need for such a detailed explanation either. This love idea was only just starting to penetrate the blackness, you know. The light had only just started flickering. Anyway, the prostate cancer operation soon put an end to any of that stupid sex business ever happening again. So, love was the only thing available now. Maybe the lady doesn't even know about the prostate situation. You can bet she would have mentioned it, if she did.

Yeah, that's why the gym girl got cuddled, alright. Just copying what the café girls were doing. The idea must have got stuck there in the brain, or something. But the lady shouldn't get too carried away, you know. After all, this cuddling idea was only a new idea. Take a fair bit of practice to get it right. Even if the light did finally switch on. Didn't mind cuddling the gym girl either. She was a nice girl, alright. Never did it again but.

"See you, Frank! Have a good day!"

There was just no getting out of the place, without being seen. Ever. Although sometimes, it was like whoever was behind the counter saw Frank coming and disappeared out the back. But that was probably just a coincidence, eh.

There're going to have a lot of fun with you.

So, back on the veranda with a coffee. Thinking about girls cuddling girls and loving each other in that way. And not the other way. Trying to drag up all the old memories, about lesbians and poofters. Didn't prove easy either. There wasn't much there, you know. But there were lesbians and poofters around, in the old life. There's no doubt about that.

But lots more information became available, after watching a comedy show on television a few nights later. Yeah. This bunch of comedians started talking about shirt lifters and carpet chewers. The live audience was having a good old laugh.

But this was another dose of new information coming in. And the understanding just wasn't there. So, on goes the computer and these words were looked up. What a shock that was. To read the meaning of carpet chewer. And only after three or four times, did the meaning truly sink in. But there was still non believe and shock. So, reading one more time had to happen.

Carpet Chewer; one woman chewing out another woman. Fucking hell. What in tarnation did that mean. But it didn't take too long, before the meaning became clear enough. And the pictures in the brain started happening. The understanding was there, alright. And so was the real shock of it all.

Shirt lifter; homosexual man. Well, that was easy enough to understand. Everyone already knew what poofters were.

This new found knowledge, clearly resurfaced some of the memories about lesbians and poofters, you know. From the old life. But they couldn't be called that anymore. Well, lesbians were still called lesbians. They used to be called dykes on bikes as well. But that was only if they rode motorbikes.

But you couldn't call poofters, poofters anymore. Or faggots. According to political correctness anyway. And poofters, didn't like being called poofters or faggots either. That was common knowledge as well. And they wouldn't like being called shirt lifters either. You could bet on that.

There was lots of information on television, you know. About all this kind of stuff. And all kinds of other stuff as well. About all kinds of things. That maybe were better off not being known about. Yeah. The head was filling up with all kinds of new information. The new life was taking off, alright. And getting bogged down at the same time. Information overload was happening. Already.

Something happened in the gym the next morning, that shook the new emotional foundations. And it wasn't even known how it all happened. Not really anyway.

"There's been a complaint made against you!"

"What! What do you mean a complaint?"

Some other gym goer reckoned they were made feel uncomfortable. Been talking more and more now, you know. The confidence had been building up, over a period of several months. Maybe some words were said, that would have been better off not said. Maybe said the wrong words to the wrong gym goer. There was still lots of confusion in there about that. But this was a new kind of confusion.

After being taken into a room, things were explained. From the other person's point of view. Ok, so maybe there were a few things said, that would have been better off not being said. That was accepted. Maybe one of the other Franks had made a quick impression and then disappeared again. That would explain things. But only to Frank. Not to anyone else. It was made clear that more care had to be taken. About what was okay to say and what shouldn't be said. And that was fair enough.

The pandemic was still a big issue at this time, you know. Masks had to be worn in the gym. And hearing was harder than usual. I mean, Frank was half deaf as it was. But no defence was put up. Just wanted the whole thing over and done with. No further action was taken. The issue was settled. Thank Christ for that. But there was devastation there for weeks afterwards. After all the progress that'd been made. Something like this had to happen. That sat him right on his arse. Fuck the gym. Never going back there again.

But after further thought, it was decided to change the times around. Change the schedule up. No further problems after that. That other gym goer has never been seen again. But Frank was severely affected by the incident. So, just stopped talking to any of the other gym goers. And that worked really well. After all, he was there for himself, not anyone else. And besides, most of them had ear plugs in, you know. So, it was figured that they didn't want anyone talking to them either. Yeah, getting smarter all the time.

"Hi Frank! It's good to see you! Having a good day? Been for your swim!"

"Yes, I'm having a great day! The water was about 18 today. Just perfect! The sun's out and there's no wind! So, how could it not be a great day?"

The talking would have kept going too. But the café girl had to interrupt. There were people lining up behind. And that was probably a good thing. Because there was still that new information about carpet chewers and shirt lifters. Floating around in the brain. Just couldn't stop thinking about all that weird shit. And imagine if something slipped out, while talking to this girl. That wouldn't have been a good idea. That's for sure. The luck was there this time, you know. And thank Christ for that.

"That's great, Frank! So, what are you having today?"

"Oh! Just the meal today thanks and the coffee!"

"And you're usual table?"

"Yes! In the corner, where I belong!"

Frank just loved saying that.

This girl wasn't the crazy dancer either, so it was no problem ordering the meal. She normally enjoyed a little chat. About all kinds of different stuff. But not today. Yeah, it was the have a little chat girl. And liking her was very easy. But she never knew about that. Oh no. Well, she probably did know, you know. I mean, the way she was looked at all the time. She knew, alright. The rest of the café girls probably knew the old fella was infatuated with all of them. They just had to know. Unless they were all stupid. But they weren't all stupid. There was no doubt about that. Well, maybe just one of them.

Yeah. The usual thing was happening. Sitting there, staring out the window. People walking around everywhere. Out and about. Enjoying a nice hot, sunny day. Little or no wind. Why wouldn't they be? And then all these thoughts, just started invading the brain, you know. Couldn't be helped. Couldn't be stopped either. They just kept coming and they were still all about shirt lifters and carpet chewers.

But thank God, they were just in there. In the head and there was no talking to anyone. Because imagine how deep the shit would have been then, eh. But there was no real awareness there anymore, about how to get into any deep shit. Not just yet anyway. Otherwise, maybe getting up and changing tables could have happened.

Or at least, moving the chair around and looking the other way. But the café was crowded and why should the normal routine be changed anyway. If people didn't like other people staring at them, then they shouldn't be walking along to be stared at, should they?

There goes a pair of shirt lifters. Yeah. That's what started going on, through the mind. These two young fellas were just walking along. Minding their own business. But they looked a bit feminine, didn't they? Well, that's what the thinking was. They both had funny looking haircuts as well. And they were looking at each with googly eyes and giggling like a couple of school girls. So, they had to be shirt lifters. That was the only explanation. And they were covered in tattoos as well.

A few minutes later, two girls walking along holding hands. Well, figured one of them to be a girl anyway. The other one, looked more like a truck driver and she walked like one too. Big lump of a thing. With tattoos on her muscled-up arms and bits of metal, sticking out of her face. And a crew-cut. Fucking hell. Wouldn't want to pick a fight with her. That's for sure. The other one was almost in a G-string and was covered in tattoos. They must be a pair of carpet chewers. Yeah. They just had to be. They stood out from a mile away. And there were lots of other strange looking people wandering along.

Then the realisation happened. It was like watching an invasion of human sized smarties or M&M's walking along. All these different kinds of people, you know. There were old memories slowly turning up now as well. Of when the only people around were normal people and wogs. Now there was just about every kind of human, parading along. Right in front of the eyeballs. Talk about a new world for the new life. And there was an alien sitting there, watching it all unfold.

Chinese. Indians. Japanese. Lebanese. Africans. You name it. And people covered up. So, you couldn't even tell what they looked like. And on a boiling hot day, like it was. And God only knows how many other types were on display. Yeah, what a different world it was now. That's for sure. But no one seemed to be bothering anybody else either. Everyone was just doing their own thing, you know. Just like the alien, watching.

Then the wondering started. Maybe it would have been better, just sitting there on veranda. Getting slowly pissed and enjoying a few, nice fat joints here and there. Staring at the trees and the birds flying around. No worries then. Or staring off into the blackness. But that wasn't recommended at all. Too much bad shit in there. Depending on what blackness is being looked into or thought about, of course.

There was the night time blackness, which was okay to look into and imagine all kinds of things. But those other black places were all inside the head, you know. And going in to anyone of those, only ever caused pain and misery. So, keeping away from them was always the best idea. But sometimes bad forces came together and the end result was plunging back in there. Back into the internal blackness. That hung on like mucky glue and just wouldn't let go. And what an almighty effort it always was to finally get free.

Yeah. This new life business and the new world, that went with it. Was all getting a bit too much. More confusing than ever. The lady, you know. She'd fucked the whole life up. There was no doubt about that now. Stupid bitch. Well, not really. That probably just came out wrong didn't it. But it was like going from one fucked up world into another fucked up world. That's what the thinking said, anyway.

Yeah. Watching everything on television was one thing. And reading about stuff in the newspaper was another thing. But to be actually in there, mixing with all the other humans. Was another thing altogether. Such a daunting thought, you know. Still avoided contact as much as possible.

But when the pandemic restrictions were on, it made things a lot easier. With the social distancing and everything. And having to stay within the local government area. And only going swimming or to the supermarket for essentials. Or to the chemist when the prescription drugs ran out. Yeah. All that made things much easier. As far as staying away from other people was concerned. Hardly any people around anyway. Hardly any cars on the roads either.

Remembering stuff about the old life was happening again too. The old life was much easier to deal with. Just like things were, during the pandemic. There was no doubt about that. Yeah. Went back to missing the old life. But the best thing about the pandemic was the pubs and clubs. They were all closed up. So, if a bust looked like happening. It couldn't happen. And what a good feeling that was. No resistance required. No GA meetings either. And the money in the bank account kept building up. But the urges came and went. Big urges they were too. With nowhere to go.

So, the urges to play poker machines were under control. For the time being. But the urges to get blotto and stoned out of the brain were still in there. Almost busting out of the dark shadows. And the fuses were under enormous pressure, you know. The ticking time bomb was just about to explode. And what a mess that would have been. But it was also a familiar mess. Suffered and enjoyed, too many times already.

So, it maybe could have been a good thing, if the inevitable explosion did happen. Because by the time everything got put back in place, the pandemic and all the restrictions could be over and things would get back to normal.

But then, a realisation popped in. An understanding was reached. If the alien was to fully accept the new life and all that came with it. Participate in maybe, some of the social activities available. Like talking to people and smiling and not mixing up what's being said, with bullshit. Then lots more changes would have to take place.

Yeah, the path ahead. Full of mistakes, for sure. Errors of judgement. Misunderstandings and the sheer terror, at the thought of it all. There was this ever-growing doubt now, you know. About everything. So, where was the lady when she was needed the most? She only turned up when she felt like it. And that wasn't fair. Especially, when the thinking was spinning right out of control. Like now.

"There you go, Frank! Enjoy!"

Lunch and coffee arrived together.

"Uh! What? Yes! Thank you!"

"Gee, you get looked after well, Frank! There're a good crew here, aren't they!"

"Yes, they are! I already know that!"

That was NG2. She was already half way back to the counter, before anything more could be said. And taking off like that would have been understandable, if it was busy times. But it wasn't busy times. So, it must have been her turn or something. To dig into the old fella. Get a conscience thing happening or something. The awareness was growing more and more now, you know. About a conspiracy between the café girls. And he was the victim. But it was in a good way. If being a victim, can ever be in a good way.

There're going to have a lot of fun with you.

Anyway, what a relief it was. To be interrupted. And just at the right time too. Just having all these negative thoughts floating around wasn't good for a new absorbing mind, you know. Better off not thinking about anything at all. Old life or new life.

"Hi Frank! I haven't seen you for a while!"

"Oh hello! How's things? No, I haven't seen you either!"

Well, that made a lot of sense. It was the smiling gym girl. Didn't even see where she came from.

"Oh great! I've been in Queensland for a week!"

"Well lucky you! And you're all tanned up too! Looking good!"

"Gee thanks, Frank! Anyway, I better go! Things are busy right now! See ya!"

"Yeah, see ya!"

That was nice and quick. But things were still not busy. Yeah, so it was a conspiracy, alright. Well, maybe it wasn't. She could have just noticed him there and decided to say hello and have a quick chat. That was a possibility. But it didn't matter. The old fella just secretly loved it all, you know. The attention that is. Yeah, couldn't get enough attention. Especially from the magic café girls. But of course, they were never going to know anything about that, were they?

There're going to have a lot of fun with you.

There were NG1 and NG2 now, you know. Two new girls who started in the takeaway section during the pandemic. Only ever been seen with masks on. Great to finally see them uncovered. At least one of them, anyway. NG2. And she was so shy when she started, you know. But not anymore. The other girls probably had something to do with bringing her up to speed. You can bet on that. Didn't take long either. Quick learners, these café girls. Both great looking girls as well. Well, all the café girls were good looking girls. And so friendly and efficient. They were just the best.

But the understanding was always there. Stop concentrating on the café girls so much and pay more attention to the new world. That was still causing all kinds of challenges and bucket loads of confusion. And it was also a known thing, that the café girls were causing much of the confusion. So, that was a confusion within itself. And that was the main reason for loving all the attention so much. After all, the old life had always been full of confusion. So, why should the new life be any different?

There're going to have a lot of fun with you.

Right. Ok. Let's just call it fun. Yeah. Getting smarter all the time.

Before this latest interruption, the last thought to go through was the fact, that it was the last generation and the generations before that. That created this new generation of odd balls. Well, they shouldn't really be called odd balls, should they? Maybe just refer to them as the new generation. Before the next generation. And after the last generation.

And judging by this new generation. Just imagine what the next generation will be like and the one after that. Fucking hell. And just when this kind of thinking was getting out of control, another line of thinking gradually took over.

It wasn't their fault at all, was it? I mean, they couldn't help being who they were. Or what they were. They were just born that way. But it was still very interesting looking at all of them. The word circus suddenly entered the thinking. But that just wasn't fair. Not fair at all. That's for sure. I mean, it's clear who belonged in a circus. Still the biggest clown around.

But really. How could anyone be blamed, for the way things were. After all, it's just the way things were, you know. Too late to change anything. I mean, once the seed is sown. Such will the tree grow. Who knows, where that one came from. It was just in there and it just popped out. Simple as that. And once something is born, it's just there, isn't it. Not like you can just send it back and get another one. Like maybe how they should have sent this alien back.

And how could anyone be blamed for watching the whole damn show either. They were all just there, right in front of the eyeballs. How could anyone not see them? Unless they just sat there with the eyes shut. Or walked around, staring straight up. As if that was going to happen. At least they all looked happy enough. Well, most of them did anyway.

"Yes Frank! You're starting to get the picture now! In a good way! Just treat people as you find them! That's the best thing to do! People are just people

Frank! And no, they can't help who they are! Any more than you can help who you are!"

Well, she just had to go and put that last bit in didn't she? And staying there like a sitting duck any longer would only give her the chance, to start up again. For sure. So, the papers got read quicker than usual. The meal and coffee went down quicker than usual. And Frank was out of there. Much quicker than usual.

The papers were always getting read much quicker than usual now anyway. The girls must have noticed the continual squinting. The papers always getting turned towards the light. Made reading much easier, the more light there was. It was on the way out one day, when the next surprise attack started.

"Were you having trouble reading there, Frank? The light could be a little better in here! Maybe the print's a bit smaller than usual today!"

That could have been the irrepressible cuddling girl who said that. But there were a few others standing around and he wasn't paying attention anyway. So, it could have been any one of them.

Yeah, there were comments like that, for a few days. But the stubborn old fool wasn't listening. But really was listening. Just didn't want to listen. Didn't want to hear, what was being said.

So, they all started wearing glasses around, didn't they? First it was whoever was at the counter. And the coffee machine. Or just standing there looking at him. Usually with reading glasses on.

"Oh, hi Frank! I've been reading so much lately. My eyes are so sore! I've had to start wearing glasses!"

Yeah, one of them said something like that. And she just knew he'd noticed the glasses. How couldn't he. They were all wearing them now. And this time, it was the irrepressible cuddling girl. Because she was standing right there right in front of him when she said it. NG1 and the serious one were there as well. But it was irrepressible who did the talking, alright. And they all had the café girl smile on as well.

And then the fuckwit who wasn't a fuckwit, just happened to walk in and stood right beside them. So, a smart comment just popped into the thinking and then just popped straight out.

"She thinks I'm only about 30 years old!"

"Well, she is wearing glasses!"

Yeah. What a smart arse. But everyone who was there got a good laugh out of it. Even a few waiting customers had a bit of a laugh.

Then it was the girls walking around, cleaning up tables. Especially one of them. They all had weird looking glasses on. But this one. Fair dinkum.

"Oh, hi Frank! I've been bumping into things lately! And I'm having trouble reading the menus! So, I've had to start wearing glasses. Do you like my new glasses?"

They were big, ugly, hot pink rimmed glasses for Christ's sake. Bigger than her whole face. She looked like a goggle-eyed gold fish. And here she is prancing around the café. Like nothing mattered. Looked fucking ridiculous. But he wasn't going to tell her that was he. There were just no words anyway. I mean, what was he going to say?

Yeah. Nothing was said about the stupid looking glasses. But from then on, this girl was the glasses girl. That always put a smile on the face, whenever she was seen walking around. But you know, she was just such a nice girl. And she was a café girl. So, she was special. Just like the rest of them were. Strangely enough, this glasses-wearing caper only lasted a few days.

There're going to have a lot of fun with you.

"Hello, I'm Frank and I'm a compulsive gambler!"

"Hi Frank!"

"Hello Frank!"

Yeah, there were plenty of hi's and hellos. Like always. There was a big grin on the face, you know. That just couldn't be helped. Been building up for days.

"Would you like to share, Frank?"

"Yeah, ok! I haven't played the machines for another week!"

"That's great, Frank!"

"Well done, mate!"

"Good on you!"

"Yes, that's good news Frank!

Yeah, it was still a week-to-week struggle for Frank now. And he looked forward to saying that, every time he started sharing. The new life was controlled by routines now. Had been for a while. And as long as things stayed within the timeframes, no busting was likely to happen. Unless, something unforeseen happened and fractured the emotional structure and caused a big spin out. But that hadn't happened lately. Resistance had been building and getting stronger.

But nothing could stop what was just about to explode. Couldn't be held back any longer.

"Would you like to continue sharing, Frank."

Well, you know. Just try and stop him.

"The worlds full of carpet chewers and shirt lifters!"

"What! What are you talking about, Frank? You can't say that!"

The controller, almost fell out of the chair. Everyone was just stunned. Then started pissing themselves laughing. Yeah. An uproar of compulsive convulsions.

"What do you mean the world's full of carpet chewers and shirt lifters?"

"There're fucking everywhere!"

One of the older female compulsives piped up. "What's a carpet chewer?"

Well, that almost caused a riot. Everyone had tears rolling down their cheeks. Even the controller had lost control. No one could say anything for a good-few-minutes. The compulsive who asked the question just didn't get it, you know. You could tell that by the look on her face. But she was laughing anyway. You can bet a few of the other compulsives, didn't get it either. But they just pretended they did. After things settled down, the controller did what controllers do best. Took control.

"Ok then, let's all just settle down and get on with the meeting!"

The room went dead quiet. No one wanted to say a word.

"Would you like to continue sharing, Frank?"

"Sure ok. I was just watching this show the other night and some comedians kept saying those words and I didn't know what they meant. So, I looked them up on the internet. And carpet chewer said; when one woman chews out another woman."

This was said really quick and everyone just sat there. Stunned again, for a split second. Then the eruption of laughter happened again. The old compulsive who asked the question was just sitting there, staring into space. What was going in her head was anyone's guess. Poor old dear.

"Ok, that's enough! That's enough! Quieten, down! Just quieten down! Are they new thongs Frank?"

"What! Oh yes, they are! They cost me $50 bucks! And the other thing they were talking about was shirt lifters! There're homosexuals! Did you know that?"

"There're poofters, mate! That's what shirt lifters are!"

There was no laughing or commotion this time. The controller was right onto it.

"Look, that's enough! Where're here to talk about gambling, not poofters! Or carpet chewers! Now let's get on with the meeting! Tell us the one about the thongs, Frank!"

The controller took control, alright. But wasn't really in control at all.

"I know what poofters are!"

That was the old compulsive. She'd brightened right up. The whole place just cracked up, all over again. Even the controller couldn't control anything, anymore. Just burst out as well. But not for very long. You have to give credit where it's due, you know. But had to raise the voice, to get things back under control.

"Come on, come on! That's enough! Frank's going to tell us about the thongs! Some of you here, haven't heard the thong story yet! So, let's hear it again, Frank!"

Honesty will come into your life if you let it.

"Ok! Well, I just went over to the mangroves to check on my plants. But they weren't there, were they! Some bastard pinched 'em! I was really pissed off, you know! So, I went for a bit of a walk through the mangroves. I noticed this thong, sticking up out of the mud. So, I went over and pulled it out. Then I saw another one. So, I pulled that one out too. Then I just kept walking and seeing thongs everywhere. So, I keep getting them. I kind of forgot about the plants. Started going for walks in the mangroves all the time, after that. Looking for thongs. Ended up with a pile a metre high, out the back."

"He used to walk in here with odd thongs on! Different colours! Different sizes! He was too miserable to even buy a new pair of thongs!"

The compulsives got another good laugh out of that one.

"Well, they were perfectly good thongs! Who cares about wearing odd thongs anyway? Not me! Anyway, I saved plenty of money!"

There was one compulsive in particular, who always got stuck into Frank. All in good fun, of course.

"What! On thongs! There're $2 a pair, mate!"

Anyone could say pretty much anything in GA meetings. And they usually did. Yeah, there was no pressure in GA meetings, you know.

"Anyway, it's good to see you with a new pair of thongs on Frank! Ok, would anyone else like to share?

"What kind of plants grow in the mangroves?"

The old compulsive wasn't finished yet. And it wasn't even her share either. She just got curious that's all. She grew plants herself. Everyone knew that. But not the same kind Frank was talking about. There were smiles all around and a few giggles here and there. Frank couldn't help himself.

"These were special plants! They only grow in the mangroves!"

"Well, what are they called then!"

This old compulsive wasn't stupid, you know. There were a few muffled laughs happening. Frank was stuck now. Didn't know what to say. But he said something anyway.

"They were mangrove plants! Anyway, who cares what kind of plants they were! It doesn't matter. Some bastard still pinched 'em, didn't they?"

"They were pot plants, darlin'!"

All the compulsives just cracked up again. The controller threw the hands in the air and just waited for things to calm back down. The poor old compulsive. She still didn't get it. Frank had a big smile on his face. He decided to explain it in real simple terms. Satisfy the old girls curiosity.

"What he means is, they were pot plants. You know. The kind of pot you smoke!"

"Oh, you mean drugs?"

Well, everyone just cracked up again, didn't they? I mean, what else was going to happen, eh. The poor old dear must have had a sheltered life or something.

"He means marijuana!"

"Oh, I understand now! That's what the hippies smoke!"

The controller, allowed the laughing and the smart-arse comments to go for a few minutes, then put the controllers foot down.

"Ok! Ok! That's enough! Now, would anyone else like to share?"

"Oh, sorry! Thanks for letting me share!"

Frank had to say that. Because that's what you said. After you finished sharing. You may already know that. There were a few more shares. But the time had passed really quickly and the controller proceeded to close the meeting in the usual way. All the compulsives stood up and joined in as one voice. Yeah. The Serenity Prayer. Here we go again.

All together now. Boring. Boring. Boring.

"To the God of our own understanding. God, grant me the serenity to accept the things I cannot change. The courage to change the things I can. And the wisdom to know the difference."

Then the hand holding bullshit thing. What the point was with the hand holding bit was never understood and never explained by the controller. Well, no one ever asked either. Everyone just did it, because that's what had to happen. Before the meeting closed.

All together now.

"Thanks for sharing! Thanks for caring! Keep coming back! The meetings make it!"

And that was that. Another GA meeting, over and done with. This was before the pandemic hit. When there were no restrictions on and the compulsives could stand next each other, holding hands.

There were never any warm and fuzzy feelings happening, holding hands with any of the other compulsives either. Standing there, feeling like a complete fucking idiot. And the bit about the God of your own understanding. What a load of bullshit that was. Because Gods always meant religion. And religion was all bullshit. Everyone knows that. But there was a liking for the GA meetings and a real need. That's for sure. So, putting up with a bit of bullshit here and there couldn't hurt, could it.

"All this religious, God bullshit! What's that got to do with gambling! And what the fuck does God know about poker machines, anyway!"

"It's got nothing to do with religion, Frank. It's just about a power greater than yourself! That's all! You don't have to believe in a God! But you need to accept the idea of a power greater than yourself!"

That's what the controller always said, whenever some non-believer challenged the concept of a power greater than themselves. And the controller never backed down either. Yeah. Knew how to control any smart-arse compulsives. That's for sure. Frank still thought it was all bullshit, you know. But just stopped saying it. Didn't want to go pissing the controller off too much. Didn't want to know about any power, greater that himself either. Not another one, anyway.

"Hello Mum! How are you today!"

"Oh hello! No one ever visits me! You're the only one who's been here today! I haven't seen you for ages!" How are you?"

"Oh, I'm fine mum! Just fine! Would you like a cup of coffee?"

Liar. Frank was never really fine. Not 100% anyway. Not ever.

"Oh yes! I'd love a cup of coffee!"

She was just sitting there in her chair. Staring out the window when he returned with the coffee.

"There you go, mum!"

But she was gone again. Off into another zone. The zone she always went to, whenever Frank was there. That's how it seemed anyway. Into a past world. An unhappy world. A world she'd never come to terms with. A world that still haunted her. A world where her world was ripped apart. The fragments were still scattered everywhere.

When Frank's father died, his mother experienced a new-found freedom she'd never known before. With her aged pension, that she could spend any way she liked. Going for little walks up to the shops was her favourite thing to do. Buying old things. Just cheap, little old things. Like cups and saucers, with pretty patterns on them. And paintings of flowers and country scenes. How cheap they were, didn't matter. She just bought what she liked.

She loved expensive antiques too. But couldn't afford to buy most of the ones she liked the best. Living within her own means was an easy thing to do. Instead of being dependent on someone else like she'd always been forced to do. Her whole life. That always belonged to someone else.

Hang on. She's coming back. Yes, here she is. She's back. But not for long. Just long enough to get it out. Then back into her own personal zone again.

"I miss Dorothy! She's my older sister! I love Dorothy! Not the other one! Just Dorothy! Where's Dorothy? I want to see Dorothy!"

Frank was just sitting there, sipping his coffee. Listening. Then he drifted off as well. Back to the time, when his mother did see Dorothy. For the first time in over 60 years.

One day, there happened a chance meeting. Maybe this chance meeting was one of those chance meetings that was meant to happen. Because it answered a lot of questions that could not otherwise have been answered. Not even known about. Certainly not by his mother anyway.

She was just wandering along. On her way to the shops, as usual. A conversation took place, with a neighbour who'd moved in a few doors up, on the other side of the street. What was actually said would be impossible to say. One can only speculate. But after a few days, this neighbour started dropping in for a coffee.

Frank's mother had a friend, who dropped in for a coffee and a chat. This had never happened before and the positive change that took place in his mother was remarkable. You see Frank's mother was never allowed to have any visitors. Friends were not even thought about.

Anyway, as it happened, this neighbour was a psychiatric nurse at a mental hospital. That's what they called them back then, you know. Mental hospitals. Eventually, after several weeks of regular visits, she asked the question.

"Do you have a sister?"

Well, the reaction was predictable I suppose. There were a few kids still living at home and Frank was still there as well. His mother was instantly stunned. She stared at this friend, for what seemed a very long time. And everyone else was staring at their mother. Including the friend. The answer came very slowly.

"Yeeesss. Yeeesss. I doo have aaa sisssteeerrr. Herrr nammeesss Dorrrooothyyy."

Then the tears came. A river of tears came. And they didn't stop for a long while.

This lovely neighbour and true friend got to work. She organised a home visit. Frank's mother was noticeably anxious for a few days, before this visit took place. And her friend was there every day, preparing her for the biggest event in his mother's life. This friend. She knew what she was doing, alright.

The big moment came. Frank's mother was sitting at the kitchen table. Calm as you like. Staring at a full cup of cold coffee.

"Hello! Hello!"

The friend was half way along the hallway, when she slowly emerged from the kitchen. The sisters looked at each other, for about ten seconds. Then ran forward. Arms outstretched and when they met, wrapped themselves up together and both burst into tears. The friend started crying. The few kids that were there, all looked at each other in amazement. Frank didn't know what to do.

But the emotions were building up, alright. Time to get out of there. So, just walked straight past them, before the explosion. Out the front door and off down the street. Wandered back in, a few hours later. There was laughter coming from the kitchen. After walking in, Dorothy jumped up out of her chair.

"I'm Dotty Dot! They call me Dotty Dot, because I'm a bit dotty!"

Then before anyone knew what was happening, Dotty Dot ran around and flung herself straight at him. Her skinny legs went around his waist. And her wiry, little arms wrapped themselves around his unsuspecting neck. Dotty Dot, gave Frank the longest, hardest hug you could ever imagine. Near chocked him to death. Giggling in his ear the whole time as well. Having a great old time of it. There had never been any hugs for Frank. Of any kind. In the whole old life. From anyone. And certainly, not in the whole new life either. But this titanic like strangle hold, made up for all that. Thought he was going to die.

"She does that to everyone! That's why we all love her so much!"

That's what the friend said, before she started unwrapping her arms from around Frank's neck. Dotty Dot was so strong you know and she just wouldn't let go.

"That's just what she does! When she hugs anyone! She never wants to let go! She hugs everyone! We have to watch her all the time!"

It wasn't long after Frank was free, that it was time for Dotty Dot to go. Everyone was looking at her. And maybe wondering whether they'd be next. So, it was time for the visit to end.

"She has a sleep in the afternoons. So, we better get going! Come on, Dot! Time to go now!"

Well, it's understandable that Dotty Dot, didn't want to leave. The smile disappeared. The frown went on the face. The bottom lip stuck out. The arms were folded across the chest. The eyes squinted and the moaning started. But the friend knew exactly what to say and she said something like this.

"You know who'll be there to see you, Dot! She loves you, Dot! And she just loves your big hugs! What will she do, if you're not there? She will be crying and saying; where is Dotty Dot? Where is Dotty Dot? So, we better go and see her, so she doesn't start crying!"

That got her attention straight away. Dotty Dot was back to happiness again. Just like that. Like a magic spell had been cast over her. Out of the kitchen she ran, giggling her little head off and headed for the front door. With the friend right behind her. No goodbye. No, see you later. No anything.

This friend later explained how she couldn't help noticing the striking resemblance between Dotty Dot and Frank's mother. And eventually the curiosity became so strong, that the question just had to be asked.

There were many more visits from the friend, over the next few years. But not from Dotty Dot. Frank's mother learnt many things about her big sister and what happened to her and what her life had been like. Some of the things she was told, may have been better not said. Because of the many emotional and mental breakdowns Dorothy suffered as a developing child.

The friend had access to Dotty Dot's medical history. And Frank's mother kept asking the questions. So, the friend kept giving her the answers. But not all at once. They were spaced out, over a period of time.

She was pretty smart, this friend and a true friend she turned out to be. The only real friend, Frank's mother ever had. Except maybe for the next-door neighbour. Who picked, her times well. Before having a friendly chat, over the side fence. Always when his mother went out with the washing, or bringing it back in. And always when his father was off doing, whatever.

Very occasionally, a sister-in-law would visit. She'd walk around 5 or 6 kilometres, just to sit in the kitchen and have a quiet coffee. The kids were told to disappear, which they always did. Frank knew to disappear as well. The private kitchen conversations that took place, usually lasted about an hour or so. And even when Frank snuck up to the door and tried to listen, there was nothing to be heard. Except quiet whispers. Like they knew someone was probably listening.

On one occasion, after all the whispering was finished, Frank noticed the distraught look on both their faces as they walked out of the kitchen. Neither of them made an effort to say anything. But they both had watery eyes. And smudgy looking patches on their face. Things got back to normal pretty quickly after one of these visits. But nothing was ever said about what they talked about. And for some reason, nobody ever asked.

One sadness often leads to another, you know. Not long after Dotty Dot's visit, she was transferred to another mental hospital. A long way away. And not long after that, the friend came with the sad news. Dorothy had passed away. That's all the friend knew. There was no mention of a funeral. Or a burial site.

And you wouldn't believe it. Within a few years after this distressing piece of sad news, the friend was diagnosed with cancer and died within a few more years herself. And Frank's mother was diagnosed with the early stages of dementia, within a few short years after that. And signs of Alzheimer's followed soon after that. She was on her way out, alright. And even the most hardened of all hearts would surely soften enough to appreciate, that if there was a time to find a little compassion and understanding, then now was that time.

And so, another rumble within the dark shadows, slowly began to get louder. The little cracks would soon follow and another rupture was on its way. This kind of emotional rupture didn't happen very often. It wasn't the same kind of rupture that happened before and after busting either. This kind of rupture was all about another person's feelings. Usually his mother's.

There were always measures in place to stop it happening at all. But sometimes the pressure just builds and builds, you know. And next minute. Emotional overload. Kaboom. What a fucking mess. And the biggest challenge in controlling these outbursts was not letting anyone else know about them. And if there looked like being a breakout, then the disappearing procedure was the best option available.

Back to the present time zone. His mother was fast asleep. Looking so at peace. Just sitting there in the chair. A little smile came soon enough. Frank never smiled much. But nothing could be done, to stop it this time. And reaching for the tissue box was necessary. Because there were tears rolling down the cheeks. And the shirt was soaking wet. How the hell was that allowed to happen?

"Oh Frank! See! You really are human after all! There's nothing wrong with letting the emotions out! Keeping them locked up, only causes more problems! You must learn to deal with your emotions, Frank! Before they get a chance to build up and cause great anxiety! There's no value in hoarding your true feelings. They will come out! One way or the other! And try and think positive thoughts, Frank! That always helps! I know you can do it, Frank! We all know you can do it!"

Yeah well. Didn't know what anxiety even meant, did he? Have to look that one up, when he gets home.

Well, she was right out to it now. Not coming back anytime soon. Easy enough to work that out. Time for a swim.

Unbelievable. Slogging away in the pool. On the last lap and there's that drunken bum from the old life. Wandering along the side of the pool. Like a lost sheep. Alongside some other useless looking character. There was a thought of a couple more laps, till they passed by. I mean, most people wouldn't be seen dead talking to these two. But no. A feeling of obligation was there now, you know.

"Hey man! What's happening!"

Deaf bastard, didn't even stop. But his mate heard something. Stopped and turned. Stared down into the pool for a few seconds.

"Hey Frank! Hey man! How ya doin? Long time, no see!"

Fucking hell. This other bloke knew him as well. Now he'd have to talk to both of them. So, out of the pool and standing beside these two ding-a-lings. Easy to tell they'd both been on the piss. Smelt like they'd slept in a sewer. Bloodshot eyes. How the hell did the recognition happen anyway. Then the other one woke up.

"Hey Frank! Doin' ya swimming, mate! Might go for a swim meself later, eh!"

"Yeah! Doing a few laps! What are you guys doing, wandering around anyway?"

"Oh, just walking, mate! Good exercise, eh! Just checking things out, you know! Havin' a look around!"

Not hard to tell what they were checking out either. Nice sunny day. Place was crowded. Bare bums everywhere. Soaking up the sun. Pair of old fucking pervs. They were getting a bit wobbly now as well. How they could even walk at all was a miracle in itself.

"Well, it's been good talking to you guys! Good to see you! I've got a few more laps to do! See you later!"

And with that, Frank was off. Usually jumped into the pool. Not this time. Dived in. Swimming faster than ever before. Get as far away from these two as possible. As quick as possible. There were heads popping up everywhere by now. Been hearing the conversation, if you could call it that.

Yeah. Back in the pool. Till these two flips disappeared. But what else was supposed to happen. Being a regular at the baths now. Who'd want to be seen, talking to these two old deros. Pissed to the eyeballs. Not a good look at all. Still couldn't remember who they were anyway.

There was another time, you know. Just about to jump in for a swim, when a voice was heard from behind.

"You going to warm the water up for me!"

Yeah, said something like that. There was a half turn. Enough to see some smiling, devious looking imbecile standing about a metre away. Staring. The answer was just spat straight out.

"What! I'm fucking sure I'm not! Fuck off!"

That left the stupid bastard, standing at the side of the pool. Looking like a stunned mullet. Well, what's anyone going to say, to a complete stranger, who just walks up and asks a dumb question like that anyway.

And besides, there'd already been enough deviates, just walking up and started talking. Like they knew who they were talking to. Telling them to fuck off, just seemed like the thing to do. No thought had to be put into it either. And they soon fucked off too. Can tell you that.

"Oh Frank!"

That'd be right. Only just got going again and she's started up. Never done that before. Not that could be remembered anyway. Interrupting the swimming routine. So, what's the problem this time?

"Maybe they were just trying to be friendly, Frank! Get to know you! Quite a lot of the regulars, do that you know. Get to know the other regulars. And you are a regular now, Frank! There's nothing wrong with being friendly, Frank! Try and remember that!"

Try and remember that. Try and remember that. As if there wasn't enough to remember already. Now being friendly to every deviate that wanders up, and wants a friendly little chat, has to happen. Fucking hell. There's no end to it all. This new life, is full of so many complications, you know. Just when it's all worked out. Something else has to be all worked out. It's just too fucking much.

Checking in with the mobile phone was always a hassle, you know. This was early on in the pandemic. So, getting pissed off, didn't happen so easy. Not yet anyway. But checking in had to be done. Everyone had to check in. One of the girls noticed Frank at the little front desk, pushing the buttons. She's wearing a vest. With 'COVID MARSHALL' written on it. She stood out, alright. Couldn't miss her. Had a look of, don't mess with me, about her. But she was friendly.

"Can I help you there?"

Before there was time to answer, she gently took the phone and started pushing buttons.

"You don't need to push so hard. Just touch lightly. You need to put your name in and your phone number and your address. And a password. If you need any more help, I'll be around!"

"Right! Ok! Thanks!"

After following these instructions, the job was finally done. Took ages. But after getting approval from the COVID Marshall, entrance was permitted. What a fucking joke. Yeah. That's what the thinking was, alright. But the COVID Marshall was just doing her job. Anyway, she was so nice. Very likeable. And without her help, there would have been no lunch at the magic café that day.

That's for sure. From that day on, she was known as the marshal girl. And Frank told her that one day.

"I like that! I like that!"

Then burst out laughing as she turned and walked away. Yeah. Just like he liked her. But she'd never know anything about that, would she. There wasn't any offence taken, when she laughed either.

"Yes Frank! You're getting the idea now! She laughed in a good way! You made her laugh, Frank! Now she will always remember you, with a smile on her face! She'll have good thoughts about you! You're learning, Frank! You're learning! Good for you Frank! Good for you!"

Well, finally done something right for a change. Anyway, there was no real need for that interruption either. Kind of figured all that out already. Well maybe not. But the lady wasn't getting the credit for everything. And she never said it in the first place, did she?

"Hi Frank! What are you having today?"

This was the beautiful one talking. But then the idea came. They were all beautiful, these café girls. In their own way. That was easy enough to work out. But if they were all called beautiful, then that would be so very confusing, wouldn't it. So different names had to be thought up, you know. Yes, knowing who was who was important.

After all, this café was the only café in the whole world right now. And besides, by the time the ordering was done and the short walk to the table was completed, the name of the girl at the counter was usually forgotten. Even if it was known in the first place. So, special names were necessary. Simple as that.

Short term memory loss, you know. A real bother. And they didn't have to know about the little, folded up piece of paper in the wallet either. With all their names written on it, did they? Yeah, getting smarter all the time.

Sometimes, one or two of the girls would walk up to the table and interrupt the lunch time. Forced Frank to stop reading the paper. Look up and acknowledge their presence. And the girls in the magic café, all had a presence. Can tell you that. Full of self-confidence.

"Do you remember our names, Frank?"

So was this some kind of test or something, was it? Had no idea what their names were. Couldn't remember. Couldn't get the piece of paper out of the wallet either. Not with them standing there. With their café girl smile stuck on their faces.

Honesty will come into your life if you let it.

Fucking hell. Gamblers Anonymous, followed him around like a bad smell.

"Uh well, not really. But if you remind me again, I'll make sure I remember next time!"

After a little giggle and a slightly larger smile, they did remind Frank of what their names were.

But you know there were already a few, whose names could never be forgotten. They were well and truly logged in. For one reason or another. And it didn't take that long, before several other names were logged in as well. Their real name and their special name.

So, after these two smarties wandered off, their names were written down on the piece of paper. One was the tattooed one. Because she had tattoos. Easy enough. And the other one was the lovely one. Because she was just so lovely, that's why.

Looking after this old fella seemed to be important to the girls. This miserable looking old fella, who just happened to wander in there one day. Only out of hospital for a short time. After another breakdown. And they were all just so good to him. Right from the very start. How could there not be good thoughts about all of them.

They must have guessed the situation straight away. Unless the lady told them all about the sad old case. That thought was there every now and then, you know. About the lady and what she was up to. Even before the heavy thinking started. About what really might be happening.

Oops. A momentary lapse of that memory was going on here now. The most beautiful girl in the world was still haunting the head space, you know. Still hadn't been dealt with. Not properly anyway. And there was no thought put into what her real name was either. Couldn't give a damn. But there were a few special names for her, alright. Yeah. Still in there. Appearing and disappearing. Like a recurring fucking nightmare.

Liking her was easy enough. The look of her anyway. But not liking her was much easier. Especially after what happened. And besides, didn't even know her. Or what she was really like as a real person. She probably had plenty of sneaky little tricks up her sleeve anyway. All these females are the same you know. You never knew what they were going to hit you with next. Especially that one.

So, what was the point of thinking about her at all. But thinking about her was still happening. All the time. There was no control over it. And that was the biggest nightmare. Staying away from her was the most sensible thing to do, alright.

"Well Frank! What are you having? Which one of your favourites will it be today?"

"What? Oh! Sorry! I was just trying to decide what to have!"

Liar. Ok then, so what was he supposed to say anyway. Hello beautiful one. I was just too busy thinking about the most beautiful girl in the world, to answer you. Still trying to work out whether she's an evil little bitch or an evil little witch or both. Or whatever she was. Don't think so.

Anyway, there was no thought put in to any particular answer. That one just popped straight out. Lucky it wasn't such a busy time. Getting there after the lunchtime crowd was a good idea. Usually about 2 o'clock. Maybe the staring went on for a bit too long.

"So, are you ordering or not?"

Obviously in a bad mood today. But the café girl smile was still there.

"Oh sorry! I'll have the favourite meal, thanks! Haven't had that for a few days!"

"Ok then! So, what favourite meal would that be? You've got a few to choose from now!"

No. She wasn't trying to be smart or anything. She wasn't like that. And that lovely smile was still there. And those beautiful blue eyes were doing the staring now. So, how could there be any aggravation. Anyway, she was a café girl. So, she could be as smart as she liked. Even if she wasn't being smart.

"Uh! The first one! Sourdough, avocado, spinach, mushrooms, tomato and relish! And butter!"

"Nuttelex!"

"Yes please! And the coffee!"

"Righto! Ok! Your usual table, Frank?"

"Uh, yes! Right! The usual table! In the corner! Where I belong!"

Yeah. Just loved saying that. The beautiful one was on the ball, you know. And always smiled and gave the thumbs up, whenever she saw him walking in or out. And Frank always smiled and gave the thumbs up back. Which was not something he ever did. But for some reason, there was always some kind of mental blockage happening, whenever it came to just talking to the beautiful one. Whenever she was just walking around the café. Cleaning up tables and having a chat here and there with other customers.

And for another unknown reason, Frank always copied what she did and that could never be worked out. Not yet. It wasn't talking, anyway. So, there was no problem. But she was getting in there, alright. Tickling the emotions. Waking them up. Yeah, the emotions. That's what usually caused the blockages. That was a known thing now. That's for sure.

And she got the heart movement going as well. But not pounding away, like a giant drum. Like TMBGITW managed to do. Just a slow, gentle, rhythmic pumping action. TMBGITW is short for the most beautiful girl in the world, by the way. Much easier to say it that way. And much less painful.

On this particular day, after ordering, some kind of eye connection thing happened. It was like the brain inflated and then deflated again. In a matter of seconds. And the chest did the same thing as well. Yeah. Another temporary eye lock situation. The internal whoa was the only reaction possible. Like what happened once before. With TMBGITW.

But this time, more gentle and smooth. Like some kind of slow-moving magnetism. Gradually drawing on the new feelings, that were never there before. And even pleasurable. There was also a gradual, drawing feeling of desire. About jumping over the counter and grabbing hold of her. Give the beautiful one a big cuddle. Let her know all about that loving feeling that was hiding inside. Just busting to get out. But not getting out. Held back by an even greater magnetism. Like a safety device. A protective shield. It wouldn't have been like all the girls did to each other either. What a disaster that would have been. Thank Christ he didn't do it. But there was still mesmerisation, for at least three days. I can tell you that.

"There you go, Frank! Get into the good stuff!"

It was her again. The beautiful one. Put the lunch down. Smiled that warm café girl smile. Turned around and walked off. There was an immediate flushing of both cheeks.

"Gee it's always good to see you!"

Yeah, managed to squeeze that out. But she'd already took off. Doubt whether she even heard it. Probably better that she didn't.

The stupid old fool, almost made a complete fool of himself. Again. Then a real shock entered the system. And admitting to the truth about it was very difficult. But truth had come into the new life now. So, it had to be admitted. Now that it was at the surface. And that truth was. That it was TMBGITW who put the strange new feelings in the chest in the first place.

But the admitting, only lasted a few seconds. Calm and order had to be restored and maintained. And quickly. Because any thoughts about TMBGITW, only ever caused mass disruption. So, forgetting about TMBGITW was always the best thing to do. But it was never an easy thing to do. And that usually caused just as much disruption. There was just no escape. And no peace. None at all.

"There you go, Frank! Enjoy!"

The coffee arrived. Gently placed down beside his lunch. Never seen this one before.

"Oh thanks! I haven't seen you here before!"

"No, I'm usually upstairs! Sometimes we come down to help out. When it's busy!"

"Oh right!"

And more would have been said as well, you know. But she was gone already. And there were only three other tables, with customers sitting at them. So, she was obviously very confused this girl. Yeah. She was called the confused one straight away. Never saw her again. Sacked for sure.

There're going to have a lot of fun with you.

After a quick skim through a few newspapers, it was time for some more perving. There were not so many g-strings around. But there seemed to be lots of people walking and jogging along. And dogging. Frank called it dogging now, after watching the same comedy show, where shirt lifter and carpet chewer came from. They were just people out walking their dogs, you know. But not anymore. Not after this was discovered.

Dogging; A slang term for engaging in public sex while others watch.

Fucking hell.

But what else was the thinking going to come up with.

Of course, there were various other meanings for the word dogging. But this one was the best. Frank thought it was hilarious.

And it wasn't boring, watching all the doggy activity either. There was every breed you could possibly think of. Being led along by their proud owners. Tiny ones. Hairy ones. Big ugly looking things, with their doggy saliva dripping all over the concrete. And some people even had two or more dogs to lead along. The thought did occur, you know. About maybe getting a dog, or two. This thought was in there, alright. For about one second.

Sometimes the walkers gave a little smile to other walkers and would even stop and have a little chat. While their dogs introduced themselves and gave each other a sniff over, while they were at it. All this was usually friendly too. Although sometimes, two or more dogs, after a short sniff. Would suddenly become aggressive and start barking at each other. And if they weren't restrained by their owners, there would have been fur and saliva flying everywhere. That's for sure. Probably put it down to a doggy personality clash. Fancy trying to work all that, doggy psychology out.

But there were more friendly encounters than unfriendly encounters in the doggy walking world. Often, one or more dogless walkers would casually walk up to someone's dog and ask if they could give their dog a little pat. Say hello and smile and have a little chat to the dog and sometimes the owner as well. Before moving on.

Strangely enough, most of these friendly dogless walkers were young girls. Or just kids in general. That was always very interesting. Trying to make sense of the doggy walking world and everything that came with it. Was a completely different world, the doggy world. To the one Frank was starting to feel almost comfortable in. Some of the time.

Like an addition to the new life. That wasn't needed in the new life and wasn't wanted in the new life. But there it was. Right in there. In the middle of the parade. With the g-strings. The tattooed people. The alternatives. That's a much better description than shirt lifters and carpet chewers. And all the other people, that looked the same.

And all the other people, who looked nothing like the same as anyone else. And all the other people who looked the same but different. And all the other people, who just looked like different people.

Fucking hell. Maybe getting this second chance wasn't such a good idea after all. But the time would soon be there again. The lady would be on about coming such a long way. Doing so well. We all have great confidence in you. And all the rest of the usual shit, that she always comes up with. Yeah. She'd be back again. Knew that, alright. And being ready for her was essential. Because he'd been ambushed enough already.

Well, before you know it. Lunch is over. Coffee cup empty. Not so many doggies walking around, with their owners. Another day almost over and done with. Afternoon nap time. Which had previously been afternoon poker machine playing time. But not anymore. Not for a while now anyway.

Time to take the twenty-minute drive back to the living quarters. Twenty minutes inland from where he always wanted to be now. Yeah, Frank had become a trendy beach goer. More like a beach bum by the look of him. Long white hair. Halfway down his back. Unwashed. Unbrushed. Full of knots. And God knows what else. And always dressed in shorts, thongs and T-shirts or singlets. Yeah, a real beach bum. A real old beach bum. Trying to look like, a real young beach bum. Yeah. A new delusion in the new life.

The dream was to move into a beachside house or unit. Walk to the baths. Walk to the beaches. Walk everywhere. Just not with any dog. That's for sure.

Although, the way so many young g-strings took such a keen interest in dogs. There was a recurring thought about getting a dog, just for that purpose. But then the reality check happened. And besides, what would the café girls think of him then. This old fool lusting after young g-strings. That nothing could be done with anyway. And using a dog for bait. No, that thought didn't stay there too long at all. And thank Christ for that. Maybe a different story but. Back in the old life.

"See ya later Frank!"

"Yeah, see ya!"

Stopped for a second and looked straight at her. Would have said her name, too. But this girl's name was always a big problem to remember. And she was such a lovely girl too, you know. But for some reason, her name just wouldn't come out. Maybe it was because she had a sister that worked there too. Frank was always getting them mixed up. The rest of the girls, always got a good laugh out of it. Eventually, they were both written on the piece of paper. Along with the names that helped him to remember. They were both logged in.

But it kept happening, even after the sister wasn't there anymore. So, that wasn't it. There was no way of working it out either. So, that's why this girl was always known as the forgotten name girl. And it was easy remembering her name then. Because some of the letters in the forgotten name girl's name were part of the name he used to remember her. Explaining how that worked would be so complicated, you know. But it worked. And that's all that mattered.

Remembered another girl's name by calling her the tattooed one. Because she had lots of tattoos. And her name started with a T. So that was an easy one. And it's already been explained about how many of the other girl's names were remembered. And sometimes songs were used. Especially rock songs from the 70s and 80s. Because songs often had girl's names in them somewhere. And when the time came to remember a particular girl's name, the relevant song started playing in the head.

Eventually, all their names were remembered. And communication happened on a first name basis. But it took a lot of doing to get to that stage. And the café girls. They all knew that Frank struggled with their names. Especially during the early stages of going to the magic café. And they thought it was funny. And they taught Frank to see the funny side as well. Only that wasn't realised, till much later.

And it was around this time that the feelings were becoming stronger. And these feelings were the ones telling him. That maybe he was starting to like all the café girls too much. And these were heavy feelings to be having. Especially for an old man. Such strong feelings of liking, for girls old enough to be his granddaughters. Fighting these feelings off was no use. And being in denial, didn't work either. The poor old battered heart was copping a hiding, alright. Yeah. Getting softer all the time.

But there was not really any feeling of being old anymore either. This new life Frank, felt like a much younger version of the Frank he could have been. In the old life. So, that's why the café was the magic café and the girls who worked there, were the magic café girls. Next, he'll be trusting them as well. And that was going to be an even bigger hurdle to get over.

There're going to have a lot of fun with you.

"Oh Frank! You're starting to blossom! You really are!"

She didn't have to put it like that, did she? But she did, didn't she?

"Hello I'm Frank and I'm a compulsive gambler!"

"Hi Frank!"

"Hi Frank!"

"Hello Frank!"

"I haven't played the machines for another week."

"That's great, Frank!"

"Yeah, well done, Frank!"

"I'm starting to remember things better now. Like names. And I'm talking to people better as well. It's because I'm looking after myself and exercising and going to the gym and eating properly. I'm starting to really blossom!"

Oh shit. How on earth did that come out?

"What was that? Blossom? Flowers blossom, mate! You must be losing it! What are you, a pansy?"

Yeah right. Set himself right up for that one. It's amazing how things can get stuck in the brain sometimes. But all the compulsives got a good laugh out of it. So, that was all good. Things then went quiet for a few seconds.

"I've got flowers blossoming in the garden right now!"

The old compulsive, just had to get that one in there, didn't she? Payback time, eh.

Yeah, what a smile she had on her face. In between laughing. Got all the other compulsives laughing again. Even the controller started up again. This next bit was forgotten about. Until that old compulsive got too smart for herself.

"Anyway, I was watching that comedy show again the other night. They got talking about dogging. So, I got onto the computer and looked it up. Do you know what it means? Well, I'll tell you!"

"I already know what it means. I've got three poodles. We go dogging all the time!"

That old compulsive was in for a shock. I can tell you that. There were a few muffled sounds of supressed laughter.

"Oh, no you don't! I'll tell you what it really means!"

The whole place went dead quiet and all the eyes were on Frank. Yeah. Just loving it. The controller looked defeated. But wanted to know as well.

"Right! Dogging; slang term for engaging in public sex, while others watched!"

What a roar of laughter erupted then. From everyone. Except the old compulsive. Just sitting there. Mouth half opened. With a look on her face, that was beyond description. Shut her right up. Teach her to get smart. Didn't hear another word out of her, for the rest of the meeting. Didn't even share.

The controller recorded everything in a book, you know. When you turned up and when you didn't. When you shared and when you didn't. Maybe put in some of what was said in shares as well. Oh well. Too late now. And when you busted. Frank was after that 90-day badge again. Yeah, if you went 90 days without busting, you got a badge. This was a big thing for compulsive gamblers, you know. Getting the 90-day badge. There was always a cake and it was just like a little birthday party.

What's said in GA meetings, stays in GA meetings.

Forgot about that. Anyway, what hasn't been mentioned so far, is that the first part of GA meetings, is when everyone picks a page out of the Gamblers

Anonymous book. It's like a bible for compulsives. That's what Frank called it anyway. The GA bible. And it was Frank's turn to pick.

"Page 47."

This was the favourite page. The heading was. How sick is sick. So, out come the glasses, and just about to start reading.

"Reading glasses, Frank!"

The controller wasn't shocked very often.

"Yeah well. Thought I'd give the glasses a go. They cost me two bucks. I noticed them at the discount chemist, where I get all my drugs from. For two dollars! Why not give them a go, eh!"

These are prescription drugs where're talking about here. The ones he needs to stay alive. Not the ones he tried to kill himself with. How's that for a turnaround?

"'Bout time mate. Now you might be able to see what you're reading!"

Yeah. Got a few laughs out of that one.

But that's ok. This compulsive just couldn't stop with the smart comments. Same one who ripped him off about the thongs. Always getting into him about something, you know. Frank had been squinting and mumbling away for weeks, when it was his turn to read. Trying to focus. Lucky for him, he'd read the bible so many times, that he'd remembered most of the words. But he still had trouble with the really small print. And this other compulsive, always seemed to pick pages with the really small print. Bastard.

Anyway, here's a few bits and pieces from the favourite page. How sick is sick. Each compulsive reads out one paragraph. Till there are no paragraphs left. Then someone else picks a page.

How sick is sick?

To dream about getting something out of life the only way possible. Through compulsive gambling. Until all finances have been lost. Gone into hopeless debt. Lost all their friends. Caused irreparable damage to the family unit.

Compulsive gamblers are victims of a disease. Just as surely as if their bodies are riddled with cancer. An addiction that slowly strips a person of all their values and self-respect. Like committing a slow form of suicide.

The victim of this addiction often or almost always undergoes drastic behaviour patterns. Like a Jekyll and Hyde personality. This sickness consumes their whole being. They no longer control gambling. Gambling controls them. They may say to themselves. Today I will not gamble. But sure enough, the compulsion takes over and the action becomes the motivation. Winning is no longer the driving force. But just being in action. Just gambling.

The compulsive gambler leaves behind them, a path of destruction. Jeopardising marriage, family, job, financial security. No thought is given to the consequences they will face tomorrow. They become a thoughtless, conscienceless, unscrupulous automaton. No longer capable of making decisions outside their gambling world.

Is such self-inflicted misery the behaviour of a healthy, well-adjusted individual? Is not such a person just as sick as the dope addict, the alcoholic, or the mentally disturbed? The compulsive gambler cannot take any pills or medicine to cure them of their illness. But they are nevertheless just as sick, as if they were slowly poisoning themselves or destroying their body, mind and soul. By any other equally destructive means.

Yeah, that was Frank, alright and he knew it. That's why page 47 was the favourite page. Written just for him. And so were many other pages in the bible. Actually, the whole bible was written just for Frank. And he knew that too. But page 47. That was the one, alright.

After reading, there was a short break. So, all the nicotine and caffeine addicts could get a fix. Before sharing started.

Oops, how did all that get in there? There was another share happening. Just popped in out of nowhere. Oh well. Might as well just go with it. No use fighting against it. When stuff wants to come out. It just comes out. And here it comes.

"Hello. I'm Frank and I'm a compulsive gambler."

"Hi Frank!"

"Hello Frank!"

"Yeah. Hi Frank!"

"I haven't played the machines for another week!"

"Oh, that's great, Frank! Well done!"

"Yeah, well done, Frank!"

"You've got it beat now, eh!"

That one got a bit of a laugh.

"That's four weeks now, Frank! Good on you!"

"Yeah thanks! I'm so proud of myself! I'm going to make it! I know I'm going to make it this time! I'm not going to give up! I just have to follow my instincts! That's all! If I just follow my instincts, I'll get there!"

"Of course, you will Frank! You've done it before and you'll do it again! Only this time, be aware of what made you bust the last time! Don't let the same thing happen again!"

"Anyway, nothing much has happened. If I stay away from people, I'll be, alright. It's always other people that mess me up! That's what I've worked out! That's what the instincts are telling me! Stay away from other people and you'll be, alright! So, that's what I'm doing!"

"Except, when I go to the gym and when I go swimming. That's different. And when I go to the café, I like it in there the most. They don't upset me in there. There're all wonderful! They kind of drive me crazy a bit. And sometimes I get confused. But I've come such a long way now. Maybe I'm in love with all of them!"

Stupid delusional old bastard. But that can happen to lonely old men, can't it. That other compulsive was sitting there, with a big smile on his face. The one that warned him in the first place. He just thought he had to go and say that, didn't he? But he didn't have to, did he? Fucking bastard. He didn't have to go and say that.

There're going to have a lot of fun with you.

"Anyway, thanks for letting me share!"

Yeah, as usual. Congratulations here. Congratulations there. Good, positive comments from some of the other compulsives. And it became like just another drug, you know. A share. Understanding looks, from all the long-termers; and looks of shock and amazement, from any newcomers. And then a very short bout of anticipation, before all the good vibes were absorbed into the psychological structure, of the emotionally tortured compulsive. Who'd just poured their heart out. And now looked forward to the flush of relief, that always followed one of these self-deprecating, brutally honest shares. To leave the compulsive once again, emotionally drained out. But usually with a big smile on their face. Till the next time. Yeah. Till the inevitable next time.

Yeah. There was always that understanding in Gamblers Anonymous, you know. That whatever's said in a meeting, stays in the meeting. And thank Christ for that, eh?

"That's great, Frank! But there are good people out there. Not everyone wants to upset you. What about us Frank? We're your friends! We're here to support you! That's what GA is all about! Group help! But also individual help. We all learn at our own pace!"

Yeah well, there was no arguing about any of that was there. Anyway, he wasn't in such a bad way this time. But all the good advice and positive feedback was never enough, you know. No, never enough.

"Anyway, thanks for letting me share."

Wasn't unusual for compulsives to repeat the thanks for letting me share bit either. And they didn't mind another round of the usual clapping and some positive comments, from a few of the other compulsives. Before the controller moved things along.

"Would anyone else like to share?"

Some of the other compulsives could be a real pain in the arse. At every meeting. Repeating their whole fucking life story, over and over again. Every time they shared. The words gambling or poker machines were rarely mentioned, you know. Even though, that's what ruined their whole miserable life in the first place and in many cases, still did.

But that didn't matter. It was their time to share. To unload, much of what was hidden in their own dark shadows. Frank knew all about the dark shadows. So, there was understanding going on. Just relaxing during these boring shares was the best thing to do. Try and drift off into some empty space for a while. Until the eruption of hand clapping and well wishes, snapped him back into the GA reality. Eventually, every other compulsive who ever attended more than a few meetings, knew all these repeated shares backwards.

By the time some of them finished, everyone in the room was almost asleep. Sitting there with their eyes glazed over. Sometimes the controller, did everyone a big favour and interrupted at an appropriate time. Tried to end the share. Sometimes it worked and sometimes it didn't. Depended on the compulsive. Sometimes when they got going with their share, there was no stopping them. They shared till they were finished sharing and that, was it?

But that's what Gamblers Anonymous was all about, you know. Getting it all out there. Whatever it was. Release the pressure. Yeah, it was the place to be, alright. For all compulsive gamblers. So how could one compulsive get too pissed off by another compulsive? When they were all just compulsives. But that happened, you know. From time to time.

And surely, if any true compulsive had a choice between sitting in front of a poker machine. Mesmerised. Pushing buttons. Or the one bigger, repeat the bet button, eh. Trawling all the favourite haunts or TAB's. Betting on line, or donating money to book makers. It's obvious where they'd rather be, or should be. But not all of them went to GA meetings, you know.

Most of them were just stuck in the cycle. Slugging it out. Time after time. Running out of money, till the next time and the next time. Because next time it will be different. The big jackpot will be hit and all their troubles will be over. But it's never any different. Action replay. Short term memory. Here we go again. And the cycle of misery and pain continues. Even Frank had worked that one out.

Well, all the shares were finished and thank fuck for that. Just the little bullshit bit at the end of the meeting and it was out of there.

All together now.

"To the God of our own understanding!

God, grant me the serenity to accept the things I cannot change. The courage to change the things I can. And the wisdom to know the difference."

All together now.

"Thanks for sharing! Thanks for caring! Keep coming back! The meetings make it!"

Still hated this bit. But not as much. Tolerated now. Only just. But what choice was there. And you wouldn't believe it. Just about to leave, when that smartarse walks up.

"I've got this spare glasses case that I never use. Thought you might like to have it."

So, he just happens to have a spare glasses case, does he? What a coincidence that is. Just how fucking stupid is someone supposed to be anyway.

"Gee thanks! Just what I need! See you next week!"

Well, there was a need for a glasses case after all. And it was for nothing, eh.

Yeah, that bastard. Sitting there smiling. Compulsives are supposed to support each other, you know. Not make fun of you. What a smart arse. And he never shares much. And not for very long either. And he's hardly ever there anyway. And when he is there, he sits there and just smiles at you. Fuck him.

Anyway, there're all probably working together. Yeah. That has to be it. I mean, the girls with their stupid glasses on. And the lady who wasn't there. In the head all the time. Tormenting the shit out of him. And this smiling compulsive suddenly turning up with a spare glasses case. It's a fucking conspiracy. That's what it is. It has to be.

"Oh Frank! Maybe you just don't know a nice friendly smile, when you see one. There are different kinds of smiles, Frank! The girls at the café smile at you all the time and you don't mind that, do you? Well other people smile too. For other reasons! Maybe he's just trying to help you, Frank! You may have misinterpreted his smiles."

"Maybe relax a little more! The GA members know what you've been through now. They just want to help you. And this other member. That you obviously are very suspicious of. Get to know him properly, Frank! You may be surprised! You may even get to like him! You may even learn to trust him!"

Yeah. She got him again. Driving home. She was there a lot, you know. When he was driving home. And what a head full that was. He's probably one of them fucking shirt lifters.

"Oh Frank! Really! Anxiety is such a negative character trait! You'll need to work on that!"

"Well. There're all over the place these days. I see them every day. You should already know that anyway. You being the new life expert and everything!"

Now she had him talking to himself again. But then he just shut up. There was a distraction. Something was suddenly getting remembered. Back to the GA bible again.

Believe us, we need all the friends we can get. So far in this booklet, we have touched on some of the dangers of recovery. This one, personality clashes, we believe, is one of the most dangerous.

So many members over the years, have left the fellowship and trundled back down that road that leads to misery. Using the excuse, whether real or not, of a personality clash with another member. That is something we do not need. As has been said before, we compulsive gamblers are complex characters. We can be very immature. We sometimes suffer from self-pity and we become resentful at the drop of a hat. Mix all these character defects and add a few more and what have you got.

Someone looking for a personality to clash with.

"Well! Who does that sound like, Frank?"

Yeah. Knew that was him, alright. But he'd forgotten about that bit. Whoever wrote that Gamblers Anonymous bible, sure knew what they were talking about. It's got all the information in it. Under every heading you can think of. And personality clashes, is one of the headings. And so is short term memory. There were just no excuses anymore. For anything. No getting away with anything either. Fuck it.

"Yes Frank! That's it! That's all it is! A little short-term memory problem. But it's nowhere near as bad as it used to be! Remember! You've come such a long way now, Frank! Remembering that you forgot, is such a huge step forward! You should be very proud of yourself! We're all so proud of you, Frank! You know that don't you!"

Yeah. Knew that, alright. Just didn't want to talk about it. And didn't want to be reminded all the time either. Just how much pressure was anyone supposed to take anyway.

Yeah. Back on the veranda. Few things needed a think through. Like what the fuck was going on. In this new life. Every time something got worked out. It wasn't really worked out at all. Gamblers Anonymous was the only place, where peace could be found. Where that lady didn't get in there. With all the good advice. Pumping up the brain. With bucket loads of confusion. Till the thinking reached overload and the headaches started up. Fucking hell. The pressure, you know. Yeah. The pressure. Just too much fucking pressure.

"I want my old life back! You had no right! I want it back! I want my old life back! I want it back now! Give it back! You fucking bitch!"

Almost leapt right out of the chair, screaming this one out. Top of the voice as well. Lucky there was only one neighbour, eh. Who never seemed to be home so, no problem there.

"Right! That does it! He's a lost cause, this one! Nothing more can be done! You must realise that now! You've done your best, dear! We all know that! But these outbursts, just can't be tolerated! Not after all the effort you've put into him! He's getting nowhere!"

"Yes, I agree! We should have cut him loose, after that last relapse! He's never going to make it, this one! He's had enough chances! We have no choice! We must let him go! For his own sake! And for your sake! As well as ours!"

"Yes! I think that's a fair analysis! There are limits to our patience! There must be, considering how many others are available! And you mustn't forget! We do lose one occasionally!"

"Oh no! Please no! He's made such significant progress! He really has! I can't give up on him now! I promised him I wouldn't! He'd be so disappointed, if I gave up now! No! I'll never give up on him! Never! I know he can get there! I just know he can! Please! Just one more chance! I'll take full responsibility!"

"I'm sorry dear! But you already have full responsibility! Remember!"

"Yes, that's right! I do remember! But he was so, very damaged! Yes, so very damaged! But there's so much goodness in him! I know there is! I believe in him! I really do! He can make it! I'm sure he can! Please! Just one more chance!"

"That's enough talking now! I think we all understand the position we are in! We must decide! One way or the other! Another chance! Or admit defeat with this one and let him go!"

"They usually only get one chance! So, I say let him go!"

"I don't know! He has made good progress in some areas! Maybe there still is a little hope there! I'm willing to give him another chance! But if he goes backwards again, then he'll get no more support from me! I'm sorry!"

"Well, I have to say! I've ran out of support for this one! I don't think he can make it! No! I'm sorry dear! We'll have to let him go!"

"We'll need to take a vote on it! All those in favour of another chance, raise your right hand! Right! So, he gets another chance! But only one more! It's all up to you now, dear! Good luck to you! And good luck with him!"

"Oh, thank you! Thank you all so much! I understand how some of you, can still have reservations! But he can get there! I know he can! I have great confidence in him! I really do!"

After this latest spinout, it was decided to check that word out. That last word she used, that wasn't understood.

Anxiety; an emotion characterised by an unpleasant state of inner turmoil and includes unpleasant feelings of dread over anticipated events, by nervous behaviour.

There were lots more explanations for the word anxiety. But after reading this one, that was enough. Because the words inner turmoil, hit the right nerve. And the word turmoil wasn't even understood. Until it was looked up.

Turmoil; confusion, turbulence, tumult, disorder, commotion, disturbance, agitation, ferment, unrest, trouble. And there were more words as well. But that was enough, to get the message through the fog.

So, the true understanding of turmoil was when the shitting himself feeling entered the equation. And the big blowouts happened and fucked everything up. And it took so long getting the structure back into a functioning state. And that was all he needed to know.

"Frank! Frank! Yes! You, need to control your anxiety! You really do! Your whole new life depends on it! It really does! You must listen to me, Frank! You really must! This is your last chance, Frank! Your last chance! You do understand that, don't you?"

Well, that was a sudden, emotionally charged outburst wasn't it. Not like her at all. She could be losing it, you know. But the anxiety was killing him. Have to admit that. She was right again. As usual. Yeah. Getting smarter all the time.

"So, no more anxiety! Ok! Got it! I'm all good in the head now! All good in the head! Thanks to you! Your always so good to me! I understand that! But I need to get some sleep right now! So please, just go away and leave me alone! We can talk again tomorrow!"

Yeah. Figured a friendly approach was needed right now, you know. She was already upset enough. Didn't want to make things any worse.

There she was in her chair. Eyes closed. What could have been dried up tears on the cheeks. Looking sound asleep. So, Frank just sat down in the visitor's chair and watched his mother. For what seemed too long. Almost went to sleep as well.

"Welfare were never getting my kids! That's one thing they were never going to do! They were never getting any of my kids! No! They weren't getting any of my kids!"

This was a shock, alright. One minute she's sitting there asleep. Next minute she's wide awake, firing off about welfare and her kids. She had eleven kids you know. Frank already knew a little about his mother's early life. After the Dotty Dot visit, she opened up more and more, about those traumatic times. And they were all traumatic. In one way or another.

There was no way of forgetting about all that sad stuff. Not after listening to the way his mother, explained it all. Little by little. In sudden outbursts of emotion. And she was never an emotional person either. Not outwardly anyway. Frank figured that the deepest, darkest secrets, hidden inside that head of hers would go to the grave with her. Kind of figured it could be the same with himself as well.

"Would you like a cup of coffee, mum?"

"Oh! Hello! No one ever comes to visit me! You're the only visitor I've had this week! I'm glad you're here!"

"Would you like a cup of coffee, mum?"

"Yes, I'd love a cup of coffee! Thank you!"

"Ok, I'll be back in a few minutes!"

That's all it took. A few minutes.

"Oh hello! No one ever visits me!"

"Would you like a cup of coffee, mum?"

"Yes, I'd love a cup of coffee!"

"I thought you would! There you go!"

"Thank you! You must have known I'd like a coffee!"

"I had a pretty good idea! So, how are you going!"

"I'm going, good! They look after me here! I like it when I get visitors! You're the only visitor I've had today!"

Well, this conversation with his mother was pretty much the same every time. And could have gone on forever.

But that didn't matter. For some reason, Frank looked forward to visiting his mother now. Maybe, because her time was running out and so was his. Well, in the old life anyway. And no point explaining anything about the new life. Wouldn't know how to begin anyway. And his poor mother, didn't need to know about all the pressure he was under. Coping with the many challenges he now faced, on a day-to-day basis.

Getting to know each other before it was too late. That's what was happening, alright. And that was enough. Frank found out about the open-heart surgery, you know. Yeah. If that operation went wrong, there'd be no more conversations with this, frail old women. His real mother. But who'd never really been his real mother. Sounds very unkind doesn't it. But it wasn't her fault. I mean, this frightened little orphan girl. Who'd struggled all her life. For her own identity. Her true self.

Yeah. She'd always lived in other people's shadows. And life in those shadows wasn't always good. And she had all her own dark shadows to deal with as well. And who knows what was hidden away in there. That's what the thinking was anyway. Just by the little conversations they'd been having and the little bits of information she'd been letting out.

And to think this frightened little orphan girl, went on to have eleven children of her own. She married a strict catholic, you know. What a big mistake that was eh. But that's another story in itself. And what a complicated and confusing story it is. Too complicated to be repeated here. Just wasn't up to it. Not up to it at all.

So, how could any mother, show love and affection and pass on special feelings to one child, let alone eleven? When there were no such qualities there in the first place. Or if they were ever there. Stunted through trauma and bullying and various other kinds of abuse and mistreatment. I mean, there was no nurturing going on anywhere was there. She had no chance, did she? No chance at all.

This level of thinking must have come with the new life, you know. Because it had never surfaced before. Maybe a few lights were getting switched on, here and there. For the first time ever. Maybe the brain wasn't completely destroyed after all. Even after several decades of self-inflicted abuse. Yes, those long, gluey, diabolical, emotionally strangulating addictions, almost finished Frank off for good, you know. But not quite.

"Oh Frank! This is such a big step forward for you! You know that, don't you! To be thinking with such emotion and feeling! Such a big step forward! I'm so proud of you, Frank! I'm just so proud of you!"

Was that her again, banging on. Not now please. Not now.

Half a cup of coffee and she's off again. There one minute, gone the next. Just like the lady. Usually, time to get up and leave when this happened. But not this time. What she said about welfare not getting her kids had triggered some more old memories. He'd only heard about these stories a few times.

After Frank's mother's, mother was found dead and the big black car took the kids away to the orphanage, it wasn't long before they were fostered out. To an aunt and uncle. They took all three of them. But the oldest one, a boy was a bit uncontrollable. So, he went back to the orphanage and later ended up at a special boy's home, for orphans. He was 9 years old. Born on 11-01-1926. So, this was 1935 we're talking about here.

Wandering around the grounds one day, him and this other kid got to talking. Just about stuff orphan kids talk about. Whatever that is. Anyway, this other kid who was a few years older, started saying how much they looked alike. And they kind of talked the same and didn't know where they came from either.

It was decided to go and ask whoever ran the place and find out if they were related. Or maybe even brothers. So, the Headmaster looks up the records. And sure enough. They were brothers, alright. They didn't even know each other existed, till that day.

Accidentally bumping into one brother was an excitement for both of them. That's for sure. But there was also talk of another brother. Not much was known about this other brother either. Apparently, he just disappeared one day and no one ever heard from him again. What happened to him was anyone's guess.

But after someone in the family did quite a lot of research, a few things were discovered. He'd joined the army. He didn't go overseas. But after the war ended, is when he disappeared. Sometime around 1945. He'd been in trouble for going AWOL four times, you know. That's a lot of times to go AWOL. Why that was is unknown. Guess he just didn't like being in the army. And why he was allowed to stay in the army was unknown as well. For many years anyway.

But according to the family researcher, he did like being in the army. Kept telling them, he wanted to be a marine. And they kept telling him, he couldn't be a marine. And apparently, he didn't like other people telling him, what he could or couldn't do. So, he got all upset and went AWOL. So, it wasn't really his fault. They should have just let him be a marine and there would have been no trouble at all.

A really weird thing happened when this same family member applied for this long-lost brother's army records. A package arrived. There were some medals and a letter of commendation. For bravery. So, how could someone, who'd gone AWOL four times and been such a pain in the army's arse, be given medals and a letter of commendation for bravery. The imagination could flip-out in all directions on that one, eh. Come up with all kinds of conclusions. But no one really knows and most likely, never will. Not even the family researcher could work it out.

But the family researcher did eventually confirm, that the package that arrived, actually contained his own father's records and medals and not the long-lost brothers. So, that cleared that little mystery up. But there will always be that mystery about the long-lost brother.

At about fourteen years of age, the younger brother was taken from the special boy's home for orphans and sent to some boys training farm. Learnt how to be a farm labourer. From there, he wandered around the country, from farm to farm. Wherever he could find work. Not much more was known about this brother either. Until the same family member, who'd already done some digging around. Did some more digging around and discovered that this brother had actually written a diary. One surprise after the other, eh. And what was written in this diary, answered a lot of unanswered questions. About this particular brother anyway.

Mentioning the entire contents here would take too long. But there are some interesting bits. Like when he says the boys training farm he was sent to was actually called the Farm School of Husbandry. He started in the dairy for two shillings a week. Or, sometimes out on the farm, for one shilling a week. And sometimes in the dormitory or the kitchen or the dining room.

Then it was from one farm to another. Milking cows mostly, and a variety of other jobs that always needed doing on a dairy farm. On the first farm he was sent to, the kids there had to make their own brushes, to clean the milking machines. The owner used to name all his cows and they were always milked in their proper turn.

They had to kill and skin all the bull calves. Then salt the skins. And they ate the meat every day. It was very tender meat and this brother could never remember being so well fed. He didn't mind being on this farm at all. But the owner died and shortly after that, the house burnt down. So, it was off to another farm.

There's not much said about this next farm, except it was another dairy farm. He slept in a room six foot by four foot. The bed was made out of old bags and there was no lock on the door.

The next farm was a dairy farm as well. The main memory about this place was the food. It was terrible. Mostly stale bread, macaroni or rice custard. Which was usually blown by flies. But he wasn't there long. Glad to get away.

Another dairy farm. He was the only kid there. And he liked this place. The people were good to him and he was starting to trust them. A little bit anyway. He'd begun to understand the feeling of being settled and relaxed. But then the owner was thrown of a horse and died, as a result of his injuries.

He says from there, he ran away with his brother. But not the brother he met at the orphanage. This was another brother. He only had one other brother that he knew of. And according to the name mentioned in the diary, it was the same brother who joined the army. But nothing more is said about this brother. So, maybe there was another brother and maybe there wasn't. And how he ended up meeting up with this brother in the first place, is not mentioned either. So, it's a mystery what happened there. No one in the family knows. That's for sure. Not even the family researcher.

Anyway, he ended up working in a pub for a short time. Then at a Seventh Day Adventist market garden. Growing potatoes, cauliflowers, cabbages and tomatoes.

He left that job and went to what he calls a camp. Where farmers would come and get workers for their farm. At one pound or twenty shillings a day. Didn't stay there long. Found another job, that paid twenty-five shillings a day.

Then for some unknown reason, he jumped on a goods train and ended up in a big city down south. And can you believe it. He joined the air force. Had to wait three weeks to get it. So, he got a job. In a woollen mill. Doing night shift. Making material for soldier's uniforms and blankets. He stayed there for around eighteen months. Pretty much a record for him. He says he couldn't give notice, so he shot through. The family researcher could never find any record of him ever joining the air force.

So, whether giving notice meant out of the air force, or from the job in the woollen mills, is unclear. But he was either in the air force for eighteen months, or worked in the woollen mill for eighteen months. Or both.

Anyway, he ended up working in a spinning factory for a short time. Then for a butcher. The owner had cattle and race horses. One of his responsibilities was making up hay fodder for the cattle. He also started learning how to break-in and train race horses.

In between wandering around and working at various places, he was a regular at a gymnasium and learnt how to box. That was in 1944.

Then for some unknown reason, he headed up the coast. Eventually got a job at a major railway station, taking and developing photographs. He says he was called a street photographer. He'd walk up to people and ask if they wanted their photo taken. But before that, he joined a boxing troupe. But that didn't last long, before he left and joined a travelling circus. But that didn't last long either.

He says from there, he ended up on a big cattle property. Drawing up to 800 head of cows and calves. This job lasted for about nine months. Then for some unknown reason, he headed for the coast.

Not long after arriving was when he got that job at the railway station. That's also when he met a girl, who he fell in love with. She was nineteen years old and already had three children. But that didn't matter to him. He settled down, after meeting up with this girl. Well kind of anyway.

He still went from job to job. At a tyre place. At a pie and sausage factory. A fence and gate place. Then another fence and gate place. Then back to the first fence and gate place.

During this time, he had 20 odd fights at the stadium. In 1952, he married the girl he met years earlier. They split up in 1954. Then in 1956, they bought a house. So, they obviously got back together. He says he got a good steady job and stayed settled in this house. For eleven years and six months.

Then it was back on a dairy farm. But he says that each winter, he headed up the coast. To the warmer weather. He stayed up there for a while. Long enough to go through a few more jobs. Next job he got was in the public service. At a council. Then in three of four pubs. What happened with the council job, is not explained. Well, there's never any real explanations about anything, is there. Especially about leaving jobs. His life just seemed to roll along. That's all.

Anyway, back down the coast. Got a job at a chicken farm. Lasted three years. Then at a marina. Then at a fibre glass place. Then at a place, that built buses. Then at another place that built coaches.

Then the next entry in the diary, is all about going on an invalid pension. Then onto the old age pension. After that, there's more information about other jobs he had along the way. And where he lived with his wife, before they eventually bought the house. Where they lived together for eleven years and six months. And they had five children together. As well as the three children his wife already had, before he met her and fell in love with her. Eventually, he moved back up to the warmer weather. Where he spent his final days.

But the last entry in the diary was the one that really stirred up the emotions. That's for sure. And this is what it said:

'Not bad for an uneducated boy.'

And this got the thinking going again, you know. Maybe the old life hadn't been so bad after all. What could be remembered that is. Maybe he should have written a diary himself.

"Yes Frank! Your old life could have been much worse! But at least you survived it all! Just like the long-lost brother did. And now you have your new life to look forward to! You're so lucky Frank! Not everyone gets a second chance! Make the most of it! I know you will, Frank! I know you will! You don't know how lucky you are, Frank! You really don't!"

"Yeah! Yeah! I know! We all have great confidence in you, Frank! I know! I know! You'll make it, Frank! You'll make it, Frank! You'll make it! I know you will! We all know you will! Fucking hell!"

Talking to himself again. Time to go.

His mother was still there, sound asleep. Hadn't moved. At peace once again. Frank got up. Sat back down. Got back up and then sat back down again. There were more memories coming and they had to be remembered.

Frank's mother and Dorothy, stayed with the aunt and uncle. Something went terribly wrong with Dorothy, as you already know. It was figured, that his mother was looked after well enough. But was never allowed to do anything she wanted. She had her own dreams and thoughts about her future. But her future was not decided by her. Not much is known about the environment she was raised in. Other than that, it was strict enough. Fair to say, she was never allowed to reach full bloom. Maybe, didn't even bud into half a little flower.

She never did go into detail about her childhood years, you know. They had always been like a no-go topic for discussion. Secretive business. Non sharing secrets of the past. Yeah. Frank's mother had a head full of secrets, alright. The occasional snippets let out during the nursing home visits became like excerpts of privileged information.

But certain other facts, did leak out from time to time. There was no chance of developing into an individual. Controlled from the start. In a strange new place. She never liked being there. But was stuck and powerless. And this trend continued into her married life. Until, the man she married was completely out of the picture and she could finally make her own decisions. Without anyone standing over her. Giving orders. No answering back. Do as you're told and all the rest of that bullying, controlling stuff. But that's just the way kids were treated back then. Especially orphans. And she learnt to understand that.

"Orphans aren't treated like the other children. There're different." She said that one day. And that was the first time, the far-away look was noticed in the sad old eyes.

The look that said, there's so much more I could tell you, but. And then the shutters came down and they stayed down. Till the next moment of weakness. Well actually, the sad old look had been seen many times over the years. Just not noticed. And certainly not understood, for what it really was. Not by anyone.

Years later, it was discovered that another, younger sister existed. At least a foot taller than all the rest. Was obvious enough. Had another father. There was still much discussion, whether this extra-long sister was actually the crying baby, trapped under the dead mother. Frank usually stayed out of these conversations. And doesn't know too many details, other than. Apparently, she was never a happy child.

Although the family researcher, did eventually agree that this sister was in fact the crying baby. And that was a good thing to know. Especially for his mother.

Ok, so what's going on here. Oh no. Behind schedule. Time to go. His mother was still sound asleep. Good time to get out of there.

"Where's your mask? We can't let you in without a mask!"

Fucking pandemic. In a bit of a mood, this girl. Obvious straight away.

"Oh shit, I've forgotten to bring it! It's in the car! I'll go and get it! I'll be back in a minute!"

Frank actually used the shit word in front of one of the café girls. Unbelievable. There was never any swearing in front of the café girls. Have to forgive him for that one. Wasn't quite himself, you know.

So, off to get the mask. Had a stack of them in the car. Always forgetting about putting a fucking mask on. Just hated putting masks on. But understood the need to put one on. Just like everybody else. One of the girls usually gave him one at the counter. But not this time. Confidently, walked back in with a mask on.

"I need to see your proof of double vaccination!"

Fucking hell. He left that at home, didn't he?

"I showed it at the gym this morning. They told me I only had to show it once and it'd be in the system!"

The thinking was that in the system, meant in the system for everywhere. Not just the gym. That's why the double vaccination certificate was left at home in a safe place. Took ages to print the damn thing out of the computer. After logging into the right app and moving from one screen to the next and typing in all the information required. Did that all by himself, you know. And it was a big deal. A big achievement. Just so proud of himself.

"Well, that's not right! I can't let you in, if you haven't got it! I need to see it!"

She wasn't going to back down either. The bitch. Frank just stood there, staring at her and she was just standing behind the counter, staring straight back. It was a stare off, alright. The girl at the coffee machine, kind of turned half way around and half smiled. Then looked at the cranky girl and then back at Frank.

"She's kicking me out!"

In shock, alright. But the girl at the coffee machine, didn't want anything to do with this one. Just turned her back. All alone this time and Frank knew it too. Gave the cranky girl one more little stare, before turning around and leaving. Pissed right off. But not really pissed off, you know. Getting pissed off with a café girl was never going to happen. Not for long anyway. About thirty seconds. That girl was doing the right thing. Just doing her job. That's all. He knew that.

And the girl at the coffee machine was the forgotten name girl. But she wouldn't forget about this little episode and neither would Frank. That's for sure.

Dropped into an Indian restaurant for take away on the way home. Hadn't had Indian for a few weeks. Liked Indian food. So, it didn't really matter. Not then anyway.

Back on the veranda, getting stuck into the rice and three curries. And got to thinking. Been going to the magic café for a few years now and that girl didn't want to believe him. Well, she probably did believe him. But rules are rules aren't they and she stuck to her guns, alright. The bitch. But yeah. So, good on her. But that feeling of being a bit pissed off kept coming back. But not because of the café girl. Was over that already. But there was still a mood hanging around.

This pandemic shit. All the restrictions. What a fucking nightmare. Getting to everyone. Only just got used to putting a fucking mask on. Now had to show proof of double vaccination as well. Everywhere you go. Yeah had a gut full of all these restrictions. That's for sure. Never did like rules but, either.

Fuck the magic café. Decided never to go back there, ever again. But then the thinking got rearranged a bit, you know. Still wouldn't go back. Not for a few weeks, anyway. By then, things will have settled back down. A few days passed. Back there again. Been for the usual swim. But couldn't stop thinking about what happened, with that cranky girl. And he was hungry as well. So, deep breath and back in he goes. With the mask on and with the double vaccination certificate. That same girl who was at the coffee machine was on duty. The forgotten name girl.

"Is she here today?"

Frank was looking around when he said that. Kind of hoping the cranky one was there and kind of hoping she wasn't.

"No, she's been off for a few days!"

What a relief that was. She must have noticed the edgy attitude or something. And she was right. Feeling guilty, you know. Which was very unusual. Never felt guilty about anything. Ever. But figured he'd upset one of the café girls. And that was playing on the mind. More than could be understood. I mean, the café girls had only ever been good to Frank. He knew that. If it had been anyone else but one of the café girls, the feeling of guilt wouldn't have even been there.

Anyway, this cranky one, didn't have a special name to remember yet. But she soon did have. From that day on, she was the COVID girl. No trouble remembering that one. That's for sure.

"I just wanted to say how sorry I was. For what I said. It was all my fault!"

"Oh, don't worry about it! She was having a bad day! With people coming in, with no masks on and having to show their vax certificates. She'd had enough! You're not the only one who didn't have a vax certificate! It was just a bad day! Don't worry about it!"

That was pretty much what she said. No wonder he liked her so much. But it didn't make the feelings any better about things. Still that idea of messing up badly wouldn't go away. But after ordering and sitting down, got the thinking going again. What this girl just said, made the realisation even clearer.

About how the luck was there. Just wandering into a café like this one. And knowing that, even when a major stuff up happened. No stuff up happened at all. Like nothing was a big deal. When the thinking was that it was a big deal. No wrong could be done. Even when something wrong was done. All was forgiven. Just like that. Like nothing happened. Smiles all round, from the café girls. All the good feelings were still flowing. And what a great feeling that was.

There're going to have a lot of fun with you.

"Yes Frank! That's the way! Keep that positive thinking up! You'll get there, Frank! My confidence in you! It's growing stronger all the time! And yes, Frank! You've been very lucky! You just don't know how lucky! Not yet anyway! But you're heading in the right direction now! So, don't worry! You'll work it all out, Frank! Eventually!"

Yeah. That all sounded good. And the mood was still right to have a listen as well. They were all so nice in there. They made the poor old bugger feel special. Always so friendly and kind. No matter what. But the best thing was how understanding and forgiving they all were. And genuine as well. Not full of shit, like most people are. Well, that's what the thinking was anyway. About most people telling you bullshit.

But the girls in the magic café were not like most people. And there was no pot or grog, controlling the thinking here either. So, there were no hallucinations going on. So, it must all be really happening. And what a relief that was.

There're going to have a lot of fun with you.

Anyway, the lunch and coffee had been ordered and paid for. So, there was nothing to worry about now. Just seated there at the favourite table. Staring out the window. Yeah. Things were back to normal. But staring out the window only lasts for so long, you know. Before the boredom sets in. Especially when there's nothing much to look at. Like G-strings for example.

Starts wondering about whether he'd actually ordered lunch or not. Taking forever. And things were kind of slow in the café as well. So, the drifting off thing started happening and an old memory started flooding in. A special memory.

He sees her coming. Hadn't seen this one for a while. And that special memory, just went floating straight back out again.

"There're a little busy in the kitchen right now, Frank! Sorry it's taking so long!"

So, there're a little busy in the kitchen right now, are they? That was interesting. The café was almost empty.

"Oh, that's ok! I'm never in a hurry these days! Haven't seen you for a while!"

"No, I've been on three month's placement."

"Oh right!"

He had no idea what that meant.

She slowly turned and walked away then. But stopped and kind of hovered around the nearby tables. Then she wandered back over. Looked down upon him with her big, round chocolate eyes and just came straight out with it.

"Do you mind if I ask you what kind of drugs you were on? When you were young!"

Whoa. That one got him by surprise, alright. There was hesitation there, straight away. But not for very long. The memory was always a tricky thing now, you know. But for some reason, the information was just there and ready to come out. Maybe too ready. But it'd been in there such a long time. Yeah, it was all such a long time ago. Well, not really such a long time ago. Just wished it was. But out it came anyway.

"No, I don't mind telling you. Not at all. There was pot, hash, LSD and cocaine. And all the alcohol as well. Pretty much got smashed every day!"

There was no need to go explaining things any further than that. She had a nerve asking in the first place.

"So, how long were you on drugs for? If you don't mind me asking?"

Yeah. She wanted to know everything. Just like the lady. They were all the same, these females.

"No, I don't mind! Started when I was about fourteen. Till I was about nineteen or twenty."

"It's a wonder you're not dead!"

133

Just the way she said that. Put a little smile on the old fella's face. And the understanding was suddenly there. About young people being curious. Especially young girls. Working in cafes every day. Serving hundreds of customers. Their self-confidence must build up over time. About asking forthright questions. And an old bloke like Frank. With a hard life, written all over his face. Must have stood right out.

What a relief it was when she never asked about more recent times. Like only a few months ago. Or was it longer than that now. Could have been, you know. Anyway, she didn't ask. But if she did, the truth would had to have come out. Embarrassment for sure.

Honesty will come into your life, if you let it.

Yeah, getting to understand more about that now.

"Well, I almost was! A few times! It's a bloody miracle, I'm not dead! Just lucky I guess!"

But in a way, he was dead. Brain dead. Had been for years. This girl didn't want to know about all that, did she? This next bit was a big surprised.

"My sister died because of drugs. Party drugs. She got a bad pill. That's what they said happened."

"Oh, that's no good! Sorry to hear it! Were you close to your sister?"

"Oh well! If that's the road she chose to take. Then that was her decision!"

The emotion was starting now. This girl was just about to bust open. Time to back off. No surprise, when she quickly turned and hurried back to the counter and disappeared out the back.

But she was back out cleaning up tables, a short time later. Still curious, alright.

"You must have been a bit wild, when you were young!"

Thought this one through for a few seconds as well. Came up with the only answer, there was to come up with. Without lying.

Honesty will come into your life, if you let it.

Yeah. Ok. Ok. Already know all about that.

"Well, put it this way. I had to take myself out of society. Or end up dead, or in gaol!"

"I hope you don't mind me asking so many questions!"

"No, that's ok! I don't mind!"

And he didn't mind now either. After all, she was a magic café girl. They could ask as many questions as they could think up. No problem at all. Where this next bit came from, still hasn't been worked out. But out it came anyway. And she didn't even ask the question.

"You know, I felt like an old car wreck, when I first came into this place. You know those old cars you see, out in the middle of some paddock. All rusted out! Dints and scratches all over them. Bird shit everywhere! Seized up motor! Sometimes no motor at all! Flat tyres! Or no tyres! Maybe not even wheels?"

She was smiling now, you know. So, he just couldn't stop, could he?

"Then I wandered into this place and you girls. Well, what can I say about you girls?"

The eyes were watering up now. Just a little. And there was warmth happening in the left-hand side of the chest. But he managed to control it all and keep going.

"You girls came along and dragged me out. Started working on me. Got me all cleaned up. Pumped up the tyres. Cut the rust out. New paint job. Reconditioned the motor. Started me up. And I'm off and running. You girls, put me back together! Got me going again! Tune me up. Every time I come in here!"

Yeah. She was having a good old laugh now. And that was a good thing. Because he may have said a few more things after that. And who knows what might have come out then. Better off to quit while you're ahead. Getting all emotional now anyway. Saying all that was almost too much. Shaking a little. Tears were on the way. About to lose it, alright. But the asking girl. She was right onto it. Knew what was going on. Maybe with herself as well.

"I better be getting back! Nice talking to you, Frank! See you later!"

"Yes, nice talking to you too! See you later!"

There were a few serviettes there. Went straight to the eyes. Just after a quick look around. Make sure no one was watching.

Without doubt. The longest conversation ever. With one of the magic café girls. It was so good to see her again. What they talked about was a big surprise, alright. For him and most likely for her as well. And they both finished up, with smiles on their faces.

Something happened to Frank, after talking to this girl. Something like feeling an attachment. Like when you relate to someone. Without even trying. It just all feels good. And everything felt good, when he was talking to this girl. And it all started because she asked a question. So, that's who she was from then on. The asking girl. But he never told her that. And of course, never told her how much he liked her either.

There're going to have a lot of fun with you.

Yeah. A human wreck, walked into the magic café the first time. Although the wreck had been listening to the lady a fair bit by then. She never goes away, you know. So, the thinking was always all confused. She just thought she knew everything. But the effort was still put in. To get the act together. To get fit and healthy. To start enjoying the new life and everything. The lady was into him all the time about that. The new life business. But she had nothing to do with repairing the wreck. Nothing at all.

But there was no real complaining about her anymore either. Not really. She'd be missed, if she didn't keep interfering all the time. But there was still the struggling, with all the addictions going on, you know. And it was no easy time. Can tell you that. No easy time at all. And the lady couldn't help with any of that. That's for sure.

Yeah, all the calm feelings of relaxation were there in the magic café. Unless the thinking drifted off, to that little fucking witch. That got stuck into the poor bastard in the first place. For no reason at all. The vulnerability was there then, you know. She took full advantage, alright. The bitch.

There're going to have a lot of fun with you.

"Oh Frank! You've got that all wrong, haven't you! She saw something good in you! Really, she did! She was just trying to help you! Getting to know the real Frank! The one hiding in there! She knew you were in there, Frank! I know you're in there, Frank! I always knew! Right from the start! Come out, Frank! I know you want to! Come out, come out! Wherever you are!"

Oh, for fucks sake. She didn't have to come up with that one, did she? She just thinks she knows everything about everything. Well, she doesn't.

Yeah right. Well, she sure had a strange way of doing it didn't she? See something good in some poor old bastard. Get right in his face. Pulverise the brain. Get the almost dead heart, pumping away. Send shockwaves through the emotional structure. Get the warm and fuzzy feelings bubbling away and frighten the shit out of him. All at the same time. Try and take over, the whole fucking new life as well. More like, pushed him further in. What a fucking hide she had, eh. Bitch.

There're going to have a lot of fun with you.

And what's the big deal about coming out anyway. That would mean living in the real world. All the time. Fuck that. Last thing that was needed, that was. Last thing Frank wanted to do. Old life or new life. Spent most of the old life, avoiding the real world. Now was supposed to spend the new life, joining the real world. And so, what's the fucking difference anyway.

Should have just stayed on the veranda. No witches, hovering around on the veranda. That's for sure. That negative thinking started ticking away again, you know. This fucking lady couldn't possibly be for real anyway. Really on his side. You must be joking. She's just trying to drive him nuts. Blow all the fuses right out. Should write that under the picture, eh. Oops, you don't know about the picture yet, do you? Well, you soon will.

"Oh dear, oh dear! You're just not getting it, are you, Frank! Not yet! But don't worry too much about it! Not now! Just give it some more time! After all, you're only just beginning your new life! I understand that, Frank! Really, I do! Just be patient! It'll come to you! You'll get there in the end! I, have great confidence in you Frank! I really do! But please, try a little harder, Frank! Try a little harder!"

Easy for her to say that. She is sounding a bit pushy too, you know. But these females always stick together, you know. Doesn't even matter what it's about. They always just stick together. And everybody knows that. Just like them café girls. Well. No. That was different, that was. The café girls were just special. That's all. And there was no question about that. None at all.

There're going to have a lot of fun with you.

But the feeling of terror. About TMBGITW. Was still in there, you know. That really was different. Like a huge picture hanging on a wall in the brain. Blocking out the old life. Larger than the new life. She was there. She was always there. Just ready and waiting. To come to life and leap out. Grab hold of the emotional strings and tie them up in knots. The bitch.

Till the internal chocking started and the poor old heart copped another workout. And the heavy breathing and all the negative thoughts, that always preceded the big busts. That send all the helpless compulsives, back to the only place they feel safe. Where nothing matters. Where reality doesn't even exist. Yeah, back to nowhere land. Seated in front of some poker machine, pushing a fucking button.

That picture had already sent Frank there a few times already. It was more powerful than the gambling, alcohol and drug addictions put together. And now it was rocking the structure again. Compromising the balance, that was taking so long to get under control. Stirring up the compulsive urges. Talk about drive a man to drink. She was like a noose around the neck. And the heart as well. Damn it. Yeah. Like one noose, replacing three other nooses. Fucking hell. There should be a law against pictures like her. Fucking bitch.

There're going to have a lot of fun with you.

"Oh, fuck off for Christ's sake, will you!"

Oops. Sorry. That one just slipped out again. I mean, there was mass confusion happening here. That compulsive should never have said that in the first place. Just look at all the trouble it's caused. Next time he turns up, he'll be hearing a few things. That's for sure.

But, then again. All the fun they were having was good fun, you know. That's with the café girls that is. That are still there. They keep disappearing, you know. Not just out the back either. Disappearing all together. Some of them turn up again and some of them don't. And new ones kept turning up as well. Just another confusion to put up with.

Missed them when they weren't there anymore. That's for sure. But he never told them that. Well, how could he if they weren't there. But that was better than if they were there and he did tell them. Imagine the situation then. Couldn't ever let that happen. So, them not being there was better than them being there. When it came to not telling them how much he liked them. And maybe that would have eventually slipped out, when they were there.

Yeah, the beautiful one, the irrepressible cuddling girl, the asking girl, the tattooed one, the lovely one, and a few others that can't even be remembered had all disappeared. Never to be seen again. He missed all of them. But not for very long. If he did ask any questions about what happened to them, he was often told they'd gone on to bigger things. Whatever that meant.

There're going to have a lot of fun with you.

But he wasn't missing that other one. TMBGITW. But if that fun wasn't there, it would be missed as well. And that was causing another kind of confusion altogether. Frank and fun. With a complete bitch. In the new life. In the real world. Holy shit. And having to admit to enjoying the fun in the first place. That was causing all kinds of readjustments. And the headaches were happening. I can tell you that.

And that's why the picture was always in the brain. To drive him fucking crazy. But he kind of loved the craziness of it all. And kind of complained a lot, when it started happening. But didn't really complain at all. Crazy old bastards, just get so used to being crazy old bastards, you know. So hard to kill off.

There're going to have a lot of fun with you.

"Oh dear! Frank! Please stop calling that wonderful girl, what you're calling her! She's not one of those at all! Can't you see that! She's one of the nicest girls you will ever meet! And she decided to help you, Frank! And all you can do is call her what you're calling her!"

I'm fucking sure he can't. And where did the nice bit come from anyway. She's the biggest nightmare in the head right now.

"Oh dear! Let's just leave it there, shall we! But at least you're starting to understand about having fun, Frank! That's real progress! I'm not so sure you'll be seeing that wonderful girl again anyway. They tell me she's gone onto bigger things."

Yeah right. Here we go again. Bigger things. That was their answer for everything. Bigger things. He was sick to death of hearing that. Bigger things. But he didn't care anymore anyway. She can go on to bigger things. As long as it's not around here anywhere. She can go where she likes and do what she likes. As long as it's not with him.

This changeover business. From the old world to the new world. Everything was going so well, you know. Now he just doesn't know what's going on. And it's all because of that girl. All because of one fucking girl.

Hang on a minute. How come the lady knows about what's going on. About her going onto bigger things. She couldn't possibly know that. Unless, there're all working together. That must be what's happening. Has to be. It's the only explanation. The café girls are killing him with kindness. TMBGITW is out to get him. And the lady is probably telling them all what to do. Just how dumb is this old bastard. He's only just starting to work it all out.

There're going to have a lot of fun with you.

Yeah. That compulsive knew what he was talking about, alright. No wonder he's always got a smile on his face. Bastard. He's on their side for sure. Yeah. He's one of them, alright.

But poor old Frank. Another realisation just hit home. He'd heard it all, over and over again. In the GA meetings.

One day at a time.

All good changes take time.

No short cuts to recovery.

And that's exactly what he was going to start doing. With the café girls. And TMBGITW. If he ever sees her again. And the lady. Just take things slow. Don't let them change the way things have always been done. And don't take any short cuts either. When it comes to working out how they all operate. And don't take any shit off them either. We'll see who gets the better of who then.

There're going to have a lot of fun with you.

But then again. After a bit more thinking went into it. He liked all the café girls. Too much. And they were changing him too. He knew that. Liked what they were doing, alright. And it was all fun. Yeah. Teaching him about fun. He knew that too. Wasn't suspicious of any of them anymore. Even the ones he had run ins with. So, it was all good with the café girls. Not that he was ever going to tell them that. But you know what. He kind of started to figure, that the café girls actually knew him, better than he knew himself. And that was right.

And if the lady's right, about not seeing TMBGITW anymore. Then all his problems are over aren't they. Well, all except for the lady that is. And she's always been the biggest problem. He didn't call TMBGITW, what he always called her either. So, that's real progress for you. The control was slipping away, alright.

Then another realisation hit. After sitting down at the favourite table. Thinking the brains out. No problem there. But forgot to order lunch. Busting for a coffee. Starving hungry as well. But going up to the counter and admitting that a lapse of memory invaded the thinking was not going to be easy, you know.

Been sitting there for God knows how long. Patiently waiting. But forgot to order. Wouldn't have mattered, of course. But consideration had entered the programme now. And it would have meant another episode of embarrassment as well. So, a decision had been made. No lunch and coffee that day. Just a friendly visit.

How this next bit arrived is unclear. Just suddenly there. Popped in out of nowhere. It was probably that special memory that disappeared when the asking girl turned up. Weird things can start happening, if you sit anywhere too long. Time to go. But the thinking wasn't over yet. Somehow the phone call was forgotten about and so was everything that happened. But it was getting remembered, right now.

Yeah. The bad news finally came. Frank's mother was in a bad way. Going downhill fast. Not expected to last much longer.

"Hi mum. Not going so well, eh."

"No. Not so well. It's good of you to come and visit me. I've had lots of visitors today. And yesterday."

She was laying there. Motionless. The breathing was slow and laboured. The eyes had a moist glow about them as she stared at this son. This lost son sitting there beside the bed, who she never really knew. And who didn't really know her either. But there was no time for any of that thinking. Not now. There were words there. They wanted to be said.

That's when the little, warm hand reached out. It was taken in the most-gentle way and the long-lost son was then drawn very close. So close, that the lips of this frail old mother, managed to reach an unsuspecting ear.

"I love you, Frank! I've always loved you!"

A huge weight lifted off, out of Frank at that moment. There was a gasp for breath and the tears started flowing. Immediately. Uncontrollable tears. The dam had busted. Finally. The pressure had always been there, you know. Building and building. Over so many years. About what was never said. But was now said. And if there was ever a time to say what had never been said, it was now. And the only response possible, happened without anything being said. But what a mess there was. A helpless, trembling mess. But in a good way.

The look of relief on her face was unmistakeable as well. Like a great suffering had finally escaped. And the little warm hand, tightened its gentle grip. But not for very long. And there was a smile there, that had never been seen before. And the eyes had a gentle softness about them. That had never been seen before either. Before they started fading and slowly closed. But they had stayed open long enough, to deliver the long-awaited message. The hand flopped back down. She was gone again. Not completely. Just gone. Maybe to that place she always went to. Somehow, the mysterious smile on her face was still there.

That was the last conversation Frank ever had with his mother. And the only one that ever really meant anything. To Frank anyway. But her last words were always there. They took a long time to get there. But once they were there. They were always in there. They never went away. Frank called on them every now and then. Because they gave him strength. A new strength, that had never been there before.

This new strength. Along with the support of the GA family. And all those wonderful girls in the magic café. Had everything to do, with progress in the new life. That had faltered so many times. Oh, alright then. And the lady who wasn't there as well. Couldn't leave her out, could he? She wouldn't stay out anyway. Not for very long. She'd already tricked him a few times. With being gone and then turning up again. Without warning or anything. Always trying to catch him out.

Yeah, this new added strength. This long-awaited mother's love. Was just as powerful. Or even more powerful, than all the other strengths put together. That's how it felt at first anyway. And now there was an even bigger picture. Covering the one already there. So, that should take care of that problem. Once and for all.

Yeah, the plan was to blot out the TMBGITW. And replace her with a picture of his mother. Then the strength that she gave him would always be there. I mean, that word love. Coming from his mother, after so many years and just in the nick of time. That had to mean something. Well, it meant everything. So yeah. That was the new plan. His mother would always be with him then. To give him strength. To help fight off the urges, that were always there. Knowing that his mother really loved him, made such a huge difference, you know. In more ways than one.

"You always go from one extreme to the other! Don't you Frank!"

And that's where the thinking stopped. Her face was right in his face. And the café girl smile was there as well. It was the marshal. She wasn't there very often now. Hadn't seen her for ages. She'd never even spoken to Frank, since helping him out that day. When he had to check in with his phone. So, how would she know anything. Anyway, it didn't matter. And there's no point trying to work it all out.

"Ah! What! What was that?"

"You go from one extreme to the other, don't you! Is that right, Frank?"

Well. Yes, it was right, alright. But it had nothing to do with her, did it. But he could never not answer a café girl, could he?

Honesty will come into your life if you let it.

It was always a real aggravation, whenever thinking was required. About telling the truth or just straight out lying. But not anymore. There was a fearless Frank emerging now. And the truth was no longer so evasive. Like it always had been. Yeah. A new level had been reached.

"Yes, I do! I've always been like that! One extreme to the other. It's probably not good to be like that. But that's what I'm like. There's nothing I can do about it. It's just the way it is!"

"It doesn't have to be that way, Frank! If you don't want it to be that way! Have a think about it! I need to go now! Bye! See you later, Frank!"

"Yeah, ok! See you later!"

An even bigger smile was there. Her pitch-black eyes sparkled. And then she was gone. Just like that. Left him there. Completely baffled. Yeah so, she turns up. Gets in his face. Tells him what an extremist he is. And then just wanders off, like nothing happened. Frank, saw the marshal girl wandering around, every now and then. Said hello and gave a little smile. And she gave the café girl smile back, every time. Never really talked much to her again. Only once. But he never forgot about the one extreme to the other conversation. That's for sure.

There're going to have a lot of fun with you.

That was the end of that little interruption. But the hunger was still there, you know. And still busting for a coffee.

"Back again Frank?"

It was the have a little chat girl.

"Yeah! Well, I forgot to order when I came in, didn't I! So, now I'm really hungry?"

The strangest look came back from behind the counter. Like a smirk, with a big smile right behind it.

"You ordered when you came in, Frank! One of your favourites. Sweet potato chips and the coffee! Haven't you got it yet?"

"What! I don't remember ordering anything!" You weren't even at the counter anyway. It was? It was?"

Couldn't even remember who took the order.

"Are you sure, Frank? I think you did! But I'll go and check!"

But she couldn't keep control any longer. Cracked right up. She already knew he'd ordered. And she didn't even check anyway. And she knew he'd been talking his head off, with the asking girl. And she knew his table got cleaned up and he didn't even notice. And she told him all that as well. And she told him about the marshal as well.

So, they were watching him all the time. But there was too much confusion to go thinking about what just did and didn't happen. There were giggles coming from out the back as well. And they were louder than usual. Or they seemed louder than usual. He could hear them clearly. Yeah, the dopey bastard had been sitting there at the table, and wasn't even there. For at least half an hour and maybe longer.

So, here's have a chat and Frank at the counter. Laughing their heads off. And what a great feeling that was. Laughing and not being pissed right off. Like he would have been. Not so long ago. This girl didn't have to know he was only half there, did she? But she would have known that anyway. But she'd never get to know what the thinking was all about would she. And none of the others would either. It had nothing to do with any of them. Or the lady. Some things just had to kept to himself, didn't they?

So, when Frank got back to sitting down, the contemplation started happening again. About getting drawn into the magic café in the first place. Yeah, the girls were all over him. Like they knew exactly what they were doing. Psychological mechanics. The lot of them. And they probably did know what the thinking was. How do they do that anyway. Get into the head. Extract all the required information. Get back out. And then come to his table. Interrupt his lunch and then tell him all about it.

There're going to have a lot of fun with you.

"There you go, Frank!"

There were two of them. NG1 and the COVID girl. Standing there, looking down upon him. With the café girl smile on both their faces. The coffee gets put down, right under his nose.

"We're using new oat milk now, Frank! We're all addicted to it! We just can't wait to see what you think!"

So, the dummy takes a sip, doesn't he?

"Umm, tastes yummy!"

What. Yummy. Must be joking. And where did that come from. But they just loved it. Well, I guess he had to say something, didn't he? But yummy. And so, what have they done to him anyway.

"When I make coffee at home, I put in two heaped tea spoons of coffee. Then I half fill the cup with boiling water. Then I fill the cup up with oat-milk and put it in the microwave for a minute."

NG1 seemed happy enough with that little bit of coffee making information. But the COVID girl, just couldn't help herself. And she was still smiling when she said it.

"You should put the water in first, Frank! Then the milk! And then the coffee last."

"What! So, I'm doing it all wrong then!"

"Yes, you are!"

"Well, next time I make one, I'll try and remember to do it properly!"

"Ok, let us know how you go!"

"Ok, I will!"

They both intensified the smile and gave a little giggle. Then they were off. Back to the counter.

There're going to have a lot of fun with you.

Then something occurred to Frank. For the first time. Talking to the café girls was becoming easier all the time. The air had always seemed thicker in the café, for some reason. But now it had thinned out. The embarrassment wasn't there as much. Not like at the beginning. When the old man wouldn't even talk to the young girls.

Probably because he didn't know how to. And at that stage, didn't even want to. Never even thought to try. Didn't mind looking at them but. No, not at all. But really just wanted lunch and coffee. None of that friendly, mushy get to know you stuff.

And the tension between him, and the COVID girl wasn't there any longer either. They were friends now and he was talking to her, like nothing bad ever happened. The little conversation happened one day. Sitting there having lunch and the COVID girl wandered up to the table.

"Hi Frank! It's good to see you!"

This was the best opportunity he was ever going to get.

"Oh hi! It's good to see you too!"

And then it just had to come out.

"It was all my fault, you know! You were just doing your job! I know that! You did the right thing! I'm sorry!"

"Oh, that's, alright, Frank! I was just having a bad day, that's all!"

Right. And nothing could stop what happened next. The café girl smile was there and so was Franks. For a few long seconds. Probably the biggest smile he'd ever produced. And then she was gone. But the warm feeling inside, lingered there for quite some time.

But openly talking to the café girls was one thing. There was no pressure there about that now. I mean, he knew all their names. He knew when to have something to say and when not to, because they were too busy. Yeah, a lot of progress had been made, talking to the café girls. Yeah, getting smarter all the time. That's for sure.

So, whatever it was with the evil little twins at the start was a difficult thing to work out, you know. Something was going on with one of them. Straight away. There was a kind of feeling there, alright. Only it wasn't all that clear, till a bit later on. Yeah, you know who we're talking about here. With the coffees pushed under the nose. Extra small meals. All the teasing and tormenting. And the verbal abuse. Looking for reactions out of the poor old bugger all the time. Expecting the complaining routine for sure.

But the stupidity, didn't run that deep you know. It was there, alright. No doubt about that. But there was determination there as well. Or maybe just plain stubbornness. Or maybe both. And they'd been hiding in the darkness for so long now, you know. All of the old life, actually. Undeveloped and unprovoked.

But they had both been activated now. Kick started. By some lady who wasn't even there. An extra beautiful, but miserable, much too self-confident, cheeky little imp. Or whatever she was. And a wonderful collection of beautiful girls in the magic café.

Should have just given up then. Right at the beginning. Before things got out of hand. Really moving along. And just so complicated. But of course, the old fella loved all the attention, didn't he? And once he got a taste of it, he was never going anywhere. Except back to the magic café. And that eventually became, every day.

There're going to have a lot of fun with you.

"There you go, Frank! Enjoy!"

"What! Oh, thanks!

And about fucking time too. But he was never going to actually say that was he. Not to one of the café girls. Especially this café girl. Because he'd seen this girl in action a couple of times already. Don't misunderstand. She was a great girl. And she stuck up for her friends. And a couple of times, it was Frank who was causing the mischief. Or at least that's what it must have looked like to this girl. Because she was right there to defend whatever girl it was that Frank was talking to. Maybe just to keep an eye on him or something. But he was just trying to be friendly, you know.

Like one day, when he was talking to the beautiful one.

"I bet you know everything that's goes on around here!"

But it wasn't her who answered back.

"Of course, she does! And she's good at her job! And she is my friend! And, you just leave her alone!"

Whoa. And she just came out from nowhere. Probably didn't even hear what was even said. Just wanted to let the old fella know, who was the boss or something. Yeah. She always got watched closely, that one. Especially after that little ambush.

146

But this happened early on, you know. When the new life had only just begun and it was still a scruffy mess, they were dealing with. In the early stages of learning how to be friendly. Especially to girls who had to be watched very closely. Well, they were already being watched very closely. That's for sure. And they were all watching the scruffy mess, pretty closely as well. So, it was fair enough that watching closely had to be done both ways.

When they got to know the scruffy mess a little better, the communication opened right up. Especially from the girl's side of things. Now he talks to this girl, all the time. And she talks to Frank.

And yes, the liking was there as usual. Too much liking actually. There was just something about her. That made her a bit different from the rest of them. And as you may have surely guessed. She was never going to know anything about that. He called her, the stick up for her friend's girl. And of course, she didn't know about that either.

But all the café girls supported each other, you know. If one got upset, then all of them had to be dealt with. But it's like they never really got upset. They let Frank know about what didn't really upset them. That's for sure. But they still had the same amount of friendliness. And the same café girl smile. And sometimes, it seemed like the smile got even bigger and warmer, the more they never really got upset. And this was always a hard thing to figure out.

There're going to have a lot of fun with you.

There was relaxation there now. Watching all the humans parading along. I mean, Frank was still an alien in this new world wasn't he. So, what else were they going to be called. Other than humans. Watching is not the same as fitting into the whole scheme of things. Integration takes time, you know. Especially for a social misfit.

"Oh Frank! Stop it! Just stop it! All this negative thinking! This, is your new life now! The social misfit no longer exists! You must believe that, Frank! Have more confidence in yourself! The changeover is happening! It's slow, but it is happening! Just believe in yourself, Frank! Be patient! I know you can do it! I just know you can! Please Frank! Try harder! Please try harder, Frank! You must try harder!"

Yeah. Right. Whatever you say. Bit of aggravation from the lady. Must be having a bad day or something. Or maybe just losing it.

What that little imp didn't realise was that, there was more to this decrepit looking old fool, than she could ever know about. That's for sure. So, the clamming right up thing happened didn't it. She'd be learning nothing. They'd be learning nothing. And the lady could go to hell. Not one reaction. Nothing at all. That was the latest thinking anyway. And it was like a repeat thought process. The best and only defence. Against an army of females. All out to get him. But it's funny how things work out sometimes, isn't it. Or don't work out at all.

There're going to have a lot of fun with you.

And he didn't call that little imp, an evil little witch either. Or a bitch. And he had the lady to thank for that. That just had to be admitted. And it was decided not to call her TMBGITW anymore either. That made things a lot easier to bear, whenever she came into view. Which still happened every now and then. Yeah. Just when he thought she was out of the picture, she'd turn up again. And she completely ignored him. And he completely ignored her as well. So, it was all good with TMBGITW, who wasn't called that anymore.

But it wasn't all good with the lady, you know. Nothing like it. If it wasn't for the lady they'd have got nothing out of him in the first place. She was working with them, alright. She was the master mind. Softened him up, before he even set foot in the café. There was no doubt about that now. None whatsoever.

"Why do you always get takeaway coffees, Frank?"

What. Where the hell, did she come from. It was the forgotten name girl. He'd already explained, all about the reason for the takeaways. At least half a dozen times. But what the hell. One more time won't hurt. They all just had to know everything, didn't they?

"Well, after I got out of hospital the last time. Just before I started coming here. I was getting coffee in the normal cups. But sometimes, I got the shakes and spilt coffee all over the place. Then one day, I got a takeaway. And I got the shakes but didn't spill any. So, I always got takeaways after that."

She never even said anything. Just smiled the usual smile and walked away. If he gets asked one more time, he'll have something to say about it. They must all have bad memories or something.

There're going to have a lot of fun with you.

The coffees still had to be in take away cups. Because the shakes were still a bit of an issue, you know. I mean, he still wasn't fully recovered from the last time in hospital. And after spilling all those coffees at various cafes, the takeaway idea soon made perfect sense. Yeah, they could shove as many coffees at him as they liked. As long as they were in takeaways.

Every now and then, one came in a normal cup. But he soon worked it out. The idea was for him to complain. But complaining wasn't in the programme. Knew what they were up to, alright. And besides, complaining would mean, that they would have a little win. And that was never going to happen. Not anymore anyway. Had to stay strong. Winning was the name of the game now.

"Oh, I forgot, Frank! You usually have your coffee in a takeaway, don't you!"

Yeah right. Sure, she did. They did trick him a couple of times, you know. Pretty sure this was the COVID girl, before she became the COVID girl. But it could have been another one. Maybe the serious one. And there was a kind of complaint put it. Just a quiet, gentle one.

"That's ok! I'll see how I go! But I really would like it in a takeaway.!"

So, off she goes with the coffee and five minutes later, she's back with the takeaway. But when he looked up, it was another one who turned up this time. The lovely one. Yeah. Not too tall. Not too short. Long blond hair and those magnetic blue eyes. Yeah. She was lovely, alright. And just as nosey as the rest of them. That's for sure.

"Why do you always have your coffee in a takeaway anyway?"

No hesitation here either. Just looked down upon him and smiled, when she said it. They all liked doing that, you know. Looking down upon the poor old fella and smiling. But he didn't mind. Just loved it, when they did that. And with the warm surge, that always invaded the system. How could he not love it and look forward to it coming the next time. Yeah, the magic café girls could look down upon him whenever they liked. Which was never often enough.

Yeah, there was a very good reason. And she probably already knew anyway. But that didn't matter. After all, it was the lovely one. And she could be looked up at all day. So, the explaining happened again didn't it.

"Well, about three years ago. I had some kind of a fit. A kind of stroke/fit. The doctors weren't sure what to call it. I was unconscious for a few days. And when I woke up, I had the shakes pretty bad. And I love sitting in cafes, having coffee with lunch. And sometimes I got the shakes and spilt the coffee all over the place. So, I started getting takeaways and I haven't spilt one since!"

That did the trick.

"Oh, sorry to hear that, Frank! But you're doing much better now!"

"Yes, I am, thanks! Much better!"

And he would have kept talking as well. But she just turned around and took off and disappeared out the back.

There're going to have a lot of fun with you.

The idea of winning the little battles against the café girls had never really happened early on. Losing was usually what happened. At everything. Only he didn't know he was losing. Because he didn't know what they were up to at first, did he? But things were different now. Becoming aware that winning was much better than losing was in the thinking more and more. And the enemies were well known by now. There was some fight in there now. Real resistance. That's for sure. Where it all came from was not even thought about. Not yet anyway.

But of course, always losing is what always happened early on in proceedings didn't it. Before any serious thinking began. When the battle was only just beginning. And before Frank realised, he was actually in a battle. A battle for control of his own mind. Which he'd never really had before anyway. But that didn't matter and it's not the point. What was left of his mind was his mind and he could do with it what he liked.

Yeah, it was a personal battle now. Against the lady who was already trying to take control. Of the new mind anyway. And she had no right taking his old mind away in the first place, did she? Without even asking. She just thinks she can do anything.

What. So, she floats around in hospitals, giving half dead people a new life. Like some kind of fucking angle or something. And TMBGITW. He'd already forgotten about not calling her that anymore. But fucking hell, you know. Zeroes in and pulverises, what was left of the mashed-up old brain. As soon as she saw the poor old bastard. And almost giving him a heart attack at the same time. And yeah, the café girls. Into him all the time. Right from the start. About one thing, or the other. But that was ok. They could do that as much as they liked.

He got warm chills just thinking about the café girls. And they got warmer, every time he went into the magic café. And they got even warmer, every time he saw a café girl and it didn't matter which one it was either. And when a conversation started with a café girl and the looking into her eyes became longer and longer, the chills verged on the hot side, didn't they? And this situation became, one of the hardest to control. And with all the smiling going on as well, it's a wonder he didn't just crack up entirely.

Normally wouldn't have bothered concerning himself, with any of this kind of nonsense, you know. Nothing about feelings had ever bothered him before.

Because there were never any real feelings there in the first place. Unless it had something to do with poker machines and all the bad shit that came with them. Like running out of money. And beer, pot and cigarettes. And food. And the internal cursing. And no sleep. And really bad thoughts. About ending all the pain and suffering, once and for all. Yeah. Frank was almost gone for good. A number of times.

But this new life Frank. With his second chance. Was a different proposition altogether. There had never been any fight there, up till now. No real resistance. Against anything. That's probably why all the addictions, ruled the old life. Because there was no resistance.

Where this new found resistance came from was never really thought about too much. But it was there now and that's all that mattered. Well, there was much more to it than that, of course. But it would have been useless trying to explain anything to Frank, about anything at this early stage of the transformation. From one life to another.

Well before Frank started eating at the café, he was drawn to the place. Every time he finished his swim, while walking to the change shed. The feeling was so strong, you know. Of going there for lunch. Instead of a number of other places around. They were all okay café's and all that. The staff were always pleasant enough. But from the very first visit to the magic café, Frank felt the warm vibe of the place. Yeah, he was caught right from the start. Hook, line and sinker.

But then he was remembering about when TMBGITW started getting her king-sized hooks into him. That changed everything. But you already know about what happened there. The thing is, it didn't end there. It just started there and went on for months. Was after just the third visit, when the war really began.

Just sitting there minding his own business, when his coffee was aggressively pushed across the little round table. Stopped, right under his nose. He looked up to see which one of the girls was obviously in a bad mood. But she was already half way back to the counter. She didn't even look back. It was her, alright. The bitch. But at least the coffee was in a takeaway. And it could have been the next day, when she blasted him at the counter. The bitch.

There're going to have a lot of fun with you.

He's not talking about her anymore. Not even going to think about her anymore. He's going to burn that picture out of the brain. Got a new life now. Well, according to that fucking lady anyway. He doesn't need any more of this shit. He doesn't need that bitch anyway. And he doesn't need the lady. He doesn't need anything. Why don't they all just fuck off and leave him alone. Except the café girls. He liked all the café girls. They can all stay there. And stay in there as well.

"Oh Frank! What a terrible attitude! Did you ever stop to think, that maybe she was just trying to get your attention? Don't forget, you were just another customer to her! At that early stage anyway! She was just trying to get to know you, Frank! That's what café workers do! Get to know the customers. So, you could have opened up Frank! Let her get to know you!"

Yeah, yeah, yeah. Alright, he had to admit, this girl was already a huge influence on him. Although, his new life had already begun, without any help from her. But, the nosey bitch, just seemed to make it her business to help him along didn't she? Took him quite a while to work that out. He missed her so much after she was gone. That's for sure. Bitch.

He missed her smile. That smile, that sent a warm current all through his body. A new sensation, alright. And she always gave out the biggest, warmest smile out of all the café girls. She was breathing new life into Frank. Bit by bit. But it took him a while to work that out as well. Actually, it took someone to work it out for him. But who cares anyway.

No, maybe she wasn't just a smart-arse little bitch of a witch after all. Always a bit slow on the uptake you know. But she didn't even know Frank and couldn't possibly know anything about the previous life. Frank had trouble remembering anything about his previous life himself. That miserable old life. So, how the hell could she know anything about it. Of course, her and the lady were probably working together. How else could she possibly know anything. Anyway, she wasn't getting spoken about anymore.

"Frank! Did you ever stop to consider, that maybe she had a previous life as well! It's about time you started to realise a few things, Frank! Before it's too late! Time's running out, Frank! Please! You must try harder!"

What. Well, that's a bit of a change up. Now, it's always you must try harder. What the hell does she expect. Anyway. No. He didn't. But this girl, you know. This one girl. She found where Frank's hidden heart was. She touched upon it and got it pounding. Pounding for her. He knew that and it frightened him so much. Just how the hell did she manage to do that anyway. He was always thinking that. Almost shit himself, whenever he saw here too. But he was never going to crack and talk to her first. That would be losing for sure. Gone, alright. But he's never going to think about her anymore.

Yes, after that episode, swore there'd be no going back there. Ever again. Couldn't handle all that lovey-dovey feeling stuff. Went back again and again and again. But you already know that, eh. Could never stop thinking about her either. But that was going to stop. There was no more thinking about that little bitch. Not anymore.

This girl, will always be special, you know. Yeah. Really just admitted that. She was the first one to ever truly reach, into that dead heart. Make contact, with the him that was really him. Frank knew that. But knowing that and telling her that was not possible. Or telling anyone else either. Oh no. That was never going to happen. And besides. Telling her would mean that she'd won wouldn't it. But there was no way, she was ever going to win. No way. He kind of did tell her eventually, you know. In a roundabout kind of way. But it was in a weak moment.

"You should have let her, in Frank! You should have let her in! She would have been the best thing that ever happened to you! Trust your instincts, Frank! That's all you need to do! Trust your instincts! Stop hoarding all those negative thoughts! Let your feelings out, Frank! Just look what that did to you in your old life! Holding all those negative feelings in! Don't let that happen again Frank! And please Frank! Please! Don't let yourself down! There's, not much time left!"

Trust your instincts, Frank. Yeah right. But it didn't happen. And yet it did happen. Well, not really. But it didn't really not happen either. He tried. He really did try. You have to give him credit for that. But it all got stuffed up didn't it. Yes, he did weaken enough to do it. If he knew anything about how to do that. Which he didn't. And he didn't know anything about how to win a girl over, either. That's for sure.

Yes, she was so beautiful, this girl. It was hard to tell exactly how old she was. But that didn't really matter, of course. And Frank decided to not let it matter. Just decided to do it anyway. But it was still a very hard thing to do. The hardest thing that had ever been done in the new life. Or in the old life either. Well, there was nothing hard ever done in the old life. Maybe a few things. Come to think of it. But not thinking about it was always a better way to not remember anything about what happened in the old life. Most of the time anyway.

So, the confidence and determination were breaking out one day, you know. Walked straight up and got in her face. Just like she did to him, so many times. Yeah. One day, on the way to the favourite table, she was noticed cleaning down one of the nearby tables. Near the back wall. Whatever got into Frank, forced this reckless action to take place. Couldn't have really been him at all. After sitting down, he got straight back up and slowly moved towards her. She saw him coming, alright. But didn't try and move off. So, he manages to get her trapped between two sets of tables and chairs.

Although, she could have slipped past if she really wanted to, you know. He gently pushed her up against the wall. Rested the right arm across her protruding chest and the hand landed on her left shoulder. She was going nowhere. Pulled her real close and kissed her on her right cheek. Explosions were happening, all through the physical, psychological and emotional structures. With her as well, as it turned out.

"You're wonderful!"

That's what he whispered into her right ear. In love, alright.

"If you say so!"

That's what she not so quietly mumbled, as she pushed him out of the way. Kind of like an inward yell, more than a mumble. The look of sheer horror on her face as she took off. Would have frightened the shit out of anybody. The explosions, instantly died right down after this unexpected reaction. Any thinking froze up and there was a dopey looking statue standing there. Staring at the wall.

All this happened so quick, you know. Too quick. Stood there for maybe a minute or two. A slow grinding started happening between the ears. Then the little giggles got the attention back. Huge embarrassment. Frank just had to get out of there. Left in a triple amount of confusion.

"Fuck her! Never coming back here again!"

Yeah. Bit of mumbling was going on there as well.

And he never did go back. For about three weeks. But you already know about all that too. But Frank could never stop thinking about this episode. It was always there. She was always there. Fucking hell was always there as well. And yes, his mother was in there as well. But sometimes, there's only so much a mother can do.

There're going to have a lot of fun with you.

Frank was just trying to show some affection, you know. Letting her know about the feelings. The ones for her. All for her. Yeah. Just following the instincts. Letting all the feelings out. That's what the lady said to do. Stupid bitch. Couldn't understand what he'd done wrong.

This girl, who'd been smiling the café girl smile for weeks. Shoving the coffees under his nose. Then walking away so quick, that he couldn't even say anything. Then one day, she hovered over him and smiled down upon him. The heart, that wasn't even supposed to be there, went berserk, alright. From rock solid to a steaming hot, mushy mess in a matter of seconds. This girl must have been some kind of a witch, for sure. That was still the best explanation. The only explanation. Yes, she had to be a fucking witch.

There're going to have a lot of fun with you.

"Oh Frank! What am I going to do with you! Really! Your rehabilitation, is taking longer than expected! But I'm not giving up on you, Frank! I'll never give up on you! You know that, don't you Frank! I'll never give up on you! I can't give up on you now! But time is running out fast, Frank! I don't know how much longer I can support you! And please, try being less recalcitrant! That's sure to help!"

Well, it was out in the open. In a crowded café. And she was kind of ambushed, you know. So, she had a right to get a little annoyed. Well yeah, really pissed off. That was judging by the look on her face. She's never likely to forget that day in a hurry. Stupid bitch.

Shouldn't be calling her that. He knew that. But what else was he supposed to call her, after what she'd just dished up. Stupid bitch. Then an old memory suddenly floated to the surface and put an end to that depressing situation.

"You are an idiot!"

Took a while to remember where this one came from. Way back, when in the public service, is when it happened. Frank got all excited one day and asked this receptionist to go for lunch with him. All because she had such a pretty face and the loveliest eyes, you could ever imagine. She almost exploded with joy. Should have known then, to change his mind. Such a big warning sign, you know. When the excitement level instantly reaches fever pitch. But there was too much inexperience going on here. Asking girls out to lunch, just never happened. But the eyes had him, alright. He was helpless.

Frank only ever saw this girl sitting at her desk, you know. Only went and talked to her, to look into those big blue, emerald, green eyes. Yes, she was so good to look at, you know. From her huge chest up anyway. And always so friendly. And she enjoyed talking to Frank. Not many people did. Especially girls. But she did. Couldn't get enough of him. Anyway, around he went to get her. The excitement was killing him. But when she stood up, she had an arse on her, the size of an elephants. Holy shit. Wouldn't be seen dead with her. Instant, automatic, verbal reaction.

"Uh, you know what. I might give lunch a miss today! Not real hungry anyway! I had a big breakfast! See you later!"

The look on his face must have told her everything. But that wasn't even thought about at the time. Because nothing was. Except getting the hell away from there. And her. Didn't want to know about anything. Just took off. Better off having lunch by himself anyway. Just like always.

About an hour later, is when the monster roared.

"You are an idiot!"

One of his co-workers had a little chat to him later on. Apparently, there'd been a big teary, girly session in the lunchroom. The poor girl was inconsolable. And all the women were on her side. Nothing surprising about that. But they wouldn't understand. Not from his point of view, anyway. One of them, decided to let the feelings be known. All of their feelings combined. And it was no surprise, who it was either. Miserable old bitch.

Well, being called an idiot was no surprise, you know. Happened all the time. But just the way she yelled it out. Right in the middle of the office. Walked right up to his desk. It was a photo finish, what happened first. The glare in the eyes, or the mouth opening up. But she let him have it, alright.

Used to be her desk, you know. And it used to be her job. But there were so many complaints about her. So, they transferred her off into another section. Where she couldn't piss so many people off. Such a cranky old bitch. The over traumatised girl got transferred off to somewhere else as well. Never saw her again.

Anyway. Eventually made it back to the safety of the back veranda.

What was that she just slipped in there. Recalcitrant. Have to look that one up later. No, better do it now. There was a serious situation, developing with the memory now, you know. It was a case of do it now, before whatever it was a case of, what was it that was going to get done. Until maybe days or weeks later. When something just popped in and confused the thinking. Especially when the lady was involved.

Recalcitrant; having an obstinately uncooperative attitude towards authority or discipline.

Well, of course. That, was it? Full understanding. Just like that. Frank was a recalcitrant, alright. Was happy enough about being a recalcitrant too. Otherwise, he'd be putty in the hands of the one girl, who got into his head and his heart. And drove him crazy a few times. And still does. Just the thought of her, still does. But she was never going to win, was she? So, being a recalcitrant was the best thing to be. As long as he stayed a recalcitrant, he'd be winning. Not her. And there was no thinking going on about her anymore, anyway. So, there was a winning feeling happening. And it was his and not hers. And that was the main thing.

Well, there was nowhere else to go was there. Not after this revelation.

"Hello, I'm Frank and I'm a compulsive gambler!"

"Hi Frank."

"Hello Frank."

"Hello Frank."

"Things are not so good! I busted again the other day!"

"Oh Frank! That's a real shame!"

"Yeah, that stupid bitch at the café again!"

"I thought she was your girlfriend?"

Fancy the controller saying something like that.

"I don't think so! I can't sit in peace and have lunch. I can't even read the paper. I, can't fucking do anything! She just comes right up and gets in my face. Whenever she feels like it. Them beady little, black eyes! Boring into my head all the time! Fucking bitch!"

If he was after sympathy from the compulsives, he wasn't getting any. They were all just pissing themselves laughing.

"That's terrible Frank! But you're here talking about it! That's the best thing to do! You're in the right place!"

The controller had the big smile back on the face, after saying that last bit. Was almost busting out as well.

"Are you ok, Frank? Sounds like she's still affecting you emotionally! That's probably why you busted!"

"Yeah, yeah. I'm ok! Of course, it's why I busted! But I'm over it now! That's why I'm back here again! Because she's back again! Driving me crazy! She won't be doing it again but! I can tell you that! How can she do that to me, anyway? I just have to trust my instincts and I'll be, alright. And that means staying away from her. The bitch. And I have to let all the negative thoughts out. Control my feelings! It's taking me longer than I expected. But I'm not going to give up! I'm never going to give up on myself!"

Poor old Frank. The picture had showed up again and he didn't even see it coming. And he thought it was her and not the picture. Dopey bastard. The hands went up as he looked up. Maybe, for some kind of divine inspiration or something. Then he just, sort of relaxed. Hands flopped down on the table. The head went down. And a deep breath was let out through the mouth. Complete defeat. Again.

This was when the controller couldn't stay in control any longer. Neither could the female compulsives who were sitting there, with stupid smirks on their faces. They all just burst out laughing again. Even louder than before. Like it was the funniest thing they'd ever heard in their whole lives.

Frank was nothing like ok. The poor bastard. She had him stuffed, alright. There could have been a more vivid description here, you know. But the use of language had been creeping into the thought processes. And it was decided to try and improve the communication skills. Except at GA meetings, of course. Say anything you liked at GA meetings.

What's said in GA, stays in GA.

"Anyway. Thanks for letting me share!"

He'd had enough. And he wasn't going to say anything about kissing her in the café was he. Imagine all the laughing and ridicule that would have caused.

"There are no short cuts to recovery, Frank! Enjoy one day at a time! Common to all compulsive gamblers is impatience. Recovery requires a different attitude. It can't be had overnight, Frank! There are no short cuts to recovery!"

Yeah right. Got that. All the other shares were shared. The God bit got said. Then the hand holding thing happened. And then it was out of there.

Talk about slogging it out in the gym the next morning. Heavier weights. More repetitions. The running machine, copped a hiding. Yeah, an extra-long workout.

There was a complaint made against him, you know. Exactly what he didn't need. Gave someone a dodgy look. And maybe said something, that wasn't good to say. There was only a vague recollection of what took place. But it did take place. Remembered that bit, alright. Another fucking nightmare to put up with.

First real catastrophe in the new life. But it was during the pandemic. And you still had to wear a mask, to even get into the gym. That was the excuse anyway. So, maybe the thinking wasn't happening all that good. But imagine trying to explain that to anyone.

Swimming was back to normal now. The picture had disappeared. Emotional structure was back in place. Everything was fine. Feeling good. Only four laps to go. Then it was back again. Not her. Not the picture. Just the thought of it all. Bloody hell. Even when he was swimming now.

So, now the swimming went to flat out level. As fast as it ever was. For about two more laps. Almost drowned after that. Swallowed a bucket full of salt water. Lost it completely.

She was probably in the pool somewhere. Pretending to be a lap swimmer. Or maybe just leaning against the back wall, staring at the waves rolling in. So, every square inch of the pool was scanned a few times. But she wasn't in there. Maybe she was watching from somewhere. Out of sight. With a pair of binoculars. Wouldn't put it past the bitch. Oops, not supposed to call her that anymore. But she was somewhere. Yeah. She was hiding out there somewhere.

Yeah. Terrorised by TMBGITW again. While swimming. One of the favourite things to do. And now, even that was getting invaded. Then it happened again didn't it. The picture was back, smiling that sweet, warm smile. Like it knew everything about him and he knew nothing about it. And that was exactly right.

"Where's your mask?"

The COVID girl again. What a pain in the arse she was. Something would have to be done about this one. Café girl or not. She must think she owns the place or something.

Lucky, there was always a spare mask in every pocket now. Never going to get caught out again. That's for sure. Took the smile off her sweet little face. For about 30 seconds anyway. Yeah. Getting smarter all the time.

That crazy dancer was getting above herself a bit too, you know. Scribbles a message on the lid of the coffee cup one day. Don't go making phone calls in my café. That's what she wrote. Stupid bitch. All he was doing was checking for any text messages. There were never usually any there. But it didn't hurt to check did it. But even that, didn't escape their attention.

"There's a special message on the lid!"

That's what ginger said as she shoved the cup under his nose. Then pointed straight at it. Made sure it was read too. Before she took off. Must have been from upstairs, this one. Never been seen before. But she had fuzzy ginger hair. So, what else could she be called, but ginger.

Anyway, here's the crazy dancer, standing at the coffee machine, with a smart arse look on her face. So, she gets the big one finger doesn't she. Then her and the other two that were there. Ginger and stick up for her friends. Start giggling their little heads off don't they.

There're going to have a lot of fun with you.

Here we are again. Before that little memory interruption. Sitting there, staring at the ocean. At least fifteen minutes had passed, before he snapped out of it. There was the coffee. In the middle of the table.

"Would you like another coffee, Frank? This one's gone cold!"

She was right there, waiting. They must have video surveillance in this place.

"What! Ah! Oh coffee! Yes, I forgot about the coffee. I was just thinking about something!"

"Would you like another one?"

It was nice eyes.

"Yes please. If it's not too much trouble?"

"No trouble at all Frank! No trouble at all! Back in a few minutes!"

That look on her smiling face. That, already know everything look. Yes, he knew what that look meant now. Unmistakeable. Unexplainable. Unbeatable.

"There you go, Frank! Lunch won't be long!"

"Thanks! I appreciate that!"

"Do you have many friends Frank?"

"What?"

But she was already gone. Took off as soon as she said it. And it wasn't nice eyes either. It was the girl called. But there was no recollection of this girl at all. Must have been another upstairs girl. Or maybe a ghost. Or maybe it didn't even happen at all. Yeah, the confusion was building. Again. What was that supposed to mean anyway, do you have many friends.

There're going to have a lot of fun with you.

Wait a minute. Something else just got remembered.

A few days earlier, there was a book left on the bench in the change shed right near the exit; called, 'How to Win Friends and Influence People.'

Maybe another one of those coincidences. But not likely. Must have been one of the swimmers who left it there. Or maybe one of the café girls snuck down and put it there. So, it was noted, alright but just ignored. The usual shower, drying off and changing routine took place. Just like always. But on the way out. The book was still there wasn't it. So, it got picked up and checked out carefully.

There was no name anywhere and no bookmark. But there was a receipt. Cost someone $19.99. Twenty bucks in other words. And it was bought that same day. It was put straight back down. Not getting sucked in this time. They'd only win again, if the book was taken. So, they weren't going to win this one. After leaving and walking a few metres, the flip went back in and picked it up again.

But the same line of thinking clicked in. This is a set up for sure. Don't get tricked again. So, the book got put back down. Out he went and walked for a few metres. Then turned around and went back in. Picked up the book. The thinking this time was. Fuck it. Whoever owns it, should have been back by now. Someone else will only get it. So, it was got wasn't it.

"There you go, Frank! It looks yummy! Enjoy!"

"Oh right, thanks!"

"Who was that girl, that brought the coffee! I haven't seen her before!"

"What girl was that, Frank!"

"The one who brought the coffee! Just a few minutes ago!"

"I didn't see her, Frank! She's probably from upstairs. The girls up there, come down and help out sometimes! And sometimes, we go up there and help out."

This was the have a little chat girl talking here and she always knew what she was talking about.

"Oh, right! Thanks! I'll remember that!"

So, now it was confirmed. There were upstairs girls and downstairs girls. Bloody hell. If that kept happening, he'd have to learn a whole bunch of new names. And figure out a whole bunch of special names. So, he could remember the real names. And just when he thought he had everything under control. The whole thing is going to start, all over again. She said, it looked yummy. And just the way she said it. There're at it again, alright.

There're going to have a lot of fun with you.

But the café girl smile was there again wasn't it. The even bigger café girl smile. So, there was something going on, alright. That's for sure. He'd seen that bigger smile before. And it usually meant some kind of trouble. For him. Then something else got remembered. A few days before the book was there. There was a short conversation at the counter, with, with, with—

Well, it was with one of them. Obviously, this was one on those times when the memory went missing. It could have been nice eyes, NG1 or NG2. Or the funny one. But she was an upstairs girl so, that was unlikely. And she wasn't that funny anyway. She just thought she was. Anyway, it doesn't matter.

"What do you do with you spare time, Frank? After you leave here?

"I just go home and have a rest. That's all!

"You must do something else besides going to the gym and swimming?"

She wasn't going to give up, till she found out either. Just like the asking girl. And with so many questions, maybe it was the asking girl. Yes, it probably was her. And he was right onto her as well. Didn't want to answer.

Honesty will come into your life if you let it.

She had him, alright and she knew it. And so did Frank. Yeah. Just about to lose again.

"Well, I read lots of books!"

"Oh right! Reading books is a good thing!"

Up to their tricks again, alright. Only this time, he knew what was coming. Well, he knew something was coming. But it happened again didn't it. They knew what he was doing, before he told them, what he was doing. And they knew what he was thinking before he even thought about what he was going to be thinking about. How do they do that anyway. Yeah, sucked in again. And it wasn't a coincidence either.

There're going to have a lot of fun with you.

Frank read that book. How to win friends and influence people. Three times. But they were never going to know anything about that. He might have lost at the start with this one. But he'd win in the end, as long as he didn't say anything. Yeah. Getting smarter all the time.

Right, this time he really did mean it. Was never going back there, ever again. There was no relaxing. The gym workouts were almost killing him. And swimming was no longer enjoyable. And they were tricking him all the time. This new life and everything in there was a complete fucking nightmare. And the magic café. What was really going on in there anyway. Maybe there're all witches. That would explain everything wouldn't it. A magic cage, full of witches.

"Don't be ridiculous, Frank! There're the most wonderful girls you will ever know! And let them know you, Frank! Let them get to know you! You're worth knowing, Frank! You really are! And Frank! Time's running out now! Please! Get your act together!"

Yeah. Ok. So, he needed to hear that right now. Well, you know. He knew that already. Them all being wonderful. Probably got a bit carried away, with the witch's bit though. Except for those two evil little twins in the first place. They were witches, alright.

Worth knowing, eh. No one had ever said that to him before and he liked the sound of it. Another thing he knew was that they knew him already. Better than he knew himself. And getting the act together. Maybe she's right about that too.

"Oh, you're back again Frank? It's so good see you? What are you having today!"

"Uh! Well! Um!"

And what was that supposed to mean anyway. Oh, your back again, Frank. Like she already knew he wasn't ever coming back. But he was back.

But there was no ordering in the frame right now. TMBGITW was going to get what for this time. He was looking all around for her. She had to be there somewhere. She was always there. But she wasn't there. She must have seen him coming and hid out the back.

"She's not here anymore, Frank!"

"What? Who's not here anymore! What are you talking about! What do you mean, she's not here anymore? What happened to her anyway?"

There were a few of them there now. Just staring. And no café girl smiles anywhere.

But it was the evil little twin, doing the talking. Hadn't seen her for a while either. And what was she doing back anyway. Right when her little mate was going to cop it. They were always together, these two. Seemed like that anyway. They were always one step ahead too. Yeah. Always that one step ahead. Or two.

Frank was beside himself. In complete shock. So pumped up. Ready to let her have it. And now, she wasn't even there. Damn. What a disappointment that was.

There're going to have a lot of fun with you.

He'd already forgotten her name, you know. So, it didn't matter anyway. If he ever knew it in the first place that is. Yeah ok, he knew it, alright. Was just about to say something else. But the evil twin was right onto it. Already knew what he was going to say, before he even said it. You'd think he'd be a wakeup by now wouldn't you.

"Oh, she's gone on to bigger things!"

"What! Oh right! I was just wondering, that's all! I had no idea what I was doing, you know!"

"Don't worry about it, Frank! It's all good!"

"Well, that's the main thing!"

She knew exactly what he was talking about too. Didn't even know he was going to say that either. Just said it. Bigger things. What's that supposed to mean, anyway. Bigger things. He was sick and tired of hearing about bigger things.

Yeah, this girl. This evil little thing had an even bigger smile on her face now. Then just cracked up laughing. Before turning around and disappearing out the back. The café girls were always disappearing out the back. They just loved doing that.

There're going to have a lot of fun with you.

He'll end up copping it. That fucking compulsive. Yeah, the emotions were all over the place right now. There was even a fleeting thought about a big repeat the bet button, you know.

But there was real hunger there now, so lunch got ordered and paid for and the favourite table was available. So, at least something was going right. And the thinking went right off, as soon as he sat down. And thank Christ for that.

Something in Frank had kept on warning him about thinking too much of these girls in the café. Females were always trouble in one way or another. They were all so young anyway. And Frank. He was an old man. Old enough to be their grandfather. They probably all just felt sorry for him. Yes. That had to be all it was. He didn't know where these warnings were coming from either. But they were coming. And they'd been there before, you know. A few times.

She meant nothing to him anyway. Already over it all. She was just another girl. Not so young either. Almost at the old boiler stage. Not even worth worrying about. Too old. Too beautiful. And too damn smart. There're the worse kind, you know. The beautiful, smart ones. So, he was probably lucky to finally get away from her.

Then the main reason came to him. Still in remission from prostate cancer, you know. Nothing much was happening below the waistline these days. So even if TMBGITW was after him. And she was. That's for sure. But, after she found that out, she'd have dropped him like a hot potato. Frank knew he knew that. Anyway, TMBGITW must have had an eye problem. Frank knew that as well. Or maybe she wasn't too bright. Stupid even. No, she definitely wasn't stupid. And definitely too smart for Frank. That's for sure. But he already knew that too.

Imagine getting all lovey-dovey with her. Rolling around in the hay, you know. Time comes. Oh, sorry darlin'. Nothing much happening down there these days. How would that go down. Not very good, eh. Could hardly even see the thing these days. Let alone use it for anything. Except peeing out of. Yeah, the shagging days were long gone. That's for sure.

But it's very interesting, you know. How the old shagging days, can be remembered much easier than many other activities that took place. Back in the old life. The never to be forgotten days. The most enjoyable, carefree days of youth. When indulging in all the pleasures of life were the only considerations worth considering. And they certainly were considered and indulged in. Especially, by this dried-up old relic.

But they were also the days when the most negative thoughts started formulating. And then carried through. Right till near the very end of existence. Till the last gasping, laboured breath. It's not the same for everyone, of course. Ending up a desperate forlorn druggist, alcoholic and compulsive gambler, who have no control of what's left of their pathetic, useless lives. Yeah. All sounds a little negative, eh. That's because it is. And if anyone should know, it's what's left of this one.

Although it wasn't realised, Frank was descending back to the dark old days. Of the old life that he thought was now left behind, forever. After all, he was well and truly into the new life now. So, there should have been an understanding of what was happening. But the dark shadows were still there. Maybe not quite as dark as they were. But they were still there. Yeah, the dark shadows just wouldn't let go. And the new thinking was still too confused to get rid of them.

And to think, there's hospitals everywhere. Full of sick and dying people and she just happened to pop in to the one Frank was in. And fill his head with a whole lot of bullshit. Just plain bad luck, eh.

And Frank was just about there, you know. Wouldn't have been much longer. Maybe a few more years, at the most. Pretty much looking forward to that final day of pain and misery. Self-inflicted, of course.

But that lady just had to turn up didn't she and prolong the agony. Give the old bastard false hope. All because of some fairy tale about a new life. A second chance.

"Oh Frank! Is this really you saying all that! After all the progress you've made! There's still a bit more fog there! You'll need to work on that, Frank! The fog will eventually lift! All of it! And the brightness of your new life, will forever blot out the dark shadows! You just need a little more time, Frank! That's all! Just a little more time! I know you can get there, Frank! I know you can do it! Please Frank! Please get there! You must get there, Frank!"

Yeah whatever. He'd give her some fog. That's for sure. If he ever got his hands on her. And she's sounding more desperate all the time now. Maybe she's the one who needs to get there, eh.

"Of course, it's me! Who else would it be! You should know! Anyway! It's all your fault I'm still here in the first place!"

Well, he hadn't talked back for a while now. And it did make him feel a lot better. Straight away. And the thinking went back to where it was before she zeroed in and caused all the confusion again. Yeah. It was about time some solid defence was put up against the lady.

There were vague memories arriving now. About girls and how things didn't work out, all that well. Wasn't sure about the details. Just knew he was far better off, having nothing to do with girls. I mean, he was an old man after all. Kept mumbling that to himself. Every time he caught himself out, staring at these young café girls. Strutting around in their tight jeans. With their mobile phones, sticking out of a back pocket. Always found that very interesting, you know. And sometimes wondered, how these girls could sit down, with a phone in their back pocket. Yeah. They were all good sorts, these café girls. But then the reality usually set in again. Stupid old, deluded fool and knew it too. Just wanting the old life back. Some of it, anyway.

"You're an old man! You're an old man! Wake up to yourself! There're going to have a lot of fun with you! Fucking hell!"

Yeah. Talking to himself again. Thank Christ, there was no one sitting at any of the nearby tables.

Shouldn't have even be thinking about girls, at his age. Not the way he was anyway. Yes, they were probably just being nice to him. That had to be all it was. Have to be more careful from now on. Yeah, he was just an old man, with an old man's body. Well, it was a rather muscled-up old man's body. With just a few wrinkles and a bit of sagging skin here and there. Had a nice pair of man boobs happening now as well. And occasionally when a mirror was noticed, took a quick look. What was there, didn't look so old at all. So, maybe there was a chance after all. As long as there was no shagging involved.

And there was a young man's brain ticking around, you know. The new life brain. All wired up with the necessary information, to live a much younger man's life. Never thought much about that before, you know. Not until the magic café was discovered, that is. Decided never to go there, ever again. Again. And this time he really did meant it. Really.

If that lady was anywhere around right now. He'd be telling her a thing or two.

"There you go, Frank! Enjoy!"

The serious one, just delivered the lunch and coffee. No little chat with this one. Always so serious looking, you know. Like she carried the world on her shoulders and maybe she did, who knows. She lets out a little half café girl smile sometimes. But never a full one. Bit different, alright. What else could he call her, but the serious one. There's always one isn't there. She was a very nice girl. And very polite. And so efficient. But no mucking around with the serious one.

Strange things can happen sometimes, you know. And what happened over the next twenty-four hours must have been one of those times. Because nothing could be remembered about what happened over the last twenty-four hours. A complete blank. Woke up mid-morning, with a cracking headache. Starving hungry and more confused than he'd been for a long time.

"Hi! What can we get you today?"

Thank God, it wasn't the evil little twin still there. There was a mood, to give her a bit of verbal. That's for sure. But that mood didn't last long. The hunger pains were killing him. But the confusion still had hold of the thinking. So, no thinking could happen. Not right then anyway.

"Uh! Well! I haven't decided yet!"

"OK! Here's a menu! Check it out! There's sure to be something on there you like!"

She was new, this girl. Full of beans. And very good looking. But all it really meant was that she didn't know what the favourite meals were. And what days went with what meals. Frank had a new thing happening with the routine, you know. It was Tuesday and that meant sweet potato chips with vegan aioli sauce and a coffee. With oat-milk and vanilla flavouring. She had no idea, this one. If she did, then no thinking would have been required. But she didn't and it was.

Just about to try explaining things to her when the always good for a little chat girl appeared from out the back. What a relief that was. This new girl just stood there, with some kind of bewildered look on her smiling face. Yeah. They were even smiling, when they had no idea what was going on. But there was much more understanding there now, you know. About being patient. So, Frank just smiled back at her. No worries. Then another new girl suddenly appeared from out the back. There were always girls appearing from out the back, you know. Often wondered what really went on out the back. Can tell you that. Maybe I already have.

Anyway, now there were two new girls, who had no idea what they were doing. So, they were called New Girl One and New Girl Two. Or NG1 and NG2 for short. Kind of figured these two had been seen before. Maybe it was when the masks had to be worn. That would explain it.

But they soon figured out what was going on, these two. Only took a few weeks. Yeah, they were both onto it by then. That seemed to be the average time it took any new girl to catch on. The fact there were hundreds of other regular and semi-regular customers, never came into the calculations at all. There was only one customer of any significance. And these new girls would soon know who it was. Still a deluded old fool.

But then it was realised. NG1 and NG2 had been in the café for a while now. How could that be forgotten. But it was forgotten. Maybe it was because masks no longer had to be worn. But that was months ago.

And then a conversation with NG1 resurfaced. About how she was off to New Zealand to work at some ski resort. But that didn't work out and she was back again. How could something like that be forgotten about. But it was forgotten. And that was a real worry.

The magic café was now the favourite addiction. And all the special attention the girls gave him had a lot to do with it and Frank knew it. They were affecting him in ways he'd never known before. Yeah. All these beautiful young girls and this one, deluded old man. Now that other one wasn't hanging around anymore, there was no pressure. The relaxed attitude took over. Well and truly over her by now, anyway. The new life was looking better all the time.

All they were really doing was talking to him, you know. Talking to this pathetic old man, who was in the real world, for the first time ever and it was freaking him right out. But he was okay with all that now. Only he didn't know that and would never have been able to explain any of it to anyone, anyway. So, just going with it was the best thing to do. The only thing to do. Whether he knew what was going on or not.

Yeah. This new world. That he still didn't fully understand. And to make things worse, he was still remembering stuff from another world. That he never fully understood either. A past existence. That was still there. But wasn't really still there. But less and less time was spent, trying to think about all that past stuff. And what a relief that was. But it was still there. It was always still there. The body weight was getting lighter, alright. But the weight between the ears seemed to be getting heavier and heavier. Carrying two lives around, at the same time. Not an easy thing to be doing, you know.

Yeah. Still reverting back to the mind-set of the good old days. The days almost completely forgotten about. Most of the time. And then into the mind-set of the new life. Sometimes, these two mind sets met up and went bouncing around all over the place. This adjustment business. To a new world. Was driving him crazy all over again. And it wasn't even his idea. One thing he did know. He'd never been so scared or confused in the whole two lives.

But he loved every minute of it, you know. Good idea or not. The confusion was difficult to handle, alright. But there couldn't be enough of it. Loved all the confusion in the brain. Always been there, you know. And two confusions at the same time. What more could be asked for. No need for any nicotine, pot, beer or LSD. When you can come to a magic café and trip right out. Or get tripped right out, by a bunch of beautiful young girls.

Still trying to work out how all that worked. And with the lady floating in and out, whenever she damn well felt like it. And TMBGITW haunting his every thought. How could things possibly get any better than that.

There're going to have a lot of fun with you.

And that fucking smart arse compulsive, of course. Can't forget about him.

Staring out over the ocean, waiting for lunch to arrive. The memories of a past confrontation started manifesting. And it was with a café girl. Another new one. Trouble with a café girl was never the intention, of course. But she started it. Not long after the other one disappeared. Frank, didn't call her TMBGITW anymore either. Just that other one. Or, the other one. He'd forgotten what she looked like already, anyway. And he was over it. That's what the thinking was anyway. Because that's what the thinking had to be.

Yeah, this new girl just turned up. Rather a tall one, you know. So that's what her name was. Straight away. The tall one. She was good looking and wore the tight jeans, just like the rest of them. But had an air of authority about her. Didn't know whether to like her or not. Did at first. But then something happened that changed everything. She started getting nosey and asking questions. Just like the other one. Yeah. Here we go again.

"There you go, Frank! Enjoy!"

"Oh, Thanks!"

This was another one of those upstairs girls and she was just busting to say something, before taking off.

"There's a new girl on today! You'll know her when you see her. She's really tall!"

What the... Another one of those coincidences. Like hell, was it? They must be all mind readers in this place. Witches can read minds, you know. But it wasn't good to let those negative thoughts creep in. Already knew that, eh.

Anyway, a short time later, the tall one just walked up to his table and looked down upon him. Smiled the same café girl smile and started talking. They must all look in a mirror and practice that smile for hours, you know. To get it right.

"There was a girl here for quite a while! Before she moved on to bigger things!"

Right. Just how much clearer did it have to get. Here we go again. Action replay. How the hell did she know about that anyway. Was onto her straight away. She was fishing, alright. These girls must all be part of a clan or something. Yeah. A clan of fucking witches.

Been checking up about witches on the internet, you know. Knew how they operated. They were all full of nasty tricks. And could get you doing things, that you would never even think about doing. And saying things, that you would never normally say. And they could even kill you. Or make you kill yourself. Yeah. They were very dangerous, alright, these witches.

And there wasn't just one or two of them either. But a whole café full of them. Or, maybe they could have been a religious mob. And that'd be even worse. And the way they smiled all the time. That just wasn't normal. Then something got said. Something that would never have been said under normal circumstances. Not in a million years. If there was a chance to think about it first. It wouldn't have been said either. But there wasn't, and it did. Because these weren't normal circumstances, were they? There was no control. Looked up at the tall one, and blurted this overpowering thought straight out.

Yeah. There was a witch controlling the brain, alright. When this came out.

"She got into my head you know!"

The smile immediately became some kind of evil looking smirk, before she exploded.

"What! In a good way!"

170

Whoa. Fucking hell. She seemed to get a foot taller, as they screamed that out. What was that supposed to mean anyway. In a good way. He'd heard it a few times already. In a good way. But, how the hell could it have possibly been in a good way. Because he's been confused right out of the new brain ever since.

After coming back down to her natural height, she bent down and got right in his face. Eyeballed him as well. But she didn't have them black, beady little eyes, this girl.

Not like that other one. Her eyes were a soft, green-blue colour. What a surprise that was. Pitch black would have been more suitable. Yeah. She did blow right up, you know. But settled right back down again. Real quick. Liked being in control this one. Easy to tell that. And that was the first impression, after she sneaked up in the first place. And first impressions are always important.

There was an answer building up too, you know. But nothing would come out. A jam up in the brain was happening. And that was interesting. Wanting to say something. But saying nothing. Because nothing could be said. So, nothing was said. Sat there, dumbfounded. Didn't even see the tall one walk away either. Wasn't seeing anything. Still scared shitless. That's why.

"Oh Frank! Of course, it was in a good way!"

"Oh no! Not you again! Fuck off for Christ's sake! Not now! I can't listen to you now! Fuck off and leave me alone!"

"What! Don't talk to me like that, mate! Who do you think you are! Talking to me like that!"

Fucking hell. There was a bloke sitting at the next table and he thought Frank was talking to him. He got really pissed off.

"Don't go talking to me like that! I come here all the time! I don't have to put up with dick heads like you!"

This guy was up now. Walking in between tables. Ranting and raving. Going completely nuts. And Frank was thinking about maybe getting up and smashing him. Shut the fuckwit right up. But then something extraordinary happened.

Just when you think you've seen everything. Something happens, right before your very eyes and blows your mind. The fuckwit suddenly shut up and pointed towards the window. Frank turned his head and straight away, saw the whole thing.

Some bloke. Completely naked. Had run in between the tables outside. There's an old couple at the table directly in front of where Frank and this fuckwit were standing. The woman is holding a little girl, about two or three

171

years old. A real little cutie. Next minute, this fucking maniac grabs hold of the little girl and starts heading off. The woman is hanging onto the little girl. So here they are. This old woman and this naked lunatic. Having a tug-a-war with this little girl, who was screaming her pretty little head off.

But within about ten seconds, the naked fella was flat out on the concrete, with a few shocked and outraged diners, pinning him down. He was going nowhere.

Frank and the other guy soon forgot about their little quarrel. No apologies or anything either. Frank spoke first.

"Well, that was interesting!"

"Interesting! He was going to run off with that little girl and rape her! And probably kill her!"

This guy was kind of short, you know. And very excitable. His big, dark brown eyes were almost popping out. Intense little character, alright. But he could have been right about this lunatic, running off with that little girl.

"Maybe we should go and help?"

"No, they seem to have things under control!"

Under control, alright. One bloke down, with one knee pressed into the middle of his back. Two blokes, sitting on one leg each. Another bloke, pushing the side of his head into the concrete. The poor bastard was near choking to death. Eventually, someone threw a towel in, to cover up the private bits.

Frank and that other guy. You know. The fuckwit. Ran into each other down at the baths a few times. Turns out, he's a lap swimmer as well. And he wasn't a fuckwit either. They got along really good, once they get to know each other a bit better. He was a bit of a talker, you know. And he got Frank talking as well and that was a good thing.

Frank was never very good at getting to know people. Still kind of hated people, without ever really knowing why. So, just to be friendly to this bloke and say hello and have a little chat here and there was a big step forward. As far as any kind of friendly relations go. Apart from the café girls that is. Reading How to Win Friends and Influence People, probable helped a little as well, you know.

"Oh Frank! Talking to people is such a big improvement for you! I'm so proud of you! I really am! You've come such a long way! Don't stop now, Frank! Don't stop now! I know you can make it Frank! I know you can make it! Keep going Frank! Just keep going! Please Frank! Just keep improving! You must keep improving! You must!"

Yeah, she didn't stay away for very long, did she? And she must have forgiven him, for telling her to fuck off as well. But Frank always had this feeling inside him now, you know. And it was a good feeling to have. Like it didn't matter what he did or said. Because he would always be forgiven, for any mistakes that he made. And he made plenty. That's for sure.

So, the café girls forgave him and now the lady had forgiven him as well. He couldn't lose, could he? Well, he could you know. Especially, with that other one. She might have been winning in the beginning. But he won in the end. Because she was gone and he was still there. Fixed her right up. And he's over her now as well. So, that was a win/win situation for him. Only, he didn't really know, when he won or when he lost. But he knew it was either one or the other. And he knew he'd won that one.

"Oh Frank! I'm sorry for interrupting again! But it's not all about winning or losing! It's about understanding! You obviously still have a lot to learn, about personal growth and development. And relationships with other people. Especially girls! But don't worry, Frank! You'll get there in the end! I know you'll get there in the end! You must get there, Frank! You really must! And soon!"

So, it must be a fucking race now or something. She can be just so boring sometimes, you know. A real pain in the arse. Anyway, usually he didn't even know he'd made a mistake at all. Until someone explained that he did. And it was quite often the girls in the magic café, who did the explaining. Only they had this way of explaining thinks to Frank, that Frank didn't realise were being explained to him.

So, he started understanding lots of things, without even knowing how he was understanding, what he was even knowing. And he wouldn't have understood anything anyway. Even if the girls did try to explain it to him, any other way. Other than, how they were explaining things.

There're going to have a lot of fun with you.

Not long after the meal and coffee arrived, the police turned up. And so did this old fellow. He was huffing and puffing and pointing. Raising his arms in the air and pleading with the officers. No doubt, on behalf of the, by now, desperate looking maniac being squashed into the concrete.

Turns out, the old fellow was the maniac's carer. Somehow, they got separated and you already know what happened then. The police seemed okay about the explanation. Allowed the carer to take control of the situation. He helped the poor fellow up. Wrapped a towel around him and wandered off with him. And that was the end of that exciting little episode.

Frank and the fuckwit who wasn't really a fuckwit, returned to their tables. But Frank decided not to talk to this bloke anymore. After all, he could have been a shirt lifter. But you already know what happened later. And how the fuckwit, who wasn't really a fuckwit and Frank became kind of friends. But not really friends. There was nowhere near enough personal growth and development going on yet, to actually have real friends. And that book had only been read once, anyway.

"Oh dear! Friends are good to have, Frank! Everyone should have at least one good friend! The café girls are your friends, Frank! They like you so much, you know! They all think you're wonderful."

"What! Wonderful! How do you figure that!"

Oops. After what just happened, it wasn't a good idea to keep talking to himself. So, there was no more conversation. Got stuck into lunch. Read a few little stories in a newspaper. About riots and people dying from starvation. Because their country was getting blown to pieces.

There was a sad story about some deranged husband, who murdered his wife and children. And some sporting hero being up on drug charges. But he soon got sick and tired of reading about all that shit. Put the newspaper back and then he was out of there.

"See you later, Frank! Have a good day!"

That was another one of the new girls. Not NG1 or NG2. Another one altogether. Didn't take her long to catch on, did it. But Frank had been talking to this girl a bit, you know. She was a vegan herself. Just like Frank. And that's what they talked about a fair bit. Veganism. But she was smart as well. A university student. Such a lovely girl she was too. A very likeable girl. And Frank sure did like her. Another one of the magic café girls, who made him wish he was at least thirty years younger. He called her the Vegan Girl.

There're going to have a lot of fun with you.

"Hello! I'm Frank and I'm a compulsive gambler!"

"Hi Frank!"

"Hello Frank!"

"Hi Frank!"

"There's another new girl at the café. Another bitch! She made me start talking about her again! Just when I'd got rid of her! Yeah. She made me start thinking about her again! So, I busted again, didn't I! But it wasn't my fault!"

"Oh Frank! That's no good!"

"Once they get in there, man! They won't let you go! I should know! I'm got two of them up here now!"

This compulsive was pointing to the side of his head, when he said that.

"Yeah! Well, I've got a few of you bastards up here as well! And I can't get rid of them either!"

She was smiling and laughing, when she said that and pointing to the side of her head as well. And all the other compulsives were having a good old laugh. Including Frank. The controller was just sitting there, trying to be in control. But wasn't in control at all. Joined in laughing, like everyone else. But controllers don't stay out of control for long, you know. That's why there're the controllers.

It was always a good thing, for the compulsives to have a good laugh. And it was quite often when Frank was doing the sharing. But that was okay. Figured after a while, that maybe that was his way of contributing to the GA meetings. Having everyone else laughing at him. Or laughing with him, is a better way of putting it. But they were really laughing at him. Not with him. And everyone knew that.

So, here was Frank. Trying to stop laughing, while everyone else was laughing at him. Feeling like a complete failure. Which he was. All compulsives were complete failures, you know. That's why Frank opened up, when it was his time to share. Because all the other compulsives, understood exactly where he was coming from. And they didn't judge him either or call him names.

Well, some of them did call him names. Insulted the shit out of him. But it was all in good fun, you know. He knew that. He liked all of them. Well, maybe not all of them. Some of them got up his nose a bit. That's for sure. But they were all still compulsives. Just like him. All part of the family. The GA family. And that was the main thing.

"Anyway, I don't want to talk about that other one anymore! And she's gone now anyway! She's gone onto bigger things. And I'll never see her again and thank God for that! And I have to stop going from one extreme to the other. It's better to stay on an even keel and just chill out. It's good to just chill out! But I have come such a long way. I have to keep believing in myself. I know it's just the beginning. I just need to be more patient. I'll get there in the end. I know I will. So, thanks for letting me share!"

There was the usual clapping and various comments, that there always was.

"Ok! Who else would like to share?"

There were several more shares. But Frank couldn't stay focused, you know. That picture was in there again. The eyes looked darker and more squinted. And the smile was wider. She just wouldn't leave him alone. And his mother must have been having one of her naps or something. Because she was nowhere to be seen. He was so glad when the controller ended the meeting.

All together now.

"To the God of our own understanding!"

Here we go. Blah. Blah. Blah.

"God, give me the strength to accept the things I cannot change! The courage to change the things I can! And the wisdom to know the difference!"

Then the stupid fucking hand holding bit.

All together now.

"Thanks for sharing! Thanks for caring! Keep coming back! The meetings make it!"

Another meeting over and done with. And thank God for that. Couldn't get out of there quick enough.

Yeah! Well! He pretended not to think about that other one. So, he didn't think about her. But he was always thinking about her. Even when he was pretending not to think about her. She was still in there, alright. Sometimes, there was no room for anything else. That's when she almost drove him mad.

There're going to have a lot of fun with you.

Driving home that night, Frank got to thinking. He was kind of hoping the lady would start talking to him again. I mean, he did tell her to fuck off the last time, you know. So maybe she wouldn't be back. Not for a while anyway. But hang on. She was back there again wasn't she. Or maybe she wasn't. Anyway, she'll be back again. She can never stay away for very long.

"Oh Frank! You're so incorrigible! But I'll never give up on you! You know that, don't you Frank! I'll never give up on you! I can't give up on you now, Frank! I just can't!"

See, I told you.

"Oh good! You're back again!"

"Yes Frank! I'll always be here for you! Always! You must know that by now! Listen very carefully to me, Frank! Have you ever considered the idea, of comparing yourself and who you are now? To who you were, before she came into your life?"

"What? Well! No! I've never even thought about that!"

Lots of people have conversations with themselves while there're driving along, you know. Anyway, after arriving home, the lady's words were still in the head. But there was no relaxing. No thinking about anything else and definitely no sleep. The television went on and off again about three or four times. There was nothing happening, while staring at the computer screen either. There was no concentration happening there at all. But he did manage one thing.

Incorrigible; incapable of being corrected or reformed.

Yeah. That was him, alright.

Right. So, it was time for a coffee on the veranda. The only option. It wasn't long before old memories were formulating again. Then becoming clearer and then rising up out of the darkness. And this darkness wasn't because the eyes were closed either. This was the deep, internal darkness. The kind of darkness, that's always there for a reason. And the reasons are not usually good reasons. And they were never good reasons for Frank. That's for sure.

Out they came, like a raging tsunami. There were flashes of light and the multitude of tiny fragments, appeared and then disappeared just as quickly. Lightness then darkness. Fragments appearing then disappearing. And Frank was recognising all these fragments. They were fragments of the early years. The very early years. The fragments that were locked away in the deepest, darkest shadows.

The fragments that were completely forgotten about. The horrifying fragments. The fragments that sent him on a journey of drug and alcohol abuse and carefree debauchery. All through the teenage years. And a life full of pain, misery and mistakes. All through the adult years. Shadowed by a never-ending desire for self-destruction. What the fuck was going on here.

Yes, now there was nothing more than a soppy, blubbering, emotional mess, sitting in the favourite chair on the veranda. Then that picture was there again. That had already reduced the brain to a pulsating mishmash a few times already. The rotten bitch. It had to have been her. What other explanation could there possibly be. Yeah. The other one was in there again and she was giving him hell.

It was revenge. That's what it was. Revenge. The bitch. Just waiting for a vulnerable moment. Waiting to strike.

There're going to have a lot of fun with you.

Yeah. Well, there was no fun happening this time. That's for sure.

"Oh Frank! That's not how it really is! Not at all! Yes, it was her Frank! It was her! But think about it, Frank! Think about it! Your old life was a disaster! There's no question about that! No question at all! But look at yourself now, Frank! Look at yourself now! Look how far you've come! Yes, it was her Frank! But she gave you the biggest and most valuable gift, anyone could give you! She breathed new life into you, Frank! That's what she did! And always remember Frank! Before you can begin a new life! You need to come to terms, with the old life first!"

"Be at peace with yourself, Frank! Could you have ever done that without her! Never! You must know that by now! You owe that girl your new life, Frank! You owe her everything!"

Whoa. What a brain full that was. The old Frank would have already downed a half a dozen cans and smoked at least two nice, big fat joints by now. But the new Frank, just wouldn't let that happen. Well, it couldn't happen could it. There was no beer or pot anywhere in the house, for a start.

Meanwhile, the tears were rolling down both cheeks. Could have filled a bucket. But you know what. After the senses came back a few hours later, he felt so light-headed, you know. Like there was a balloon sitting on the shoulders. Not the giant boulder that'd been carried around, all through the old life. How that happened was just something else that had to be worked out. The lady might have to explain it; next time she turns up. Because there were no ideas happening. None at all. Just mass confusion. Again.

Back to the nursing home. Like there was no control about where the memories were heading. Just had to go with it. Completely forgot about this little conversation. But it must have happened. Anyway, it was better than putting up with all that other shit.

"Hi mum, how are you going today?"

"Hello Frank! Thanks for coming to see me! I've already had two visitors today! It must be my lucky day!"

There was a nurse in the room, checking up on a few things. She looked at Frank and shook her head from side to side and he knew what that meant. Anyway, it was only ten o'clock in the morning.

"Yes, it's your lucky day, alright! Would you like a cup of coffee, mum?"

"Oh yes, I'd love a cup of coffee!"

So, out he went to get the coffees. Always the same routine. It wasn't unusual to end up sitting there, watching his mother and having a coffee by himself. But not today. His mother was ready for a conversation.

"So, Frank! Tell me what you've been doing with yourself? No one tells me anything anymore!"

He'd never seen her so excited before. And wanting to know what he'd been doing. What a shock that was. Frank had never been close to his mother, you know. They hardly ever spoke. What an opportunity this was. To open up about what he was doing in his new life. I mean, what would be the point of dredging up the old miserable memories. When his poor old mother was in such a fragile state and nearing the end of her days. This is what was going through the head as he started talking.

"Well, I've been looking after my health!"

"Oh, that's wonderful, Frank!"

They must have had her on new medication or something. Or accidentally overdosed her. She was sitting there in her chair, with a big smile on her face. And her eyes were sparkling. And her mouth opened, like she was going to say something but she never said anything. So, Frank just kept on talking.

"I've been going to the gym and swimming and getting a suntan and going to this great café!"

"Oh, that's wonderful, Frank! What else have you been doing?"

Then she clapped her hands and let out a little giggle. And still with the big smile and the sparkling eyes. Yes, she was pumped full of something, alright. That's for sure. But what the hell. She was the happiest he'd ever seen her.

"Well, I've turned vegan now! Yes, I've been vegan, for about six months!"

This bit of news got her attention. Changed the whole mood in an instant. From a joyous, enthusiastic, childlike old women. To a very serious, concerned looking old women. She took a grave look at her son and there was no sparkle in the eyes anymore, either.

"A what, Frank? A vegan, did you say?"

"Yes, mum! A vegetarian!"

"That means you don't eat any meat, Frank! How can you live, without eating any meat! That's the silliest thing I've ever heard in my whole life! Everybody eats meat, Frank! You can't live without eating any meat!"

She even raised her voice as she said all that. And that was very unusual. His mother had always been such a quiet, gentle soul.

"Well, it was all because of the cancer, mum! All that radiotherapy! It messed my insides up! So, I had to change the diet around! That's how it all started!"

"What cancer? When did you ever have cancer? Why didn't you tell me you had cancer? Nobody tells me anything anymore! I'm your mother! I should have been told you had cancer!"

This was the first time that Frank had ever known his mother, to ask so many questions. She didn't finish her coffee. But he hadn't finished his either. It seemed like a time out thing was happened here now. They'd both stopped talking and were just looking at each other. No more words were coming. An uncomfortable feeling was creeping into both of them. The air in the room was getting thicker and thicker. The communication was finished and they both knew it. Just like old times.

And there was no point, reminding her about being told about the cancer. Best to just let it go and that's what happened.

"I'm getting tired now, Frank! It must be time for my afternoon nap! Thanks for the coffee! I'll see you next time!"

How time flies, eh. But it was still only just after ten in the morning. Frank watched his mother struggle to get up out of her chair and walk the short distance to her bed. He thought about offering assistance, but he thought for too long. Yeah, she was already in bed. Turned over the other way, with her back to Frank and asleep. Or, pretending to be.

Remembering all this was not a good thing really. Frank liked his mother much better, the other way. Not knowing what the hell was going on. And drifting off, to wherever she drifted off to. This for real conversation business was far too complicated and difficult to deal with. He should have known better, than open up about the new life in the first place. She just didn't get it, did she? Nobody else got it.

Only the café girls. The lady. And the other one. Well, after what the lady just told him, she really shouldn't be called the other one anymore. She actually meant something to Frank now. She deserved some kind of respect, I suppose. Yeah, he just had to admit that now. So, it was back to calling her TMBGITW again. That should make things right.

It was useless trying to explain anything to his mother anyway. Always had been. Gave up on it, years ago. Anyway, she wasn't herself. Drugged up to the eyeballs, by the look of her.

And Frank was getting tired now himself. All this remembering gets exhausting, you know. Tired enough to wander off to bed. Was late. About 11.30. But he slept like a baby. For too long. Set the alarm on the mobile phone, alright. But forgot to put it next to the bed. Left it in the lounge room. Didn't hear it go off. Got up. Felt like shit. Gave the gym a miss. No breakfast. Already hot outside. Turned the computer on. Couldn't concentrate. Turned it back off again. Made a coffee. Back on the veranda. But not for long. Emptied the coffee cup, over the railing. Decision was made.

"Oh, hi Frank! It's good to see you! It's the first favourite meal day today, isn't it?"

She knew it was. But she liked saying that. And he liked her saying that as well. He'd just done twice the laps he usually did. So, he was hungry, alright and exhausted.

"I'm just great, thanks! I've been for a swim! Yes, it's the first favourite meal day today! Any chance of a double shot of coffee?"

Liar. Felt even worse. Completely fucked. And she didn't even ask how he was either.

"Sure Frank! A double shot it is! Frank wants a double shot of coffee!"

She yelled that out so loud. The whole café would have heard her. Bitch. No, no. Just joking. A few of the kitchen staff took a quick look out. And there were a few giggles coming from out the back. Nothing unusual there. The girl at the coffee machine was little miss bright eyes. Because she had lovely bright eyes. That sparkled, every time he looked into them. And she had a bushy ponytail as well. And so fit. Bouncing around, like some kind of athlete.

So, it was a choice between bushy ponytail or bright eyes or maybe bouncy. Decided on little miss bright eyes. Such a lovely girl. Anyway, back to the girl who was taking the order. Who'd just embarrassed the hell out of him. The head was just busting to let this one out.

"Do you think I'm an offensive person?"

This was a surprise, alright. Got her attention. Took the smile off her face. Stuck for an answer. For a few seconds.

"Offensive! Of course not, Frank! That's why we all like you so much!"

Can you imagine, how that made the old fella feel. Now who had the smile on the face.

"I was down at the pool. Talking to these two old drunks. One of them must have looked at someone the wrong way! And maybe said something, that he shouldn't have said! They can still get a bit cheeky sometimes, you know! These old bastards. Anyway, this girl gets up and walks up to the three of us. And she looks straight at me! And she calls me a dirty old man! And it wasn't even me that said anything. And I wasn't even looking at her, or her friends. There was about five or six of them."

"She was probably just a bitch. Don't worry about it, Frank!"

The smile got even bigger. But a café girl, just used the bitch word. There was always an awareness about not using the bad words in the café, you know. And one of the girls, comes out with the bitch word. Well, I'll be. Better not mention which girl this was either. Wouldn't want to embarrass her. Or get her into any trouble. After all, there was never any swearing coming from the café girls. Except this one time. Well, not that was known about anyway.

From then on, there was no more talking to these two dickheads. Frank had become immune to all the g-strings by now. And he never would have bothered talking to any of them anyway. And he'd learnt, not to even look in their direction. So, he didn't even see them. Didn't hear them. Didn't want to know them. It was like they weren't even there. And they weren't.

Yeah. Things were all finally under control, as far as the g-strings were concerned. And now these two drunken bums could end up ruining everything. And get him into all sorts of trouble. After all the progress he'd made. It would have all been for nothing. So, fuck them.

Been talking more and more now, you know. The confidence was growing all the time. And that was all because of the café girls. One day they would be told, how great they all were and how much he really, really, really liked them. But today wasn't that day. And thank Christ for that, eh. But the day would come. That's for sure. So, the mind was at ease again now. As long as he only talked with the café girls, everything would be ok. And avoid those two useless old alcoholics. There was no choice now. None at all.

And then a new dawning came. The whole new world was full of spies wasn't it. Down at the pool. That was probably another one of those setups. They were all working together. Even those two old drunks could have been in on it. Just pretending to be pissed.

The thinking was already starting to think that way anyway. About spies being everywhere. But now there was no more thinking required. Because that's what was happening. Extra care had to be taken now. Yeah. The war had been taken to another level. So, no one could be trusted. But he'd never trusted anyone anyway. So, it wasn't difficult putting this adjusted mind-set into operation. A new plan was necessary. Yeah. Getting smarter all the time.

No more talking to anyone. Anywhere. About anything. No more eye contact. With anyone. Don't even get near anyone. No. There was no choice now. Either that, or go to another pool. But then the spies would probably turn up there as well. That's how spies operated you know. So, no one could be trusted now. Not anywhere. They were everywhere. Yeah. Spies everywhere.

Especially any new girls who turned up at the gym. Yeah. They'd be in there for sure. Looking so good in their gym gear. Prancing around. Like they owned the place. They had to be watched extra closely now. Well, you know. Watched. As in kept away from. Don't let them get near you. If they appear at a work station next to you. Pretend you're finished and move somewhere else.

And whatever you do, don't go talking to any of them. Don't get caught again. Just stick to this new plan and everything will be fine. Just talk to the café girls. The rest of them are just too dangerous. There're all out to get him. Knew that now. The only place that was safe was the magic café.

But they were probably in there too, you know. There were windows everywhere. Probably knew when he was coming. Watching him walking up from the baths. Wouldn't put it past them. They always knew what he was thinking as well. Didn't know how they did that. But they did it, alright. Yeah. They had to all be witches. And spies. And they were all out to get him. Yeah. Getting smarter all the time.

Well, what a relief it was. To have all that worked out. The lady was probably organising the whole thing, you know. She'll have to be watched more closely as well. Well, not actually watched. You can't watch someone who's not even there, can you? Maybe, just not listened to as much. Yeah. Just stick to the plan and everything would be fine. But it was hard to believe any of the café girls could be working with the spies. No, they wouldn't do that. Not the café girls. Well, not all of them anyway.

"Oh, bad luck, Frank! Your tables not available today!"

"What! Oh right! Well, I'll just sit at that one over there!"

But he'd already claimed his table. She knew that. Just joking around. The café girls were always joking around with Frank now.

There're going to have a lot of fun with you.

Yeah. Knew that now. So, no reaction. None at all. So there. Well, there was one reaction. Just gave the café girl smile back, turned around and took off. Just like they'd been doing. Ever since he walked into the place. Two can play at that game, eh.

Frank sat down and immediately stared out the window. The ocean was calm. There were sailing boats in the distance. Yeah. One, two, three, four, five. Five sailing boats. And lots of people wandering around. But there was distraction, going on in the head.

"Hey Frank! How you going? You look a bit tired!"

"Uh! What! Yes, tired! I'm a bit tired. Maybe I've been doing too much! I'll have a little rest when I get home."

Doing too much thinking was the problem. And tired of being interrupted, every time the thinking got started.

"Oh right! You'll be ok Frank! Just chill! Just chill out! Maybe you're better off not thinking about things too much! Sometimes, the more you think about something, the worse it gets!"

So, it's happened again. Now the chill out girl was in his head. But that's what he did. Straight away. He chilled out. The chill out girl had cast her magic spell again. How does she do that, anyway. He was going to say something back. But she'd already wandered away. Cleaning up a few tables and straightening up a few chairs.

The café girls were always doing that you know. Wandering around and straightening up tables and chairs. Cleaning up the messy tables and spraying them before wiping them over. Most of the customers, just sat down, ate their lunch, and talked their heads off. Got up and walked away. Leaving all their mess for the girls to clean up. And they were always still smiling, that lovely, warm café girl smile. Amazing.

So, now that he was all chilled out, the thinking started up again didn't it. This time, it was all about some programme on television. About how humans evolved from monkeys. And how they were our closest relatives. This was very interesting information to be hearing. And seeing. Right there, on the television screen.

Because the memories were there, about how all the humans were started by just two people. Called Adam and Eve. Some God created them and they got the whole human race going. These were very old memories, you know. And very strong memories too. Now, they were there and being remembered. From way back, when he was a little boy. But there was nothing said about any monkeys, having anything to do with it. That's for sure.

And then the thinking moved to all the people, walking along the promenade, who were supposed to come from only these two people. This Adam and Eve. But that just didn't seem right. It would have been brothers and sisters. Having kids together and their kids having kids with each other. And maybe even this Adam and Eve, having kids with their own kids and maybe even with the kids of their own kids. And that just didn't seem right either.

The perving. No sorry. Not perving. Looking. The looking had been going on for a long time now, you know. And how all these different people could have come from just two people, just didn't make any sense. Even to someone who was still adjusting to a new life in a whole new world and who didn't really know too much about anything. Especially, what was called human evolution. That's what the old guy on the television called it. Human evolution.

And with all these people wandering along, almost completely naked. It was easy enough to see that, they were nothing alike. No two people were the same. There were so many different shapes and sizes and colours, you know. And they were all supposed to come from just two people. Yeah. It was beginning to seem more and more unlikely. That only two people could be responsible.

More like millions of them. From all over the planet. Frank knew all about planet Earth now and all the countries. Television was a great thing to watch. Frank learnt everything from the television. And from reading newspapers. Yeah. Knew lots of interesting stuff now.

Monkeys seemed like a better explanation. There were these programmes that got watched. Called documentaries. And it was the same old guy, talking about chimpanzees and how they were our closest relatives. Considering all the different shapes and sizes and colours that were on display, not to mention the carpet chewers and shirt lifters, here and there.

No. No. No. Didn't take long to forget about not calling them that anymore did it. What should have been said was—all the variations on display. Genetic variations. The old guy, talked about that a lot too, you know. Genetic variations.

But the mind kept wandering and certain bits of information were missed. Although, enough was heard to get the general picture. No, no. Not the picture. Any other word but picture. Story. Yeah. That's better. Story. Yeah. The story of human evolution.

Then everything about all these humans wandering along the promenade became perfectly clear. They were all monkeys. They had to be. There could be no other explanation. Monkeys with clothes on. And monkeys with almost nothing on. That old guy, made perfect sense. Knew exactly what he was talking about, alright. Only a short amount of thought was necessary, before conformation in the brain happened. Yeah. Getting smarter all the time.

They were all monkeys, alright. And Frank was one of them. He might have felt like an alien. But he was one of the monkeys as well. Just had to admit that. Especially after looking into a mirror. And sometimes in the change room at the baths, there were monkeys with hair all over their bodies. No wonder so many of the monkeys covered their whole bodies with clothes. Especially the older monkeys, who seemed to have much more hair than the younger ones. But Frank had hair all over his body as well, so he was one of them, alright. Just a dumb arse monkey, like all the rest of the dumb arse monkeys.

Well, not all the monkeys were dumb arses, you know. But it just felt good calling them that. Not that he wanted to be just a dumb arse monkey either. And if he had a choice, he wouldn't be. But then what would he be, if he wasn't just a dumb arse monkey. Figuring that one out was going to take quite some time. So, just the idea of thinking he was an alien was a far better idea, than admitting to being just a dumb arse monkey. Yeah. Getting smarter all the time.

And the biggest giveaway, you know, was with the fingers and toes. There were stumpy little feet with even stumpier little toes. And long skinny feet, with long skinny toes. Just like the monkeys have. Especially chimpanzees. So, some people looked more like monkeys than others.

And maybe there were some other animals involved, other than monkeys. But the old guy didn't say anything about that. So, maybe there wasn't. Or, maybe he just didn't know. Anyway, it didn't matter. All that mattered was that all people were monkeys. And they came from monkeys. And all their children would be little monkeys.

And so, human evolution would always be filled with monkeys. And it was a good feeling to have all that finally worked out. Except, Frank still didn't feel like a monkey and he didn't want to be one either. But he was. And it didn't matter how much thinking went into it. Because the same conclusion was always arrived at. The new life was full of monkeys and he was one of them. And that was that. But it was a much better idea to call everyone a human. That's for sure.

And the humans all being so hairy, you know. Especially the older generation. Hairy legs and arms. Hairy chests. And under the armpits. Except for most of the females. They have this habit of shaving all the hairs off their legs and from under the armpits. And they were much better to look at too. Except for the carpet chewers. Oops. That should be lesbians. Most of them, didn't bother shaving anything. Except sometimes they were bald.

But you know what. Sometimes two of the most beautiful monkeys would walk past, holding hands. Smiling and talking away. And the thought was always there then. About whether they were lesbians as well. Or just female monkeys, who were in love with each other. Like it was explained one day by the irrepressible cuddling girl. And it was the same with the homosexuals. Easy enough to spot most of them. But some of them. You wouldn't even know they were homosexuals. Unless you heard them talk. Then it was obvious. Voices squeakier that a hinge, that needed oiling.

And then a thought came, about calling the café girls monkeys. But that just didn't seem right. And they probably wouldn't like it either. So, they weren't called monkeys. But all the other humans were. Because Frank didn't care so much about them.

And it was a weird feeling you know. Watching the girl monkeys with other girl monkeys and boy monkeys with other boy monkeys. Wandering around. Just like everyone else. Nobody seemed to pay any attention. Or even notice what was going on. Except the alien sitting there. Absorbing all the monkey behaviour. In the new world. That he didn't really belong in. And he never would either. And there was no explaining why he never would. It was just a feeling. And it was getting stronger all the time.

And at the same time, trying to match things up with what was remembered about this kind of thing in the old life. But there was no matching up happening. None at all. So, now the thought process was altered. And it had to be altered. To suit living with the monkeys in the new world. And that was. Boy monkeys will be girl monkeys and girl monkeys will be boy monkeys. Well, some of them anyway. There were others, who didn't look like boys or girls. And some of the hairstyles. Bloody hell. There was more than one alien monkey in this new world. That's for sure. Yeah. Getting smarter all the time.

"Are you an observer, Frank?"

Looked around and here's the dancing girl, smiling at him.

Honesty will come into your life if you let it.

"What! Well! Yes! I am an observer! It's just what I do! I like watching everything out there!"

Yes, he'd been caught at it. Got him good and proper. Whether she meant to or not, didn't matter. Been observed by an observer. Bit of a bother, that was. But she was never going to know about the thinking, was she? About them all being monkeys and her being a monkey herself. Just imagine what her thinking would have been, if that one leaked out. Yeah. Getting smarter all the time. Lucky there was nothing else there to say. But the dancing girl had already danced away. And thank Christ for that.

"There you go, Frank! Enjoy!"

Normally, after they say that, they go wandering away. But not this time. Could feel the presence. Looked up. Oh no. The tall one. Looking down upon him. And the café girl smile was there as well. Sometimes that meant everything was fine. But sometimes it meant trouble. Like what was going to get asked. Or happen. Or, what was on the menu, this time. The verbal menu that is.

Wasn't any fun trying to figure out what was coming in the beginning. When the café girls were always smiling and saying nice things, to this miserable old guy. For no reason at all. But after a while, the interest picked up a bit and eventually ended up fun. Yes fun. But that took a fair while, as you already know.

"You must have had a troubled childhood, Frank. I'd cry if you told me about it. I'm sure I would!"

She'd cry, alright. Cry her fucking eyes out. Lucky, he didn't say it like that to her but, eh. And she was never going to find out anything anyway, was she? What a nerve anyway. Just who did she think she was. Saying things like that. And she didn't even ask, either. She just said it. Just like that. Just how stupid was the poor old sucker supposed to be anyway.

All she had to do was ask. And he would have maybe told her a few things. And she probably would have started crying. Right then. In the middle of the café. And that would have been fun. Watching the tall one cry. Instead of just standing there. Hovering, like some intellectual know it all, or something. And it would have been another win as well. But the thinking missed out on that opportunity, on this occasion.

"You don't have to tell me anything, if you don't feel like it, Frank!" But I understand how difficult it must have been for you."

Yeah. Sure, she did. But she did sound like she did. So yeah, they were mind readers here, alright. Clamming up was the only thing to do now. That should get rid of her.

"Oh look! There's a dragon fly! Right there, on the glass!"

Wasn't going to be that easy, was it? But there really was a dragon fly there. And she pointed one of her long skinny fingers at it. Frank, just hated long skinny fingers. Especially this monkeys long skinny fingers. But took a quick look anyway.

"Yeah, it's a dragon fly, alright! Wonder how it got in here?"

Big deal. A, dragon fly. Well, he had started talking more now, you know. So, it really shouldn't matter who to.

"It must be a sign!"

What. What kind of a sign. Signs weren't really thought about much, you know. And here was one on the glass, just above Frank's head. And it was a dragon fly. Probably a bad sign if anything. With a name like that.

"Well, I'm not very good with signs! And what kind of a sign is a dragon fly anyway?"

"I'll be going now, Frank! Try and remember what we spoke about!"

We. She must be joking. She did most of the talking. She's worse than that bloody lady. And then she finally wandered away. Couldn't help checking her out either. Looked good from behind, alright. But then she half turned and caught the old fella at it. And that café girl smile was there as well. So, it was all good. Even with the tall one. Back to relaxation and a good look out the window. But not for long.

Yeah, another one's got into the head. Sneak attack. Unnerved him, alright. But nowhere near as bad as before. Nothing could match that other one. TMBGITW. That's for sure. But things were upset again now. Emotional pressure was building. There wasn't much time either. And this wasn't one of those funny situations.

This was serious business. Of course, he had a troubled childhood. This whole episode had a huge negative affect, you know. Been a while since anything was taken so seriously. But a troubled childhood is a troubled childhood, isn't it. Then something happened, that surely saved the emotional eruption. That was only seconds away.

The girl who found him must have noticed the troubled look.

"Hey, Frank! It can't be all that bad!"

The chill out girl again. Just at the right time too. Because it was coming out, right now. One way or the other.

"I got a real bad start in life, you know! I didn't grow up properly! I had lots of problems!"

"But you're ok now, Frank! So, just chill! Just chill out!"

Yeah. What else could he call her, but the chill out girl. She was always telling him that. To just chill out. And right then. It was what he needed to hear. That's for sure.

These café girls had to be working together. In pairs. Or, it could have been just another one of those coincidences. But even if they were working in pairs. And it wasn't another one of those coincidences. That was ok. Because it was all about Frank. And interaction. And adjusting to the new life and everything that went with it. Which was a never-ending learning experience. But the lady never mentioned that, did she? Well, not that could be fully understood anyway.

Right, another lunch and coffee over and done with. Time to go.

"See you later, Frank!

"See ya, Frank!"

"See ya, Frank!"

There were a few more see ya's as well. All said with the café girl smile. But there was no mood for any answers back.

Yeah, bright eyes bushy tail, nice eyes and NG1, all there together. And maybe have a chat and the forgotten name girl.

There're going to have a lot of fun with you.

In the front door and straight to the computer.

Dragon Fly; The Totem of the Dragon Fly, holds the insights of adaptability and transformation. They are spiritual creatures. Connected to light and change. When you see one, be reminded of these qualities in yourself. Perhaps you are in need of more lightness and joy in your life. Or perhaps it's simply time to take a moment to be consciously grateful for the lightness and joy, that you do have.

Yeah. It was a sign, alright. But how did she know that. And how did she know all about Dragon Flies anyway. She had to know. It was probably a plastic one, you know. And she probably stuck it on the glass, when he wasn't looking. She was tall enough to do that. Could have been another one of those coincidences as well. But not likely. Another set up for sure.

Yeah. Just another set up. But you know what, that was only one of the meanings for Dragon Fly. There were lots of others. But this one was the first one that came up. So, it's the one that got read. And there was no one looking over the shoulder, when it got looked up either. So, how could it be another set up. But there was a big headache coming. So, that's where the thinking had to stop. The pressure was still there. Computer goes off. The head was just pounding with confusion. Again.

Yeah, stayed away for at least another week. Then wandered back in, like a lost puppy. A week was about the limit.

Knew by now, there was no use fighting against the urge. The, magic café urge. Frank was addicted to the place and he knew it.

Been noticing the looks, you know. Looks of disapproval. Took a while to work it out. Yeah. Was the coat, alright. Always bought the clothes from St Vinnies. Anyway, the favourite coat. Grubby old thing. Had it for over twenty years. The favourite item of clothing. Never getting rid of it. And it didn't matter how the café girls looked at him. But that feeling of disapproval was always there. Every time. And there was no café girl smile either. Frank loved that old coat. Was like an old friend. But he loved the café girl smile too. And they were his friends. So, it was a real dilemma. That's for sure. And the controller's words kept repeating themselves as well.

Frank stopped wearing that favourite coat, a few weeks later. But couldn't make the decision to throw it out. Just couldn't do it. Back in St Vinnies and found a few hoodies that were a perfect fit. They were $5 each. Except for one, that only cost $1. That was because when checking the pockets, found a $2 coin in one pocket and a $2 coin in another pocket. Been a lucky day, alright. Had a big win on the pokies. Yeah. Busted again. And a spending mood was happening. Even bought some new socks, underpants, tracky pants and singlets. The cheapest ones anywhere. But yeah. Busted again.

Next time in the café. Could feel the girls looking at him. Straight away. Kind of made a bit of an entrance. Get the attention. They didn't need to say anything but one of them did. Came around from behind the counter and stood right next to him. These girls seemed to take it in turns of doing that. Standing right next to him and smiling. Some of them even went as far as putting a hand on one of the shoulders. And sometimes, gave the back a little up and down rubbing. Just loved it when that happened.

"Gee you're looking good today, Frank! Are they new clothes?"

"Uh yes! I decided it was time to update my wardrobe again! So, I lashed out! What do you think?"

Yeah, asking for some positive feedback. Things were looking up.

"Hey, check out Frank's new clothes!"

Yeah. That's right. Tell the whole fucking place, why don't you?

Now there were a bunch of café girls surrounding him. But they didn't need to know, that all the clothes came from Vinnies, did they? A charity shop, within walking distance from where he lived. Well, there was no need to go telling them that was there. Didn't get told last time either. And they didn't have to know everything this time, did they? But they already knew that, of course. And the figuring was that he knew that they knew. But decided not to know it. Yeah. Getting smarter all the time. Anyway, it was something else to talk about. Besides all the normal stuff.

"Good on you, Frank! You look great! Now, what are you having today?"

"Just the usual meal! It's my favourite."

"There're all your favourites now, Frank! So, which one is it going to be today. Oh, I forgot! It's the first favourite meal day today! Sorry about that!"

Yeah. That's right. Always ordered the right meal, on the right day. The gym at 5.30. Home for a rest and breakfast. Always weet-bix and a banana. On the computer for an hour or two. Then change into the swimming gear. Get the towel and change of clothes. Which were always neatly placed on a lounge chair, right next to the front door.

Same number of laps in the pool. Into the change sheds to shower and change. Back to the car, for the wallet, phone and sunglasses. To the café. Claim the favourite table, if it was available. Order. Quick chat to whatever girl was on duty and sitting down, staring out the window.

And all this happened within a certain time frame. And there were never more than a few minutes difference, each day. A real creature of habit, alright. Felt safe and secure, when nothing had to change. Liked routine. Needed routine. Yeah. Frank's daily activities were controlled by routines.

All the girls knew that, and nothing ever had to be asked. About what meal had to be had on what day. But sometimes it was. Because every now and then, they tried to trick him. They knew he got confused very easily. And he knew they knew and he didn't like it either. But Frank just loved it, when they tricked him. But not as much as when some new girl was there. Who didn't know anything about what was going on. Yeah. Some real fun happened then. Till she got saved by one of the other girls.

"Well, we have a new vegetarian meal on the menu, Frank! Vegan nachos! Everybody loves them! Would you like to try them?"

"No thanks! I'll just have the usual!"

"Oh, go on Frank! Try them! We'll all addicted to them!"

"No, I don't think so! Not today thanks!"

"Oh, go on Frank! Give them a try! You'll love them!"

"Oh, alright then! I'll give them a go!"

There was no real desire there, you know. Didn't really want to. But he did, didn't he? These girls were starting to have such a big influence. That's for sure. Too much. Resistance was weakening, alright. But it was a great game. Everybody got a laugh out of it.

"How were the nacho's Frank?"

"Loved them! There're, the new favourite thing now!"

"We knew you'd like them! Now you've got another favourite! How many is that now, Frank! About four!"

That's how he found out about sweet potato chips as well. Had to be talked into having them the first time. Loved them too and they soon became the new favourite. So, then there were three favourites. And that was enough. But it wasn't enough. Because now there were four.

"It's good to change things up a bit, Frank!"

So, for several days after that, vegan nachos were ordered. Then a swap to the sweet potato chips for several days. Then back to the first favourite for several days. Until one of the girls suggested he mix it up a bit more. But it wasn't the same girl who'd already suggested it. But he did it anyway.

"Hey Frank! You've had the nachos three days in a row! The sweet potato chips are really nice today!"

Which meant why don't you have sweet potato chips today. Finally worked out how they did that. Well, not really knowing how they did it. Just knowing they were doing it and he was doing what they were not really telling him to do. Because they were saying things in a way, that made him do it.

So that's what he did. Had one or the other meal, every day. And before too much longer, never had the same meal, two days in a row. Didn't realise it at the time, but these café girls were in heavy training mode. And Frank was the trainee. Took ages to finally work out what they were doing. But they knew exactly what they were doing, alright. Yeah. And now he knew it too. But always decided not to know it. Yeah. Getting smarter all the time.

You know, even when it was all worked out, nothing was ever said. Not by him or the girls. They all knew that he knew and he knew that they all knew. And they knew that he knew that they all knew. But that was the best thing about it. These café girls were now the favourite addiction and Frank couldn't get enough of them.

There're going to have a lot of fun with you.

That comment was always there, you know. But in a good way. Next time he sees that smart arse compulsive. He'll have to thank him.

"They care about you, Frank! They care about you! And why not have some fun along the way! You don't need to be so serious all the time! Lighten up a bit, Frank! Have some fun with them! Let them know you're having fun! Talk to them about it! They'd like that!"

She just wasn't up to date with this one, was she? Fun was already happening. Not often he gets one up on the lady. But telling the café girls what they were doing to him. She must be joking. Why would he do that anyway. Having too much fun. Telling them would just ruin the whole game. Yeah. Getting smarter all the time.

Fact is, the old Frank, didn't know anything about having fun. Especially with girls. Well, that's not quite right. There was lots of fun with lots of girls back then. But not necessarily in a good way. They were full of tricks back then, you know. Dirty tricks. He knew that. He didn't quite know how he knew. Just did. But this was the new Frank we're talking about here. The new life Frank. The second chance Frank, who loved all the fun. And in a good way. Now that he knew what it was. About having fun in a good way that is.

Oh fuck no. How the hell was this allowed to happen. Anyway, it happened and this is what happened.

After all, he did go up to her and kiss her right in the middle of her right cheek. In the middle of a crowded café, for God's sake. And he did whisper into her right ear!"

"You're wonderful!"

"If you say so!"

Wait a minute. He's not going through all this shit again.

But yes, TMBGITW was in there again. Causing the usual havoc. His mother had let him down again.

194

And then something else was remembered.

It was after the kissing episode. A few more days of darting looks, here and there and avoidances of direct eye contact. And deliberately looking in the opposite direction, if she came anywhere near him. Before the main Frank, rose to the surface and decided to end all the bullshit. And settle this business, once and for all. Yeah, the main Frank. He'd had enough.

Went up to her at the cash register. Stood right beside her. And it was like there was this force behind him, pushing him along. So, there was no real choice about being next to her. But there was no one there telling him what to say was there. And it wasn't what he would have said, if he had more time to think about it first.

"I really do appreciate it, you know. All the help you've given to me. And all the feelings I have now. That you gave to me. And all these feelings! There're all good. For you!"

Fucking hell. Embarrassment all round, you know. They both went bright red in the face. Nothing more could be said. Even if there was a script to read off. Complete shutdown again. Emotional malfunction. Again. Couldn't take anymore. Turning around and taking off was the only option. Leaving TMBGITW just standing there, staring straight ahead. At nothing. Smiling. And not the usual café girl smile, either. More like the dopiest girly smile imaginable. While slowly turning an even more dark crimson colour. And not knowing what to do either. Or what to say. For a change. Dumbstruck, alright. Frozen to the spot.

This could have been noted down as another win, you know. But that wasn't even thought about at the time. Because nothing was thought about at the time. Only the idea of getting the hell out of there. There was no winning or losing, going on here. That's for sure.

On the way out was like a hurried walk of shame. Everyone in the place, heard every word of it. Didn't even consider whispering. Not after what happened the last time. All the eyes were on this poor victim. A few of the other girls were standing around. But it was the closest one that said it:

"See you later, Frank!"

Then the giggles started up and seemed to get louder and louder as the exit got closer and closer. Fastest the legs had ever moved. Ever.

There're going to have a lot of fun with you.

Yeah, the heat was up. Through the whole body. Temperature, at boiling point. Getting the hell out of there, happened even quicker. Especially after hearing the, see you later Frank bit. And all the giggling. And it was the chill out girl who said it. The only time she never chilled him out. Not the time for it anyway. Wouldn't have even penetrated the solid mood of embarrassment.

The imbecile, turned up the next day. There was a bunch of them there, behind the counter. Having a good old girly session. Yapping away. With a little giggle here and a little giggle there. Just couldn't help themselves. When they saw Frank approaching, there was an immediate evacuation. Out the back. In about two seconds.

Except the one girl, who made him kiss her like he did. She was just there, leaning up against the coffee machine, smiling at him. With a look that said. Come over Frank. Come to me. Come and talk to me. And Frank. You know what. The bonehead almost did. Wanted to, alright. That's for sure. But just couldn't do it. Suddenly, snapped out of the trance. Out of the danger zone. And thank God for that. Just in time too. Turned around and took off again.

Something unexplainable happened. An internal mechanism thing. Connected to the emotional structure. Complete systems malfunction. General shutdown. Depending on which way it's looked at.

Yeah. All the Franks were going nuts. There was complete madness approaching. Get me the fuck out of here. Was coming from all over the place. Maybe all the Franks got together, you know. And saved the poor old bastard. Before the laser beam hit again.

No lunch at the café that day. Or for several weeks after that episode. Guess all the Franks, just shit themselves. That's all. Well one of them did anyway. And lucky for them, it was the main one.

There was another girl, cleaning a table half way between the counter and the door. Rushing past her happened so quick. All that was seen was the smile. Yeah. A huge smile. Covering her whole face. But she still managed to get it out.

"See you later, Frank!"

And there were a few customers, here and there. Smiling as well. Everyone in the place was smiling and laughing at him. Frank just knew they were. Could feel them all staring at him. Yeah. Out of there, like a frightened child who'd just seen a ghost. Or a monster. Or something even worse.

There're going to have a lot of fun with you.

Driving home, the thinking started. Full blast. About being locked in with some girl. Long term. But he couldn't let her win, could he? That's what it was really all about, you know. Not letting her win. No, that could never happen. Only suckers get locked in. TMBGITW or not. And remembering how old he was and how young she was.

Well, maybe not so young. That extra bit of beef was a dead giveaway, you know. But getting locked in was getting locked in wasn't it. And getting locked in, just wasn't in the programme. Never in the old life. And now it was certain. Never in the new life either.

And there was nothing much happening down below either. And that would have mattered. What the hell was going on. It could never happen. No. It was never going to happen. Anyway, being just so fucking ugly as well, you know. Wouldn't help matters would it. And she was so beautiful. It just wouldn't work. That was obvious. It was all just a stupid head game.

"Oh Frank, you're still so negative about everything, aren't you? She's such a nice girl. And yes! So beautiful! She's the best thing that could ever happen to you! Look how far you've come Frank! And it's all because of her! You know that, don't you, Frank! You can't give up now! Don't give up now! I'd be so disappointed, if you gave up now, Frank! Please don't give up now, Frank! Please don't give up now!"

The lady's sounding more and more desperate all the time now, you know. But yeah, TMBGITW. It was all because of her. Her, is when the whole fucking nightmare started. Knew that for sure. But kind of loved her as well, you know. More than, kind of didn't.

And that was the worst thing, to have to admit to. Didn't want to know it. But knew it. And the heart knew it even more. And that was even worse, than the worst part. Having the heart saying one thing, but the brain saying something else. Wished he'd never even seen her.

But the thinking, just did some kind of turnaround or something. Everything then became clear. That wasn't needed to become clear. But came clear anyway. From the grubby clothes, to good clothes. New shoes. Regular shaving. Deodorant. All cleaned up. No drinking. No smoking. And no big fat joints. She had him by the balls, alright.

Then this big thought hit the new brain. Maybe the lady and TMBGITW were in cahoots, you know. After all, they were both into him about the same things. First it was the lady in the hospital who wasn't even there. Then it was

197

TMBGITW. And now it was both of them. And all of the other café girls as well. And all at the same time. And that fucking blabbermouth compulsive. I mean, what chance was there. None at all. They had him fucked, alright. Right from the start.

There're going to have a lot of fun with you.

But Frank, you know, wasn't really in any mood to go thinking about thinking about anything. Too emotionally distraught right now. Confused out of the brain. So disappointed with the weakness within himself. And now totally aware that this girl, who only worked in a café was just so much smarter. Well, they all were, weren't they? And he didn't like that at all. And yes, she frightened the shit out of him, alright. Not the rest of them. Just her. Bitch.

There're going to have a lot of fun with you.

Frank decided then, never to go back there ever again and this time he really did mean it.

This big emotional breakdown happened then you know. The biggest one ever. Started shaking. Tears rolling down the cheeks. A complete, fucking wreck. Pulling over had to happen. And you wouldn't believe it. Right in front of a pub. Frank had been in this pub several times before. So, a decision had to be made. But there was no real decision made at all. The force was a familiar force. And the resistance just wasn't there.

Yes, back to the poker machines. The only real safe place there was. Safe from the world. The human jungle and all the other monkeys swinging around in there. Knew his way around in pubs. And of course, safe from the lady and TMBGITW. They obviously didn't like pubs, because they were never in there, when Frank was there.

And it was like he'd gone back to where he was before all the new life business took over the old life. Yeah. Back to where he belonged. And the mind started racing. And the main confusion was trying to decide what had happened already and what hadn't happened at all.

But as soon as he settled down in front of a machine. Fed a note into the slot and started pushing the big repeat bet button. Everything became clear. Because nothing was clear at all. Because nowhere land had come to the rescue again. And it didn't take long to get there either.

So, now it didn't matter whether anything was clear or not. Because no one gave a fuck when they were in nowhere land, did they? To hell with the lot of them. Yeah. To hell with everything. Such a relief to be back in there again. Like returning home. After a long and tiresome journey.

No more funds available. Fucking hell. Pissed off again. Head booming. Not with music. Just bells. Well, there was a kind of music there too. In the background somewhere. But it wasn't really music. Just fucking noise. Back in the car. Then back on the veranda.

The last thing that was needed was coffee. Yeah. So, after three cups, the thinking was really fired up. Been going to GA for a while now. Hadn't played the machines for over three months. So pleased with himself and all that. But now, there'd been another fuck up again. And he'd have to front up, at the next GA meeting and let it all out. Yeah. It'd been a while, since the last bust. But what had to be done, just had to be done. There was no getting out of it.

Honesty will come into your life, if you let it.

But it was always interesting, listening to all the other compulsives and their stories of self-destruction. Heartache and pain for themselves and all in their world. They become like pariahs. Lying, cheating, pathetic, helpless souls and soon this helpless soul would be back in there with them again. Where he belonged. With another failed episode to share. So, things were bad. But they weren't all that bad. Could have been worse.

No one was ever alone in GA, you know. This realisation, always made the feelings feel better. Especially about himself. Knowing there were plenty of others out there, just as far gone. Years of addiction to the dreaded poker machines had taken a heavy toll on many monkeys. Yes, and he was only one of them. He felt at ease with these fellow monkeys. At first that is. The thinking was getting a bit rearranged, by this stage. Too much coffee does that kind of thing, you know.

Didn't mind hearing the same stories over and over again either. New members, after sitting through only one meeting. Never to be seen again. No, never back again. Didn't sleep properly for several days, after this latest bust. Lost all the money he'd saved up. Feeling like shit. Thinking like shit as well.

One of the repeated GA sayings was to maybe hand over the life to a greater power. Fuck that. No way that was going to ever happen. Maybe they think, there're God or something. Had to get out of the place. Decided never to go back to GA, ever again. Just didn't belong there.

But the controller was always saying that God and religion had nothing to do with GA. It was all about a power, of your own understanding. That you had to let into your life. This statement always hit a nerve in the brain. Got the attention, alright. There was already a huge awareness about powers getting into his life. That were greater than him. And they were all female. That's for sure.

Then something was remembered. That was probably not a good idea to be remembering. There was a sock full of Acapulco Gold seeds in the house somewhere. Yeah. Grow some plants again. Blow the mind right out. To where it used to go. Where there was none of this new life shit to put up with.

So, the big search began. Turned the house upside down. They were in there somewhere. But the exhaustion set in. Giving up was the only result. Someone could have snuck in and stole them. But then it was spotted. On the floor. Sticking out from under a lounge chair. Been kicked there one day. Out of sheer frustration. Been off the grog, you know. And the pot. And the smokes. This was just after the lady turned up and forced him to tip all the beer down the sink. And put all kinds of new ideas into the head. Before he knew what he was in for. Poor bastard had lost all control at that stage.

A folder, full of documents and award certificates from the working days in the old life. Soon forgot about the seeds. Checking all this stuff out was bringing back the memories, alright. But a few pages fell out, didn't they? And they weren't documents or award certificates. It was a real shock, when the realisation happened.

There was a time, when a little boy was born. Into a family. There's no need to explain who's little boy he was. He was such a beautiful soul and so unaware of the real world. He was a disabled little boy. And Frank often visited his home and spoke to him. About many things.

Over several years, this disabled little boy, impressed everyone who got to know him. About how intelligent he was and how determined he was to live his life, as well as he could. As an individual. Regardless of his many challenges. Always smiling. And he knew lots of jokes. Made everyone laugh. Yeah. He was a real little joker, alright. Frank liked him and admired him. And so did everyone else.

One day, he handed Frank several pages. The ones that fell out of the folder. By now this disabled little boy had become a disabled young man. And he'd typed out a story about his life. And he handed these pages to Frank and asked him to write a story about his life. Unaware maybe, that he'd already told the story of his own life. Better than anyone else could have ever told it.

So, here's Frank holding these pages and remembering the promise he'd made, to this disabled young man. A promise, that he'd never kept. And it played on his mind and just wouldn't go away. So, what else was there to do, other than tell it now. And it's going to be told exactly as the disabled young man typed it out. Word for word. So, here it is.

My life started in the year of 1975, and of course I started as a little baby like everyone does. So from then on till I was about 3 years old, my parents had to look after and care for me as good as they could. They changed my nappies, bathed me, put me to bed and all sorts of things.

But when I reached the age of three, I guess you could say I started to become a real person. And I started to do many more and different things, like I started to go to some parties and I use to try and roam around with others in our street where we lived and play games. So I would say that I had fun at that age even though I did not really know what was going on in the world. When my fourth birthday came up though, it made mum think a little. Mum was wondering whether I should be sent to school after the next Christmas. So she thought and thought about it, till the time came when the decision had to be made, and the decision was to send me to school. So I actually started school one year before I should have started. Because they say these days that you should not tart school under the age of five, but when I started it was not as vital.

So from the first day of school in the year of 1989, I went to school. In that first year of school, I just did as all the other kindergarten people do, that is do as the teacher said and play with friends. So I had to keep doing that till the end of that year, for that time anyway. Then the Christmas holidays came up, and I just had to find things to do at home for six weeks. And for four of those weeks I was good, but for the last two weeks we had what we did not particularly like, and what we did not expect. That I started to shake sometimes. And I also did other strange things. So In about the last week of the holidays, they ended up taking me to hospital. So when I got to the hospital, the nurses took me to a room, and did a blood test straight away. After doing the blood test they came out to mum and dad with some not so good news. That was that your son unfortunately has diabetes.

It wasn't only diabetes that I got at that time unfortunately. I one day was taken to the eye doctor, and he told us that I besides having diabetes, I also had an eye problem called optical atrophy. So that meant that I had the two problems, the eye problem and the diabetes to live with. It wasn't only me but mum and dad also had to get used to how much each food was worth, when to give me sugar and just diabetes in general.

So while I was in hospital, the nurses and sisters instructed my mum and dad in what would have to be done, and what they would have to look out for, what could happen and what couldn't be eaten.

So they were told about what to do, and they sort of instructed me; till I got a bit older. So I just sort of did what mum and dad told me for quite some time, seems that I had diabetes.

But I must say that from that age of five when I first got diabetes, there has been many diabetic clinics, camps, and all sorts of different things like in which I have participated in, and have enjoyed them. Besides all the activities I have had with the diabetic foundation and different places, I must tell you that also my family with me went roller-skating, temping bowling, to the show, to pictures and many other places at times. Also during that time, I had trips in and out of hospital, and I was in hospital that often, that the hospital nearly seemed like a second home.

Although, if the hospital was classified as a real home, you would have millions of mothers, and you would not have the same amount of fathers by any means. So from there I just took life as normal, but had to look after my problems too, with my parent help. During that time too, I also with my mother's help got a pen-pal and her name was Mary. So Mary and I wrote to each other for around two years.

Then I remember one year, it was at Christmas, I was going on a diabetic camp, and just by coincidence it happened that my pen-pal who also was a diabetic was going too. So just with hearing that news it made me feel excited, because I knew I was going to meet my pen-pal on a camp. But when the time came for the camp to start, we got there and saw each other and looked at each other and weren't too happy. So after that fortnight away, we were literally finished as pen-pals.

So then we were in wonder of what I could do as a hobby, so mum went around and some of her friends gave her ideas of what might be a good hobby for me to do. Then someone said to mum, have you thought about y.p.t and mum did not know what that was at first, but she was told it was an acting class, and was told where it was held. So mum ended up wringing up about the acting class, and that Saturday mum took me down to the uniting church, to the young people's theatre class.

After that class, I went home and I told mum that I quite enjoyed that activity. So I kept it up for around three or four years. But then too we were told by a doctor that I now had epilepsy. So for my epilepsy I was put on a tablet called Tegretol (500 mill of it).

So that gave me more to remember, because that meant now that I was also on the Tegretol, that of a morning I had to have insulin and I also had to take 500 mills of Tegretol.

So me having to take those two things, insulin and Tegretol, continued for quite some time. But during that time, there also was many different places I went for different activities. But seems that I now had three problems, it did make it harder than what it was earlier, but we managed.

Then it was one time after having those three problems for around 11-2 years, I was in hospital again. The reason I was in hospital this time was because every night when I went to sleep, I started the night just about perfectly, but half way through the night my dad had to come into my room and either wake me up or resuscitate me, because I was either stopping breathing or very close to it. And that started being and went on for quite some time. So dad did it for all that time.

And during that time when I was having trouble sleeping, when we went to the doctors we told them about it, and they tried to help us, but it still continued. So that continued for quite some time, till one time when dad was worried with what was going on, so he told the doctors, and they got me put into hospital again, for a reason we did not know at the time. But that night when I went to sleep, the nurses watched me and what went on, and then they realised what problem mum and dad were having, and what problem I was in for.

So in the day time after that night, when mum and dad came up they were told what the nurses saw and what problem it was: sleep apnoea. So the next night they tried what was the only thing that would work, the C. Pap Machine. And that was a mask which sort of came in and helped you breathe if you stopped. And they figured out that that worked for me at that time, so they got a machine and sent it home with me for me to use at home.

So I used the C Pap Machine for some time with mum and dads help, and the doctor came to our rescue if something was to happen that none of us could fix. But it was after about two years of being on the c. pap machine, that dad started noticing me going through pretty well the same trouble of stopping breathing during my sleep. So the C Pap Machine had stopped doing its job. So when we went to see the doctor next, my dad told the doctor of what problem he was having during the night, with the machine.

So, the doctor looked at the problem carefully, and he eventually told us after looking at the problem closely, that the machine wasn't now doing the job for us. So we had to think carefully, because there was one thing that we could do which many people had gone for, but there also was another thing we could do which no body had gone for yet. The first thing we could do which was already in use by some people was to get wires put pretty well all over you, and it made you not be able to talk properly or basically do anything properly. But the other way was to have an operation where they put a hole in your neck and put a tube down the hole.

So I thought about it for some time, and I did not at all like the result of the first thing I could do, so I decided to be the guinea pig of the tracheostomy. So I had the tracheotomy put in, but it was for a reason that no one else had had a tracheotomy before, and that reason was to sleep at night. Because after having the tracheotomy, I had to hook up to a ventilator each night, before I went to sleep, so then it would breathe for me at night.

So after finding out I had that problem too, I myself was hoping that that would be the last problem to hit me, because four problems, I thought, were enough.

Even though I do have those problems, I must say that my brother is good because sometimes he takes me even though I have the problems, out to putt golf, or tempine bowling, and we may go to other places.

But I myself do still do things myself to, because of a Saturday I somehow get from my home, and I go to a big shopping centre, and other days I say at home and have good times inside, because not long ago bought myself a CB radio. And I have made lots of friends on the CB radio.

At home sometimes, my brother and I want to do things together, so seems that when I was young and had a bike of my own, seems that I had a few problems on that bike because I fell off it and other things happened; we eventually bought a tandem.

A tandem, for those who don't know is a bike that they use to use for two people. So we got one of them, so now my brother can take me around when I want to ride. And I must also say that we at home have a pool table, and that pool table I bought for the family, and I love the game when I get a spare moment.

And so that is about all I can remember of my past there, Frank, and I hope you can make a good story out of what information I have given you.

The way in which this all started, that is my life, is that firstly mum and dad got married in about the year of 1972 to 1973. And then as with most couples they have good time together especially while they don't have any children to worry about. So mum and dad went through that stage and had the good times with just their mothers, fathers, brothers and sisters, then in the year of 1975, it was on the second of June, that I came around.

And I was born as normal and lived just a normal little one life. It was when I started school, that was when I was four, and in the year of 1980. I started then even though it actually was a year early.

It was then after that first year of being at school, that I started to have a little trouble, because about half way through the Christmas holidays in the year of 1980; I started showing some symptoms of what we did not know at the time. But it was a little while after the symptoms started to show, that I was taken to hospital, and we were told I was getting diabetes, and I at that time only had 24 more hours to live.

Yeah. That was exactly what his little disabled mate wrote. And there was an obligation there now, you know. This story just had to be told. And Frank realised that, more than ever. And he also reaffirmed in his own mind, that he could never have told it any better. So, he didn't even try.

And a great burden of responsibility had been lifted. The promise had now been kept. His disabled little mate, sadly passed away within a few months of handing Frank his life story. It was like he must have known, that his short life was just about over.

Frank's feeling of relief, to have finally kept his promise was indescribable. But he needed to be left alone now. For a good while. No interruptions.

Talk about being, snapped back to the present.

"Frank! Frank! I've been trying to get in touch, for quite a while now! There was just so much static! I couldn't reach you! And you can't just sit there all day, Frank! Watching videos, eating that terrible food and drinking coffee! You need to get up and do something!"

"The lawn needs mowing! And the kitchen sink, Frank! You need to get yourself some cleaning products! Give it a good going over! It's disgusting again! You need to wipe it clean every day! You need to be consistent! Come on Frank! Get up! Get up and get going! You were doing so well too! What's happened, Frank! What's got into you! You need to get motivated, Frank!" Come on! Get going!"

Oh, for fucks sake. Is that really her. Back again. With all her usual shit. Do this, do that. Blah, blah, blah. Next time he'll have to remember to turn the volume up. Full blast.

That's where the idea came from in the first place, you know. How to get rid of the lady. When she wasn't wanted around. Filling the head up with garbage. Just, turn the volume up.

And then she had to go and have a good look around didn't she? Noticed all the empty cans. And the old frying-pan full of butts and roaches. Fucking hell. He was in for it now.

"Oh, Frank! What have you been doing! Just look at all this mess! This is so disappointing, Frank! So disappointing! And just when you were going so well! I did expect a little relapse or two. Every so often! But this is just ridiculous, Frank! You've regressed so badly here! I'm, not so sure you can come back from this! This is a catastrophe, Frank! Don't let me down, Frank! Please don't let me down!"

Well, none of that was any good. That's for sure. Then everything went dead quiet. She was gone, alright. And thank Christ for that. She can go and turn someone else's life upside down, for all he cared.

Yeah. She'd never been so pissed off before. That's for sure. Never that bad anyway. But she'll get over it. She always does. There was a fleeting thought about telling her to just fuck off and leave him alone. That worked once or twice before, you know. But he thought better of it. She'd only come back again. Yeah. Only a matter of time and she'd be back again.

Maybe she already knew he was going to tell her that. Because she was already gone. Before he even thought about saying anything. Always one step ahead. Yeah. Always that one step ahead.

Regressed; return mentally to a former stage of life or a supposed previous life, especially through hypnosis.

Yeah. That's what happened, alright. Back to the old life. Just like that. Didn't take much for that to happen did it.

Hypnosis; a mental state of highly focused concentration, diminished peripheral awareness, and heightened suggestibility. There are various techniques that experts employ for inducing such a state.

So, the lady had the poor bastard hypnotised. That explains everything. And she was an expert, alright. No doubt about that.

Suggestibility; the quality of being inclined to accept and act on the suggestions of others.

So, that's what's been going on. And it wasn't only the lady either. TMBGITW and the café girls were all into him. Right from the start. Yeah. There've all got him hypnotised. Been fucking him around. Right from the very start. And here he is. In some new life. In some new world. Struggling to understand any of it. Didn't have a clue half the time. And there're all sitting back watching him and, laughing their fucking heads off. And he had no control over the situation. None at all.

There're going to have a lot of fun with you.

He'd been robbed. That's what happened. They took his life off him and left him floundering around in some place he didn't understand. Yeah. Another nowhere land. And it wasn't even his fault. And it wasn't getting any easier. In a nowhere land that he didn't understand. Not like all the other nowhere lands. At least he knew where he was in all the other nowhere lands.

"Oh! Stop it, Frank! You're talking nonsense! You had no life, before we came along! You know that! You've come such a long way in your new life! And now you're throwing it all away! So, you just have a think about that, Frank! Have a long hard think about that! Oh please, Frank! Have a good long think about what you're doing with your new life! For both our sakes! Please, Frank! Please! Get your act together! Before it's too late!"

Right. She was back quicker than expected. And full of such aggression. Fucking hell. She could change moods, alright. Long hard thinking, eh. Frank had never been any good at long hard thinking, you know. But he understood the message. Clear enough, alright. He got it, alright. The brain was still burning. What's with the, we bit anyway. There couldn't possibly be more than one of her, could there be. No. There just couldn't.

A few hours later, you wouldn't have known the place. The whiz bins were full. Frying pan emptied. Cleaned and back in the cupboard. Sink was sparkling. There were cleaning products available now, you know. How she missed that one, he'll never know. Carpet sweeper got another run. Then sheer exhaustion took over.

Yeah. Ok. I know. I know. She'd won again. She always wins in the end. Every time. But he doesn't want to talk about that any more.

"Oh, hello Frank! You're back! We thought you were gone for good! It's so good to see you again! Now, what are you having today?"

Yeah, gone for a few days. Could have been longer. Maybe a few weeks. The mind had been kind of half vacant for a while now. And the half that was there, ached badly. But it was good to be back, alright. Drawn back like some magnetic force got hold of him. Resistance was futile. He'd heard that one somewhere. Probably on television. Or maybe on one of those videos. Before the lady turned up and woke him up. And blasted the shit out of him again.

It was the have a little chat girl. And things went back to normal. Like nothing unusual happened. Café girl smile and a little chat. And nothing was mentioned about TMBGITW. Maybe, she'd forgotten all about that. No, she knew, alright. They all knew. But they all said nothing. And he didn't say anything either. Yeah. Getting smarter all the time. But the head was still booming.

Yeah. Should have told her to just fuck off again. Have a few more beers. And a nice fat joint or two. That would have pissed her right off. But she'd just come back. Keep on and on and on. Till he got up. And he always got up. Yeah. She'd won again.

Then another realisation, hit the brain. Like a bomb exploding. Frank was losing all the wars now, you know. And they were all against females. Fucking hell. The headache got even worse after that thought bubble exploded.

There're going to have a lot of fun with you.

"So, what are you having, Frank?"

"Oh sorry! I was just trying to remember something! Uh, I'll just have the vegan nachos. And the coffee. Thanks!"

"The nachos are not on the menu anymore! Sorry about that!"

That'd be right. Just when he gets used to something, it gets taken off the menu. Only gone for a few days. Or, maybe a bit longer. And everything's changed. There were a few more seconds of contemplation.

"Ok then. I'll have the favourite meal then!"

"Which one, Frank! The first one? The second one? Or the third one?"

Okay. Right. Another decision-making time. She was just standing there. Café girl smile on. Ready to tap the buttons.

"How about the sweet potato chips and the coffee!"

"Sure, Frank! No problem! Been for your swim?"

"Yes, I have! The water was almost warm today. It was colder in the middle. But when the waves crashed over, the water was warm. So, the water was a few different temperatures. And it was a bit rough as well. I like it when it's like that! Bit like being in a washing machine. So, I only did half as much as usual. Three hundred metres, instead of the five or six hundred I usually do! I was stuffed when I got out!"

What a bloody chatter box. And he would have kept going as well.

Bit like being in a washing machine. What a stupid thing to say.

"Gee, sounds like fun! So, where are you sitting today? Usual table?"

"Yes, why not! The usual table! In the corner! Where I belong!"

And the talking didn't want to stop there either. On a roll, alright. But the, have a little chat girl was looking straight past Frank. Like he wasn't even there. No more little chat today. And the look was still straight past him. So, Frank turned around and noticed a line-up of customers, all the way out the door. Some of the looks weren't too friendly at all.

But he still hadn't swiped the credit card. Not even out of the wallet. After that was done. Head down. Quick turn to the right and straight for the table. No looking back either. And you know, he never even claimed the favourite table when he walked in. And it was the only one vacant as well. So, maybe his luck was changing and it was going to be a good day.

The usual scene outside. All the monkeys wandering everywhere. But then a wheel chair went past. With a carer behind it. There were lots of disabled monkeys around, you know. Getting pushed along in wheel chairs. Not that it was noticed as much before. But after finding those pages that his little disabled mate wrote out, these individuals stood out more than ever.

Often you would see them in the pool. Splashing around and making unusual sounds. But they were sounds of sheer joy. They were excited about being in the water, letting their feelings out. Expressing themselves as much as their condition allowed. Sometimes their carer's were right in there with them and sometimes they stayed on the side of the pool. Keeping a close eye on things.

And after it was noticed, about how many of these disabled monkeys were around. And it wasn't just a few either. Or one seen every now and then. They seemed to be everywhere. And apart from that one incident with the naked one trying to run off with that little girl monkey, they were always well behaved. They enjoyed being out in the community. See that easy enough.

"Oh Frank! There may still be hope for you yet! But please stop calling the humans monkeys! They wouldn't like that at all!"

That put an end to that little contemplation didn't it. She always picks her moments well doesn't she. Thought maybe she was gone for good, after that last blow up. But no. Here she is, butting in again. She just can't help herself. But at least she didn't stay long. Just long enough, to mess the thinking up. But they were all monkeys, alright. So, that's one thing she wasn't up to date with.

Then a thought just popped in, out of nowhere. The lady was never around at all, when the music was blasting away in the car. Yes, that was the answer, alright. When she wasn't wanted around. Turn the music up. Full blast. Teach her to just pop in and out whenever she felt like it. If there were any wars to be won at all, new strategies had to be employed. And this was a beauty. She won't know what's hit her. Or what's going on for a change. What a great plan.

Too bad he wasn't in the car right now. That was her favourite way of interrupting, you know. When the poor bastard was just driving along. Listening to the favourite music. Total relaxation. Then like a rock to the head; in she comes and dive-bombs the thinking. Starts yapping away. Driving him fucking crazy. But not anymore. She was in for a big shock, alright.

Because part of this new plan was to only have the music at half full volume. Then when she comes crashing in. Turn up the volume to full blast. The smile just wouldn't leave his face, after thinking that one up. Worked, alright.

Yeah. In the car. Music pumping away. There were discs and a stick. With 1960s and 70s rock music. All the favourite stuff. Remembering where these things came from was never fully realised. And videos of the good the bad and the ugly. Magnificent 7. Clint Eastwood spaghetti westerns. Beverly hillbillies. F troop. Green acres. Loved all that stuff. There were only vague memories, of people dropping in on him from time to time. After the cancer operation.

This was long before the lady even turned up. So, she couldn't possibly know anything about it. And that was a good feeling to have. Knowing about something, that the lady didn't know anything about.

On a Pink Floyd disc, there was a song called 'Braindead.' This was the all-time favourite song by this band. All because of the one lyric. There's someone in my head, but it's not me. Well, there'd always been other people in Frank's head, you know. Besides all the Franks. But that was in the old head. In the old life. Now there was a new head in the new life and there was someone in there as well. That wasn't any of the Franks. Because it was the lady who wasn't there.

But she was there, alright. And TMBGITW was still in there as well. And the café girls, of course.

But it was always, alright for them to be in there. Always liked it, when they were there. Although, there was still that suspicion, you know. About them all working together. The spy net-work. But that was better off not thought of so much. So, it wasn't thought about at all. For most of the time, anyway. Yeah. Getting smarter all the time.

Always wishing the lady wasn't there was usually the main wish. So glad when she wasn't there. Because she always had plenty to say. Too much. But it was always stuff, that was good for him to hear. And that was getting to be understood, more and more.

Although, she was a real nuisance sometimes. But in a good way. So, whether it was a good idea to have her around all the time was a bit hard to work out. So, if she was only around some of the time, that would be okay. And things were usually okay. Unless she was there too much. And then she was just a pain in the arse. But she never got told that. Not that can be remembered anyway. But he was used to her now, you know. After all, she'd been there, on and off, for a long time.

Yeah. She was a real sticker, alright. Still there. Even after getting told to fuck off a couple of times. She was just another aggravation, that had to be lived with. Didn't really mind all this new life business now either, you know. Starting to get used to it. But if it had been known the lady was always going to be tagging along, it would have been a different story. That's for sure. She was worse than a king size fucking doppelganger. He just loved the word doppelganger. Another word from that English comedy show.

Doppelganger; a biologically unrelated look-alike, or a double, of a living person. In fiction and mythology, a doppelganger is often portrayed as a ghostly or paranormal phenomenon and usually seen as a harbinger of bad luck. Other traditions and stories equate to a doppelganger with an evil twin. In modern times, the term twin stranger is occasionally used.

Yeah. That was her, alright. A fucking doppelganger. Perfect description.

And TMBGITW was still in there as well. He just knew she was. And she would have known, she was a pain in the arse sometimes as well. No, not sometimes. All the time. Unless she really was stupid. But she wasn't stupid. She was nothing like stupid. That's for sure. She was probably another doppelganger.

But she was the best thing that ever happened to him. Frank knew he knew that now. And he'd never forget it either. Not with the lady always reminding him.

When the music was up, the lady was gone. And that's all that needed to be known right now.

But enough about the lady. And TMBGITW. And any other doppelgangers, that were hanging around. They'd been in the head too much lately. Where all the videos and movies came from was the thought of interest now. But that thought didn't last long. The way Frank ended up in a house that he owned was now doing a lap around. The thinking always took a sharp turn, whenever TMBGITW got in there. There was an instant burst of pressure that erupted. And it had to be dealt with immediately. Or else anything could happen. And it was usually bad. For him.

Like a huge bust and days of emotional and mental torture. And sometime weeks of it. And more miserable shares at GA. And he'd had enough of all the shit she caused. So, another strategy had been developed. To keep her from sending him crazy. She was never going to win, you know. Never.

"Sorry for the wait, Frank! It's been so busy today!"

Yeah. Knew he'd heard something. And here was the stick up for her friend's girl, smiling down upon him. Just standing there, with the coffee. The place was almost empty. She was in no hurry. And she still hadn't put the coffee down. Saying something seemed like a good idea.

"So, how have you been going!"

"Oh good! It's my birthday today!"

And that's when the coffee was placed down in front of him.

"Dare I ask how old you are?"

"21."

"Oh right! A big birthday, that one!"

"Sure is!"

"I hope you're not going to party too much!"

"Oh, maybe a little bit. I'm going out to dinner with my boyfriend! And then it's out with the other girls from here. To have some fun!"

"Okay! Well, have a good birthday!"

She seemed happy enough with that little conversation. And so did Frank. No emotion involved either. Just straight-out conversation. For both of them. The communication barrier, that had only recently been penetrated was completely gone now. How that happened wasn't really understood. But it wasn't there anymore and that's all that mattered.

"I better be getting back. Your meal shouldn't be too long!"

"Okay thanks!"

And off she goes.

Anyway, that all started in the weirdest way, you know. Ended up with his own property. After watching that elephant struggle out from behind her desk, Frank retreated back to the office and ate lunch as his desk. Was the officer in charge, you know. Yeah, that's right. The officer in charge of a whole section. Well, he wasn't really in charge of anything. The staff, just let him think he was in charge.

They made all the decisions. And that suited Frank just fine. They had this way of letting him know what had to be done and then, making a few suggestions about how things could be done. And then waiting for him to repeat the right suggestion. And then thanking him for making the right decision. And of course, they were all females. No surprises there, eh.

Anyway, the phone that never rang, rung. It was only ever used to ring head office and get logged into the mainframe computer. So, when it rang everyone just looked at it. Then they looked at Frank. And the real boss, just couldn't keep her mouth shut any longer.

"You're the boss! You answer it!"

So, he did. And the conversation, went something like this.

"Hello!"

It was a real estate agent. Apologising for the wrong phone number in their ad in the newspaper that day.

"Are you a real estate agent?"

The agent, admitted to being a real estate agent. Frank, usually had to be told something a few times, before full understanding was reached, you know. But you probably already do. Anyway.

"Have you got any 20-acre properties for sale?"

The agent explained, that his agency only sold or rented out, residential properties.

"Oh ok! Thanks for the call!"

And that was the end of that. Till a few days later. When the phone that never rang, rung again. And the same thing happened again.

"Hello!"

It was the same real estate agent. He'd been playing golf and started a conversation with a property developer. Who'd just subdivided a big block of land. And a 22-acre lot was still unsold.

"Yes, I'd be interested!"

So, to cut a long story short, this property developer got in touch. Offered up a deal, too good to refuse. It wasn't completely understood, why it was too good to refuse. It just was. Especially after a solicitor got involved, and said it was a good deal. A very good deal. A deal too good to refuse. And so, the purchase of this property was finalised. And what a big thrill it was. To own a property. And start a significant change in the life style.

Very secluded. The driveway in was a roundabout trip. Up and down a few sand hills, around a few thick tree trunks and through some clumps of salt bush. Then a sharp turn to the right. Down a moderately steep, uneven gravelly, slope and onto open ground. Took about half a minute.

There was a five-bay shed, with two clear spaces for cars. An old tractor that came with the purchase, occupied another one. A work area with benches in another one. And a pile of what looked like junk in the far end.

The house was actually an old radio shack. Two tiny bedrooms at one end. Lounge room in the middle. Then the kitchen and bathroom. Loved the place straight away. But the thinking was a woman would never live there. But there was no woman involved. Not a permanent one anyway. So, there was no problem there.

The shack had been moved there years before. Put down, about 50 metres from the shore line. Then came about 20 metres of mangroves. Before the open water. The young fella, who used to live there, dropped in one afternoon. To pick up a few things he left behind. Climbed up into the ceiling, to get whatever it was. Came down, with a small box and a big smile on his face. Next minute, a joint was lit up in the lounge room. And the conversation started. And lots of things were learnt about the place, that were very interesting to know.

Smoking pot had been out of the lifestyle for several years by this stage. But there was no resistance or refusal. And the joint was passed from one to the other. Just like old times. And it wasn't the only one. Several were rolled up and smoked. One after the other. They both ended up, right off their faces.

The exact conversation that took place, can't be remembered in detail. But this is the best recollection available, of what this young fella came out with. Because he did all the talking.

Like how a few people, from a nearby suburb, adjusted their horses there. And paid cash. And one of them was a girl. And she was very friendly. But sometimes she had no money. But she also liked smoking pot. So, a special deal was done and the problem was solved.

And sometimes, she brought a few of her friends with her. And they all got off their faces. And sometimes there were big parties. And just about all the young people from the nearby suburb turned up, and got completely pissed and stoned out of their brains. And eventually, he got to know all of them. Really well. Especially all the girls. Well, that was his story anyway.

This young fella was always laughing as he was talking. His bloodshot eyes looked like popping out, every time he got excited. And that was every time he started talking. Which was all the time. But you know, he had to move back to the same close suburb, when the property got sold. He quietened right down, when he came out with that bit. And it also put an end to the lounge room conversation.

Before he left was when he handed over a matchbox. It was full of seeds. And what was said was easily remembered.

"Acapulco Gold, man! Best there is! Take 'em! They're yours! I've got plenty!"

So, they were taken, of course. Simple as that. Couldn't be helped. Frank knew all about Acapulco Gold, from the old days. This young fella, brought the memories of the old days, flooding back. But that just wasn't needed right then. Took years to get over the old days. The old days, almost caused complete annihilation. Yeah. Acapulco Gold. Never forgot about that Acapulco Gold. Taking the seeds was a big mistake, alright. But that's just how it is sometimes. Just took them for old time's sake, anyway. That's all.

Then the remembering became even clearer. This young fella made a big impression, you know, "Come and I'll show you how to catch fish!"

Half way to his route, when that came out. The excitement had started up again. Off he went towards the mangroves, with guess who, following along behind. And struggling to keep up.

"They come in with the tide! Big fuckers! Use these little crabs for bait!"

And he rolled over a half-rotted log, about a metre long. Crabs everywhere.

"See them holes! That's where the big fuckers are! Use the fish heads to lure em out! But ya have to be careful! Big fuckers el take a finger off, if you're not careful!"

He loved saying that, you know. Big fuckers. Everything was a big fucker. Yeah. This young fella was a complete maniac. And still laughing all the time. But he was friendly.

"You just sit and watch 'em come in. Only a foot deep, when they come in. Big fuckers! Just, use the little suicide hooks!"

This was the fish he was talking about now. Not the big fuckers, that lived in the holes. There was an old railway sleeper with each end, jammed in between the trunks of two mangrove trees. How he managed to get that in there seemed impossible. But it was there so, it must have been possible.

"I've still got some plants growing over here!"

Next minute, he's off again. Back to the edge of the mangroves. There were little tracks, cut through the salt bushes. With a cleared area in the middle. Bricks stacked up about three high, with a big plastic bucket on top. With a few steel spikes, holding them into position.

"I had to do that, because the high tide moved em around. Tipped em over! You have to water them, with the bore water!"

Right. So, after all the showing was over with, they both wandered back over to the shack. The young fella had quietened right down now. Got a bit of a serious look on his face.

"Don't suppose you'd mind, if I drop in and check the plants. Every now and then. You can help yourself too. If you want. Just don't take too much!"

Well, how could he say no to that. When he was enjoying being stoned again. After such a long time. The feelings were all good. He'd have agreed to anything.

"Sure, you can!"

"Thanks, man!"

And within about 30 seconds. The hand shake took place. The see you later bit was said. He was in his suit and he was off. Never to be seen again. And the plants never got touched either. Not by the young fella anyway. Took a few weeks, before they did get touched.

And so, it all started again. Ever so slowly. On and off. Every so often. When the mood was right. But never during the working week. Only on weekends. And not every weekend either. And there were often gaps of months in between relapses. And about three years on one occasion. Or maybe two. But it all started again.

About ten years later was when it happened. Driving the forty-five minutes to work. Still in the public service. Suffered a massive epileptic fit. Crashed into a few cars. Woke up in hospital. Ended up medically retired. Couldn't function properly for several years after that. Weird thing was it was during one the longest straight periods.

Frank hadn't touched alcohol or pot or the dreaded poker machines, for several years. How many exactly, is hard to say for sure. But it was a few years, at least. Maybe longer. Living the straight life. On top of everything. And then it all came crashing down. Again. Just like that. The deep depression set it. Again. And it didn't take long either. Not long at all.

And that's when the poker machine addiction really took a firm hold. Again. Then came the binge drinking. Again. And before long, there were more buckets hidden in the salt bushes. Because the memories were there again. About the Acapulco Gold and how it always calmed the nerves. And there was lots more need to calm the nerves. And the matchbox full of Acapulco Gold seeds was soon empty. But the awareness was there. To build up another supply. So, the matchbox idea was replaced with an old woollen sock. And this sock was soon full of seeds.

Wasn't long before the lack of money was the main reason for concern. There was none left. All the savings were gone. Desperation had set in now. As well as the deep depression. A very bad mix. Thank God, there was always plenty of pot available. Or complete madness would have taken over. Yeah. Smoking pot was the only thing that saved him.

Laying around everywhere was lots of old stuff. Irrigation pipes and sprayers. Lengths of heavy-duty aluminium. Bits of steel plate. Wooden cabinets and some old power tools in the carport. And all kinds of farm equipment. Including the old tractor. And all this stuff, came in very handy. But not for any purpose they were made for.

When the medical retirement happened, is when the pension started. And it's also when decisions were even harder to make. Big confusion was there all the time. Even remembering very simple things was a challenge. But ways to get more money, to satisfy the cravings for more poker machine action were never far away.

The epileptic medication dulled the senses, you know. Slowed the thinking right down. To almost no thinking at all. The thinking had always been a problem to begin with. But now, the daily struggle to function at all was the biggest problem. Although, there were times of perfect clarity. And during these times, various items that were laying around got sold.

And eventually, everything that could be sold for cash was sold. After placing ads in the for-sale section, of a few newspapers and one country magazine. And as soon as any money became available, it went straight into the poker machines. And on cartons of beer. And on takeaway food. Mainly fish and chips and hamburgers. Frank ended up as fat as a house.

Been warned by the doctors, about not drinking any alcohol, while on the medication. And there was a message on the box as well. But that didn't stop the frequent loading up. Until the realisation happened. Functioning while taking the medication was hard enough. But functioning on the grog as well was almost impossible. So, one of them had to go. And luckily, it ended up being the grog. Wasn't completely stupid, after all.

Then the time that had to come, came. Nasty letters from the bank. They got ignored for as long as possible. Then forgotten about altogether. Forgot all about paying the mortgage as well. Still over $100.000 in debt. Forgot about paying any bills as well. Forgot about everything. Except playing poker machines, and smoking pot. And stuffing the junk food down, whenever there was money available. Yeah. The grog sent him over the edge. But the pot, didn't seem to affect him in a bad way. Just got the mood right and brought on the munchies.

So, here's the latest lifestyle scenario. Hanging out for the fort nightly pension. That just happened to get deposited into an account with the same bank, that sent the nasty letters. Wastes the lot, when it comes. The addictions have taken over. Again. Nothing of any value was left to sell. Not eating properly. Not sleeping well. Always confused. Super depressed. Smoking copious amount of pot. Always hungry after a few joints. Yeah. The munchies were always there. Walks around in circles, mumbling away.

Hated walking out to get the letters. Always bills and reminders to pay bills. But the worst ones were from the bank. And there was one in particular, that did the trick. After the realisation crashed in. That the bank was now in the mood, to take the property. Desperation time. So, an interview was organised with the bank manager. The agreement was. The bank, will ease off with the demands for the mortgage payments. For a few months. Till the property got sold. But only for a few months.

So, the property goes up for sale. The estimated value was less than $200 thousand. Fucking hell. That just wasn't enough. Nowhere near enough. The brain went into overdrive. After paying the bank. The real estate fees and the solicitor's fees. There'd only be peanuts left. Even the dullest of dull brains could work that one out.

There was a plan required. And that required a lot of thinking. And the thinking was always a slow process. But eventually the plan was there. In the brain. As clear as anything could ever be clear in this particular brain. But this clearness only came about, after about six or seven, big fat joints of the good stuff. Yeah. The good old Acapulco Gold was going to produce real gold. And so, the new plan was there.

And what a plan it was. The best plan ever. And Frank thought it up, all by himself. Well almost.

Two real estate agents, looked on is disbelief, when it was explained to them, how much was needed. And how much the property had to be put on the market for. Another agent was contacted by phone. Knew the property and the approximate value. And things were explained to this agent in detail, as well. But that didn't matter one bit. Same result. You won't get that much for it. Sorry, can't help you. But the calculation had been done. And the plan was the plan. And that was that.

So, they either put it on for the required amount or, other agents would have the opportunity. So, other agents got the opportunity. And it was always the same result. As in, you're joking. But there was no joke involved here. And there was no changing the plan. And real estate agents. They can be very persuasive, you know. But the thinking, when it was there was that these agents were only interested in a quick sale. So, they could collect their commission. And they couldn't give a fuck about the life-or-death situation here. So, fuck the real estate agents.

The whole situation was just causing a double dose of deep depression. So, long walks and lots of mumbling took place. For days, then weeks and eventually for several months. But it wasn't always around in circles. Frank often walked the several kilometres to the ferry wharf and took a trip across the harbour. Walked along the sand on the beaches. Out along the ocean break wall. All around to the ocean baths and then through a huge park and around to the next ocean baths. And all through the streets of the city. And various beachside suburbs as well.

There were several occasions, when sleeping on the beach or somewhere in a park was necessary. Or in some shop doorway. Because the exhaustion set in. And the thinking got confused. And lying down and falling asleep had to happen.

And it had to just happen right then and there. And forgetting about having a house to go home to, happened too often. Sometimes he was away for days and sometimes a week or so and sometimes even longer than that.

The bank became like a big black cloud. Followed him everywhere. Threw down thunder bolts of lightning and roared like thunder. That's what went through the head. Every time he got one of their letters. And it got much worse, after they were opened. So, they stopped getting opened. But occasionally, on one of the walks. There'd be an unscheduled visit.

Yeah. Drop in and say hello. And have a friendly chat to the bank manager. If they were available. And there were some great excuses thought up, you know. For not responding to requests for information, about how things were going with the sale of the property.

That's because nothing was happening, about the sale of the property. But that's not what the bank manager heard. On these occasional visits, it was usually a case of there was two or three different offers for the property and negotiations were taking place. Right at this moment. And it would all be settled shortly. And the awareness was always there, to change the story up a little bit. So as not to arouse the suspicions of the bank manager. And this seemed to work for a while. Till that next final nasty letter came. Time's up. Oh, fuck no.

But then the luck changed didn't it. It was on the following Sunday afternoon, of all times. Walking along the main street. Stoned out of the brain. Head down. All hope gone. And then, an hallucination happened. But it wasn't really an hallucination at all. After a few blinks and some slow thinking, the realisation became clear. It was a sign. Propped up on the footpath. In front of a Real Estate Agency. And the sign says, open. The name of this agency is not important. They were open. On a Sunday afternoon. Surely, that had to mean something.

Frank wanders in. The immediate attention and the friendly smile had to mean something as well. All the vibes were good. Straight away. And the youngish receptionist was so nice looking too. And there was no resistance, when the idea immediately came to start chatting her up. But that was never going to happen. Too quick on the uptake, this one. Didn't get the chance. The conversation, went something like this.

"Hello! Can I help you?"

She was at the counter by now and the smile had eased off a bit. Then disappeared. And the facial expression changed, to a more serious look. Maybe she suddenly realised, that maybe this bloke had walked in by mistake. Looking tired and untidy. Maybe thinking, he was half pissed and completely off his face. And she would have been half right. Not about being half pissed. But he was off his face, alright. But she was only a receptionist after all. So, it didn't really matter what she thought did it. Ok then bitch. Down to business then. If that's how she wanted it.

"I've got a property! And I want to sell it!"

Stupid girl wasn't sure whether to believe him or not. Just kind of looked stunned for a few seconds.

"Oh! I'm sure we can help you there! I'll just get you name and the address of the property!"

Yeah. The mood had brightened right up. And all the required information was pouring out. But before she could even write down anything, this old fella appeared from behind a screen and strode up to the counter. He'd already heard enough. After only a five-minute conversation, this bloke, his off sider and Frank were in a fancy kind of car and on their way, to check out the property. Was just like one of those things, that was just mean to happen. And it just happened. Like a dream, that wasn't really a dream.

And Frank, you know. Sitting there in the front passenger seat. Felt like someone real important. For the first time, in a very long time. Well, for the first time ever. Yeah. Felt like a movie star. Cheeks warm and flushed, with a big smile on the face. Yeah. There was a good vibe happening, about this whole situation. Right from the start. And that proved to be exactly how it all worked out. Except maybe when that receptionist, came to the counter and turned sour all of a sudden. But even that didn't stop the good result, that was on the way.

Turns out, a developer had a cool 5 million to invest. And he knew this real estate agent really well. Took about fifteen minutes to get there. Went for a wander around the place. Stopped out in the middle of the property. Didn't even want a look inside the shack. And who could blame them. Well, it wasn't really a house, was it? They could tell that easy enough.

What a surprise it was when the agent, didn't even argue about the amount required. Or the amount it had to be put on the market for. In order to get the required amount. After the agents and solicitor's fees were taken out. And that figure was only made up, by some desperate character. In deep shit with the financial situation. With no real option, but to go for the big pay-out. The big jackpot.

Yeah. The amount was just an imaginary figure, you know. Plucked out of nowhere. After a prolonged session on the weed. Yeah. When the head was floating in space and reality had broken away. Got lost in its own space. And once this figure was locked in. There was no way of readjusting it. The plan was the plan. And nothing was going to change the plan, was it?

So many people in the real estate business. Pointed out the craziness of the plan. But desperate people, do some desperate and ridiculous things at times, you know. And this was one of those times. Reality wasn't in the frame here at all.

Anyway, the agent's and solicitor's paperwork got signed. The solicitor, then did whatever solicitors do. And getting this done, required extra-long walks on both occasions. Because there was not enough petrol in the car, to make it into town and back. So, the for-sale signs went up. And the waiting game began.

Meanwhile, the shack became an even more dangerous place. A stick was needed to turn the lights on and off. Because there was now a huge split in the corrugated asbestos roof. And when it rained, water came pouring in. Down three walls in the lounge room.

The carpet got soaked and stunk for days. And the shack was sinking on one side. And when the high tides were on, the water reached up to the shack and you could hear it lapping on the underside of the floor boards.

And not only that. A hole had been cut through the fibro lining of the lounge room. And half a sheet of corrugated iron was removed, from the outside wall of the shack. A concrete slab was put down and a chimney bricked up. To above the height of the roof. Took a few weeks to do all this. Because nothing was ever done in a hurry, you know. Things had to be thought through properly. So, there was no fuckups.

Logs for the fire were dragged out of the mangroves with the tractor. That wasn't an easy thing to do either, you know. With them stuck in the gluey mud and having to dig holes deep enough to get the rope around. After the tractor got sold, a rope was tied around the back axle of the car and that's how the logs were dragged out. And this kept things nice and warm. And just in time. Because the nights were always cold, no matter what time of the year it was. But it was a big sense of achievement, when the first fire was lit up. That's for sure.

Yeah. Some rabbits burrowed underneath the concrete slab, didn't they? One night, when it was freezing cold and the fire was roaring away. An almighty crack was heard and suddenly, the chimney had moved away from the shack. By at least half a metre.

What the fuck was that. But it didn't take long to work it all out. After the cold air came blowing in and fully woke him up. Been so comfortable, sitting there in the old lounge chair. Soaking up the warmth. Now up and just standing there in shock. Shivering. Frank evaluated this new situation for a few minutes. The only decision that could be made was eventually made. Into bed, and disappearing under the dirty, old, doona covers. And the pile of dirty, stinking clothes, piled up on top of them.

Next day, after the normal morning routine. The already prepared thinking was put into action. Some long, half rotted tree trunks were dragged out of the mangroves and used to prop up the chimney.

So, the chimney didn't fall over and the gaping hole in the wall was patched up with tin. And the fireplace was in operation again. That very night. Just like normal.

There was only one problem. Every time the fire was lit, the shack filled up with smoke. Before it started going up the chimney. But it didn't matter. Because being warm was the main consideration. And besides, coughing up a bit of smoke here and there wasn't a big problem. And didn't last long. Had been happening for decades anyway.

Another potential problem was whether there was enough petrol left in the tank, to drag out the required number of logs. But there must have been. Because the job got done. And this problem was only thought about, after the job got done. So, there was no worries about that.

"There you go, Frank! Enjoy! You look worried! And that cough doesn't sound so good! Are you ok?"

"Uh! Yeah! Yeah, I'm ok!"

Another upstairs girl. Didn't know her. Never seen her before. And there was no coughing going on. And there were no worries about anything, either. Well, maybe there was and maybe there wasn't. Anyway, she was gone. Before anything else could be said. But she was another mind-reader, alright. These interruptions, always caused a shift in the thinking, you know.

So, here's the lifestyle update. A cigarette, first thing in the morning. TV's on. A few coffees. Toast, if there's any bread. A joint or two. Always plenty of pot available. Then over to the mangroves, for a few fish. If the tide was coming in. If not, a look in the freezer. If there were no frozen fish left in there, it was down to the local shop for takeaway. If there was any money available. Sometimes there was and sometimes there wasn't.

The young fella left some fishing line, wrapped around a stick and a few hooks in a bucket. Tied to a mangrove tree, with wire. There was also another bucket, hanging down under the sleeper. With its handle tied onto the sleeper. With wire. Everything that was tied up was tied up with wire.

The big thrill was sitting there in the middle of the sleeper. Legs dangling down. Watching the tide slowly come in. And when it did start to really come in, down went the line, with a little mud grab hooked through its guts. And it was excitement, watching the big fuckers snatch the little crab and take off. The water was only about a foot deep when the big fuckers started to appear. Just like the young fella said. And it was a real struggle, hanging on to the line, without it slipping through the hands. They were big fuckers, alright. And very powerful.

The freezer, always had a few fish in there. Most of the time anyway. So, food was never a real concern. Most of the time anyway. As long as you liked fish. And fresh fish were always better that frozen fish. They were only ever thawed out, if there were no fresh ones available. And the munchies were really bad. Or if there was no money. For takeaway.

And the money situation was usually a bad one. Especially now. There'd been none for a while. But there was money in the bank account. Several thousand dollars. Only, it was a matter of time, you know. And no thought was put into time right now. Not real time anyway and how it passed by.

So, it passed by very quickly. And there'd been three fortnightly deposits into the bank account. Only it hadn't been realised. The thinking had been locked in. About there being no petrol in the car and no available money. And there was nothing else to be thought up. Except the constant thought about being in a bad situation, with no way out.

Yeah. So, Frank was lost in this fog of no further thinking about the real money situation and that was probably a good thing. Because if the thinking had been there, the money would have soon vanished. So, it wasn't really there anyway. And besides, there was no room for any more thinking.

But there was plenty of room for the imagination to get completely out of control and that's what happened. First, this brilliant idea came into focus. There was an area between the shack and the mangroves. Covered in dead grass. And there were always hot ashes in the fire place. Especially during the cold months of winter. And it was the middle of winter right now.

So, the plan was to tip these hot ashes into the dead grass and wait around long enough, to make sure the grass got lit up. Then take off for a long walk. By the time he got back, the old shack should be burnt to the ground. The place was insured you know. For a few hundred thousand. So, the thinking was to collect the insurance money and then still sell the property for the full amount. After all, a developer wouldn't want the old shack and would probably only bulldoze the thing into the ground.

And no one would live in it anyway. Too fucking dangerous. And what a clean-up that would be. Yeah. Collect the insurance money first and then sell the property. So, the plan was all worked out. The ashes were tipped onto the grass. The fire started up and off Frank went for an extra-long walk. There was over-excitement happening, for the first time in many months. Years even.

But you wouldn't believe what happened. There was this bloke on the next property, who'd been working on his boat, on and off. For about six months or so. And he just happened to turn up on this particular day. Saw the smoke and went to investigate. He managed to put the fire out, didn't he? Fucking dickhead.

An hour or two later, wandering along the front of the property was when it was discovered. No fire. No smoke. And the shack was still standing. The fire had reached up to a metre from the back of the shack. There was no reason for it go out. Still, plenty of dead grass. Dried out leaves and twigs and sticks here and there. What the fuck went wrong.

"Hey mate! I just started working on the boat, when I noticed the smoke. So, I came over. Got here just in time. Another ten minutes and the place would have gone up!"

Well, Frank just didn't know what to say, did he? A mixture of shock, disappointment and being really pissed off had invaded the thinking. While he was standing there, staring at this fucking dickhead, who'd just ruined everything.

"Lucky it was only a slow burn. Just creeping along. I managed to put in out, with that old piece of iron."

This bloke was just so pleased with himself, you know. Fucking idiot. But he had no idea what he'd just gone and done. Fucked the whole plan up. And he hadn't been there for months. And it wasn't even his property. Just had his boat there. Fucking idiot.

"Gee, thanks mate. Lucky you turned up when you did!"

Fucking idiot.

"That's ok! Glad to be of help!"

And with that, he put his hand out for a shake. Smiled and only said one more thing. Before he turned around and walked off. Glad to see the back of him, alright. Fucking idiot.

"Better get back to my boat!"

Yeah, fuck off, you idiot. It's more than understandable, that the mood took a backward direction from this point. Things went from bad to worse very quickly. There were terrible thoughts entering the equation. Very intense thoughts. Thoughts of self-destruction. And they just couldn't be stopped or even slowed down.

The first one was heading off to the doctors. The same one he'd been seeing, since he was a little boy. Explain how he was going over the edge. Maybe get some antipsychotic drugs. Or some sleeping pills. Take the whole fucking lot at once. Then head over to the mangroves and set up a death by accident scene. Yeah. With the feet caught up in the roots of one tree and the head banging into another one, on the way down. Scatter a few thongs around in the mud. Wouldn't take long for anyone to work out what happened.

Or maybe if no one found him, he'd just rot away and get eaten by the little crabs. Or maybe by the big fuckers, when the king tides were on. And by then, the clothes would be all rotted and the bones would get washed away and he'd just disappear. Nothing left there at all. And no one would ever know what happened to him. And he liked that idea the best. To just disappear. Off the face of the earth.

Then the bank could do what they liked with the property. Fuck the bank anyway. And fuck the real estate agent. And fuck that developer. And fuck that bloke and his stupid fucking boat. If it wasn't for him, everything would have all worked out. It was a good plan. It would have all worked out. A record number of joints were rolled up and smoked, during this extended thought bubble, you know.

But sometimes things work out and sometimes they don't. That was a well-known thing by now. But then another idea came. There was a heap of rope in the carport. Heavy rope. Bundled up in one corner. No one wanted to buy it. And the carport was put together with big beams. So, the idea was to hang himself from one of these beams.

Frank dragged the rope out. Made the noose up on one end and climbed up on a bench and put it over one of the beams. Got an old box to stand on. Set it at the right height. Tied the rope off, to another beam. Back on the box. Put the noose around his neck.

Right. Here we go. The excitement was there again, alright. But this was a different kind of excitement. The excitement of finishing this miserable life. Once and for all. Should have done it years ago. So, here's Frank up on the box, staring at the ground. Ready for the end of it all. Just busting to get it over and done with. The pain and misery of just being alive. Yeah. The end couldn't come quick enough. But then the thought about a suicide note entered the thinking. People always left a suicide note, didn't they? So, the noose came back off and it was back inside the shack for a good thinking session.

Smoked a few more joints and thought about what to write in the suicide note. And this proved to be a difficult thing to do, you know. No words were coming. Only tiredness was coming. And then sleep. And it was many hours later, before the need for a piss woke him up. And the munchies were there again, demanding to be satisfied.

And while standing there pissing on some ants, is when the noose was noticed. Hanging there. Silently ominous. And it was slowly remembered what was in the head, earlier in the day. But that was earlier in the day and now the deep-seated desire for self-harm wasn't so great. So, it didn't happen. But the rope could stay there. Just in case the attitude took a turn for the worst. And that was a known possibility.

Frank just loved pissing on the ants, you know. Ever since the toilet stopped flushing properly. When the button got pushed, the flush happened, alright. But the refill water wouldn't stop refilling and spilt out all over the floor. So, that put an end to using the toilet. Shitting wasn't a real problem. Just required a walk over to the mangroves, with a roll of toilet paper. And sometimes an umbrella.

The next few months were a complete fucking nightmare. An unnecessary nightmare. If the realisation about money in the bank account, came to the surface. More thousands had been deposited. But if that realisation did surface, several other nightmares would have surfaced to replace the existing nightmare. So, one nightmare was far better than several other nightmares. That's for sure.

More and more trips were taken into the mangroves. Either to catch big fuckers, or try to. There was a bit too much fumbling going on now. And the concentration just wasn't there anymore. Looking for thongs, even became too much of an effort. So, it was just aimlessly wandering through the stinking mud, with not much or no thinking happening. Took many hours of every day. But always smoking a joint. And places were sometimes identified as good to set up the rope. And end up dangling down beside the trunk of a mangrove tree.

Yeah. A few more months passed by, before the developer started showing some real interest. The phone calls began. And every now and then, one got answered. And this new development, caused a major shift in the attitude. But there're a cagey lot, these developers. Especially when they know, there's no way anyone else was going to get sucked into buying the place. Not for the outrageous asking price anyway.

The estate agent kept dropping hints about reducing the price. But was told, that wasn't going to happen. Because another potential buyer had come on the scene. Some guy from England, turned up one day. Just got divorced. Wanted a new life in Australia. Had plenty of money as well. Or, so he said. Called in a few times. But not to the real estate agent. Wanted to pay cash, without any agents involved. Said he'd pay the legal fees as well. And he'd pay the full asking price. No problem. The guy was a God send, alright.

So, after much internal discussion, there was a phone call made to the agent. He got really pissed off, when he heard that bit of news. That's for sure. He didn't say he was pissed off or anything. But he was pissed off, alright. Tell that by the way he was talking. No more Mr Nice Guy. Raised his voice a bit too. Even became a bit aggressive.

There was no way of understanding anything of what he said either. The whole system just shut down immediately, if someone started raising their voice or getting aggressive. Simple as that.

But there's always a catch isn't there. This guy, wanted to turn the place into a fish farm. But he had to get a positive feeling from the council. About the chances of that happening. But that didn't happen. The poor bloke was devastated. Had everything worked out. Even had plans drawn up. The last time he turned up had tears in his eyes and apologised for all the inconvenience he'd caused. Never saw him again after that. So, another phone call was made.

"That English blokes gone. The council won't say he can do the fish farm. So, now that developer can have it."

There was dead quietness, on the other end of the phone. For a good few seconds.

"Oh, I see! Well, that's unfortunate, Frank! You'll have to leave it with me! I'll be in touch, if there's any further interest from anyone. You may have to consider dropping the price. Substantially!"

Then the phone went dead. Didn't like the way he said substantially either. Came across as a bit of a smart arse. But he had the upper hand now. And he knew it, alright. Fucking hell. There was an immediate turn for the worst. And the rope came back into the equation again. Time for another session on the Acapulco Gold and a long walk through the mangroves.

A few more months passed. The agent had contacted a few times. Dropping the same hint about lowering the price. Another letter from the bank. The final warning. The last final warning. The very last final warning. Just about to do, what banks often do. They'd heard enough bullshit already. Time had finally run out. There was nothing good happening at all. There was even consideration about altering the plan now as well. Yeah. Lowering the price. The panic stations were approaching fast. Well, they were already there, weren't they?

And the attacks of paranoia, just wouldn't go away. The rope was still hanging there, you know. Still offering, what seemed like the best solution. Yeah. The one solution to solve all the mounting problems. At the one time. Just a little step and crack. All over. And it was considered many times. Depending, on how much pot had been smoked and what time of the day it was.

But the idea of that suicide note was still the cause of much consideration and confusion. So, every time the decision was made, to finally end it all. Another decision was made to, not do it. Not until the suicide note problem was taken care of.

Yeah. Panic and paranoia had set in, at the same time. Like a gluey slime pit in there. With no one showing interest in buying the property. The bank breathing down his neck. No money, or so he thought. Dopey bastard, still hadn't woken up to that situation. Credit card maxed out. Nothing more to sell for cash. No petrol in the car. No takeaway. The big fuckers had gone off the bite. Freezer was empty. Smoking joints all day, didn't help either. The munchies were a constant pain in the guts. And all those thawed out frozen fish had given him a pain in the guts already. He was fucked, alright.

And when the limits of all endurance finally peak, it can only mean one thing. A very bad result. There was a major blowout on the way and there was nothing Frank could do to stop it. So, the suicide note started getting more thought put into it. And after days of constant agony about using all the right words, it was finally completed.

'To whoever finds this lifeless dangling body first. Please forgive me for the inconvenience, but I've had enough of this fucked up world. And now there's no hope left. Not for me anyway. Everything I do never works out. No one cares and I don't care either. Not anymore anyway. I've got nothing left. I'm starving hungry. Flat broke. The cars out of petrol and the bank's taking my house. So, I might as well be dead. And I don't give a fuck what happens now. Sincerely, Frank.'

Yeah. The feelings were all in the right order now. So, when the next time came to get up for a piss, the suicide note idea was no longer a problem. All the words had been written down on a piece of paper. And would be left in a place, where someone was sure to find it.

Maybe nailed to the post. At the same level, where the head would end up. Or a little higher. Yeah. That was the plan, about ending it all. And this was a good plan. The best plan in relation to letting everyone know just how pissed off he'd been. All his fucking miserable life. And no one gave a fuck. Didn't really want to be eaten by crabs either, you know. Or the big fuckers.

But you wouldn't believe it. Something extraordinary had happened. That wasn't known about yet. Everything had just suddenly fallen into place. Several days before this end-of-life decision had been made. The biggest decision that had ever been made and all for nothing. And all the agonising over what to write in the suicide note. All for nothing.

Luckily, another series of short delays in the thinking happened. Every time Frank was on the way to the rope. For the final act. It was back inside for another final joint and then usually back under the covers. For a little rest. And maybe a little thinking about the suicide note. And maybe how the words could be changed around a bit. Or a bit taken out or, maybe a bit more put in.

But some things are just not meant to happen are they. And some things are. Simple as that. But it still had to be explained a few times, before it became clear enough to fully understand, what did happen.

Bang! Bang! Bang! Bang!

What the fuuuuck.

Bang! Bang! Bang! Bang!

Yeah. There's someone banging on the fuuuucking door. Probably them fucking Jehovah's Witnesses again!

"Fuuuuck oooffffff!"

Bang! Bang! Bang! Bang!

"Frank! Frank! Wake up Frank! I've got some good news!"

Yeah. It was the real estate agent, alright. Couldn't understand a word of what was said. But figured he'd recognised the voice.

"What the fuck do you want?"

"I've been trying to reach you for days, Frank! The phone wasn't getting answered. So, I thought I'd drop in! There's good news, Frank! Very good news!"

Yeah. Yelling his fucking head off. But when the words, *good news*, finally sunk in, is when the movement started under the covers. Took five minutes to open the door.

But the thinking was still a bit scrambled, you know. It was probably someone from the bank anyway. Pretending to be a real estate agent. There wasn't any interest in talking to anyone from the bank was there. There're all rotten, miserable, lying cunning bastards anyway. And there wasn't any interest in talking to anyone anyway. No matter who they were. But he was up now, so the door got opened.

But the thinking was still under the covers. In dream land. He was out walking around in the mangroves. Smoking a joint and looking for thongs. Or maybe trying to catch a big fucker. And always casting a quick eye back over towards the rope. And that thought was always in there and then not in there and then in there again. And there was something about a suicide note coming to the surface. And that remained the dominant thought till the door got opened.

He did catch the odd mud crab, you know. The only food that was available, for several weeks. And they tasted good to. And he didn't lose any fingers. Had to dig the rotting fish heads out of the garbage, to use for bait.

And if he was inside, he was usually out to it. Didn't, even hear the phone. And wouldn't have answered it anyway. But he sure did hear the bangs on the door.

So, the mostly still asleep, miserable looking, half-starved, scruffy occupant, opened up and stared out. Blinking away. Trying to adjust the eyes to the light. But the focus wasn't the best. And he'd already forgot it was the real estate agent.

"What the fuck do you want?"

Didn't get many visitors. Didn't want any visitors. Especially now. The real estate agent, immediately took a backward step. But got over the shock greeting soon enough. And what he was looking at as well. Because an absolute horror show of a human was standing there, right in front of him. The conversation went something like this.

"Hello, Frank! I've been trying to get in touch for a few days. Got some good news! The developer is still complaining about having to pay tomorrow's price. But he's decided to pay the asking price anyway! The full amount, Frank! So, that's a bit of good news!"

"Yeah. Yeah. Good news. What was that again?"

Pretty much the same thing was repeated again. From got some good news. Frank was kind of half-awake by now. And it finally became clear. It was the real estate agent.

"So, it's sold then?"

The agent raised his voice a little.

"Yes! That's right, Frank! It's sold! For the full asking price! Congratulations!"

"Yeah. Yeah, thanks. So, did you say the full asking price?"

The agent raised his voice a little more. Frank didn't like it much when people raised their voice. But he just knew by now, that something good had happened. So, he had to suffer it. For just a little while longer.

"Yes! The full asking price, Frank! He's still complaining about paying tomorrow's price! But he's still going to buy the property! For the full amount!"

He was almost fully awake by now. Enough to understand the significance of what he'd just been told.

"So, it's sold then!"

"Yes Frank! It's sold! Congratulations!"

"Well, I'll be fucked!"

Yeah. Fully awake now.

Good news. He must be fucking joking. Just saved the poor old bastards life and didn't even know it. Things moved along quickly from there. Was like a dream come true. The big jackpot was on its way. Yeah. Brightened right up by now. The stubborn patience had finally paid off. And just in time. And the thought about some suicide note. What was that all about, anyway.

"Couldn't lend me a twenty, could you? I'll pay you back! Need petrol for the car!"

What a nerve, eh. But he did need petrol for the car. So, it was no bullshit. But the agent got this funny look on his face, didn't he?

"I tell you what, Frank! I was going to stop for petrol on the way back. I've got a jerry can in the boot! How about I go and fill my car up and the jerry can. And then I'll come back and get you started!"

"Okay. Sure. Thanks."

What a great real estate agent. And that's exactly what happened. But he would have preferred the twenty bucks. The Gerry can gets emptied. The car gets started up, then turned off. All ready to go there. And during all the talking, there was always a step or two taken towards the agent, you know. The excitement of it all had taken over. And the agent was always taking a step or two further away as he was talking. But that wasn't thought about at the time.

The agent didn't muck around, putting the Gerry can back in the boot and starting his own car up either, you know. He just wanted to be gone now. But managed a few words, out the driver's side window.

"Frank! Don't forget to drop in as soon as you can. There's, a few things to sign. And you'll need to sign a few things at your solicitors as well."

The agent just couldn't control his excitement. You'd swear it was his property that just got sold.

"Yeah, right! I'll do that!"

"It took a while, Frank! But we got it sold for you! And for the full asking price! Congratulations, Frank! Congratulations!"

And that was that. Off he went. But you know what. On the way to the car, he did take a quick look at the rope a few times. Silently dangling there. Grabbed his attention, alright. Took the big smile off his face as well.

"That's just there to frighten them Jehovah's Witnesses away! That's all that's for!"

Blurted that out, straight after the agent's third look at the rope. While taking the short walk to his car. And he was taking big strides too, not steps. But the rope was of no more interest, you know. And within a few minutes, there was a phone call to the bank. And didn't that create a feeling of great satisfaction. And relief.

Wasn't till the next day, after all this new information was absorbed fully, that the decision was made to get going. And there hadn't been a minute of sleep either. There was a continual surge of positive energy. Rising up from the deepest depths of depression, paranoia and total defeat.

There were things to be done. Big things. Like a new car. New clothes. New everything. Maybe a few trips overseas. Always wanted to do that. Yeah. Plenty of joints got lit up. Lots of plans were made. The head was spinning right out. And the munchies were in full attack mode.

After getting cleaned up, paid a visit to the real estate agent and the solicitors. Signed whatever had to be signed. Went to the bank. Figured there could be something in there by now. What a shock it was. There'd been lots of fortnightly deposits. That amounted to several months-worth of bingeing. Just couldn't believe that.

"What the fuck's going on here! Is this a mistake?"

The bank teller, didn't like being spoken to like that either. But she checked it out.

"There's been no mistake, sir! That's the correct amount!"

"Well, I'll be fucked!"

So, the maxed-out credit card gets topped back up to the full limit. Couldn't remember the last time that'd ever happened. Took several thousand out of the equation. And then it only took a few seconds, to make the next big decision. Withdraw every dollar of what was left. Bucket loads more coming soon. No worries there. Then straight to the nearest takeaway.

Two Hamburgers, chips, a large bottle of coke and a packet of smokes and a lighter. The munchies settled right down after all that was scoffed down. Fully pumped up and ready to go. Lit up a smoke and straight to the nearest pub. Just a few hundred metres down the road. Couldn't be helped. The head was pumping. The legs were in overdrive. And there was already a fifty, curled up in the right hand.

Just busting to start pushing that repeat bet button again. It'd been a while. Too long. The cravings had taken over, alright. Here we go again. Wallet was almost empty, before the big win came. $1800. There was a rupture in the thinking then. Frank knew what had to be done, alright. Straight away. And it took a lot of courage and determination to pull out at this stage. That's for sure. But it had to be done. Before it was too late. It's amazing what influence a little experience has on the thought processes, you know.

Filled the car up. Half a dozen cartons of beer. Half a dozen bottles of all the favourite hard stuff. And some extra bottles of the most favourite ones. Like Southern Comfort, Vodka, Drambuie and Bourbon. Enough canned food, to last at least a few months. Few dozen packets of smokes, all kinds of biscuits and a half a dozen cartons of coke. The car was loaded up all right.

This new episode all started around ten or eleven in the morning, you know. By around five that afternoon, broke again. Fucking hell. Shouldn't have started up again. Still had some fifties left. Should have called it a day. Quit while you're ahead. Have another crack tomorrow. Should have known better. Should have.

Should have. Should have. Didn't even stop to think. You fucking dickhead. You've done it again.

So, here's the developed situation. A bucket load of available funds. Overflowing excitement and enthusiasm. And some smart thinking to go with it. Yeah. A belly full of takeaway. A car full of supplies. Tank full of petrol. But somewhere in there, the back on the button thing happened again. Like an automatic part of the programme. Loaded up with fifties one minute and then flat broke the next. Fucking idiot.

Yeah. Should have stopped, when there was a wallet full. But super Frank had been released again and had a great time. Till the funds completely dried up. And then fucked off again. Like what always happened. Leaving the poor, stupid bastard wandering around in misery land. With the internal cursing happening. And the deep depression closing in.

Fucking hell. It's happened again. You idiot. You fucking idiot. But at least a little forward thinking had happened earlier and the car was loaded right up. So yeah. Back to the shack. A few beers. A bottle of the good stuff. Couple of joints. Relax. A few coffees and a packet of biscuits. Bit of a rest. But no. No rest. That's just not how it works. Once the lunatic gets out with a wallet full, there's no stopping him. The mind goes blank. The damage gets done. And cleaning up the mess, usually takes around two weeks. Yeah. What a fucking nightmare.

A few days went by. Well, some days went by. Could have been two or three. Maybe a week. There was no condition there, to count anything. Not even empty beer cans or bottles or roaches. Mind was in no function mode. Frank was just sitting there, munching away on a piece of toast. With a thick coating of butter and vegemite and a slice of cheese. One of the most favourite breakfast foods. Along with a few good strong coffees. With three sugars.

That's when the clearer thinking started, you know. About what the fuck just happened, over the last few days. Or however long it was.

Yeah. That's right. The phone call came. Cheque was ready to be collected. That got things moving in the brain again. The uplift in enthusiasm, that was badly needed. But, after years of experience, it was also a known thing. That driving a car, after days of boozing and smoking pot was never a good idea. So, the trip to pick up the cheque would have to wait till the next day. And this realisation was very difficult to accept. It was decided many times. Take the risk. Go right now. Cash the cheque and get back into it. But the most sensible decision, won out in the end.

But there was restlessness going on. No peace at all. Agitation had taken over. So, there was a long walk needed and that's what happened. Through the mangroves. Looking for thongs. Looking for crab holes. Big enough for a big fucker to hide in. But mostly just slogging it out through the mud. With big dreams in the thinking. About a big fat cheque and what could be got with it.

From this point on the programme gets a little hazy, you know. Sleep, waking up, getting up, coffee, breakfast. Must have all happened. But not much recollection was happening at all. From the solicitor's office to the footpath was like an out of world, floating experience, you know.

But, to cut a long story short. Here's Frank, standing in the middle of the footpath. Staring at a cheque for several hundred thousand dollars. There were lots of possibilities, coming slowly. Then they all started bouncing into one another. And then the shitting himself feeling won out in the end. The knowledge was there. That if something smart wasn't done with the cheque and quickly, something terrible would eventually happen. Like going broke. In a very short period of time.

Headed straight for the bank. Yeah. You guessed it. The same bank, that was sending all the nasty letters. Six-month term deposit. With a fee if taken out early. The heavy burden was lifted. This was well before the days of Gamblers Anonymous. Although, there was already a stack of GA cards. Kind of collected them, you know.

Yeah. The poker machines would have copped a hiding. And the big jackpot would have soon evaporated. So, what was done with the cheque, just had to be done. Smartest thing, that had ever been done. Besides answering that phone. That no one else would answer. And answering that one phone call, changed the whole life. In many different ways. Could very well have saved the whole life as well.

The one thing, that was left out of the calculations. Was once the property was sold and the time came for moving out. Homelessness was the result. Hadn't even thought about that. Luckily there was a member of the family, who'd just been divorced. Had three kids. Worked shift work. Needed a babysitter, every second week. And some board money would come in handy as well. So, the deal was done.

There were lots of people getting divorced, you know. And this realisation was always drifting around. And so, another negative thought was forever lodged in the dark shadows. Never, ever get married. Whatever you do. Just don't get married. And Frank never did.

But these baby-sitting times were good times, you know. While they lasted. And they lasted about six months. And the kids didn't need to know, about their babysitter being off his face or too pissed or hung over, to think straight, most of the time. They were only kids after all. But they were good kids and still are. And with kids of their own as well.

Frank was always good at pretending, you know. About being completely sober. And straight. Knew what was going on, alright. Could fool anyone, as far as all that was concerned. Even himself. But all good things come to an end as they say. And after scanning the real estate market for a few months, a suitable house was spotted. In one of the better suburbs. With views all over the city. The asking price on this property had been lowered three times. And that's what caught the attention in the first place.

Anyway, an even lower price was offered. In cash. And although the real estate agent said there was no chance of the offer being accepted. It was accepted. So much for real estate agents, knowing what's going on. They obviously didn't know anything about plans. Not the ones thought up, by someone who thought up plans. That had never been thought up before. They had no idea. And so, a new chapter began. From the swamp, to the city heights. And now, that was the new favourite saying.

"There you go, Frank! Frank! Frank! Wake up Frank!"

"What! What did you say?"

"You were a long way away then, Frank! Where were you?"

"Uh! Well! Um! I was just thinking about how much I like all you girls here!"

Didn't even mean to say that. The thinking was obviously all mixed up. Should have woken up completely before saying anything. This girl almost busted out of herself, when she heard it.

"We all like you too, Frank!"

Then she turned around really quick, took off and disappeared out the back.

It was one of the upstairs girls. Only seen her around a few times. Didn't even know her name. Or her real name. That could by why she got brave enough to say what was said in the first place. But the extra big café girl smile was there. The eyebrows went up a little. And her eyes were just overflowing, with that warm and kindliness look. That he was already so used to. And addicted to as well. The thought was there, to say something back. But she was gone so quick, you know. Not enough time to say anything. The focus hadn't readjusted enough yet anyway.

And when it did, there were at least three of them behind the counter. All with their backs showing. Having another one their little girly sessions. There was no giggling either. Oh good, lunch. Sitting right there in the middle of the table.

"Hi Frank! There're a good crew here, aren't they?"

NG2. Where the hell, did she come from.

"Yes, they sure are! I already know that!

And he already knew there were no secrets between them as well. And the words would have kept coming too. And he would have let her know, that he knew all about how they operated. As a crew. That's for sure. Just in the mood now. But she was already half way back to the counter. Too slow again.

There're going to have a lot of fun with you.

Yeah. Yeah. Yeah. Knew all about that.

The place was almost empty, when he left. No girls anywhere. It was like that sometimes. And dead quiet as well. And it was missed when the, see you later Frank bit wasn't heard on the way out of the place.

There're going to have a lot of fun with you.

Back in the car and heading home, for an afternoon nap. There was still no remembering about where all the music and videos came from either. Someone came around with them. But there wasn't much contact anymore. And it happened in the old life. So, it was okay to forget about it altogether. And that's what happened. They were rediscovered during the house cleanouts. And that's all that mattered.

One of the greatest thrills now was stopping at traffic lights. Music blasting away. Mostly the windows in the other cars, went up straight away. But lots of other drivers would start tapping their steering wheel. Other times, an arm would come out the open window and a hand would start tapping the side of the car. Or reach up and start tapping the roof. There was always a big smile, when other drivers appreciated the music choices. Usually, rock and roll stuff. There were also some really filthy looks, of course. But there was no caring about that. It kept the lady away. So, what else was there to care about.

Yeah, the lady never showed up, when the music was up loud. Knew how to get rid of her, alright. Only thing that ever worked. It was often when driving around when she turned up, you know. But this was his way of winning. The only way of winning. But it didn't last long. Eventually, she worked out her own strategy. And it was in between discs, when she managed to pop in. Now she was winning again. It wasn't fair. But there was nothing to be done about it. Nothing at all. And he knew it.

The café girls were just as bad. Interrupted the thinking, whenever they felt like it. By now, it was beyond doubt how they were all working together. What the hell was going on anyway. Still hadn't worked it all out. Why can't people just leave him alone. Just leave him alone. But they didn't leave him alone. And he was kind of happy about that and kind of unhappy as well. But more-happy than unhappy. So, it was all good with the café girls.

It was always all good, with the café girls. Especially when any of them, interrupted the thinking. And they could interrupt the thinking whenever they liked, which they did anyway. That's just the way it was now in the magic café and was fully accepted and appreciated.

But the lady, you know. That was another story. She always pissed him off. Even when what she said, made sense. She never let him work out anything for himself. Advice, advice, advice. That's all he ever got from her. And she never gave up either. There was no getting rid of her. Ever.

Even blocking her out with the music, didn't work. She even figured out a way around that. Sneaking in between discs. When he was just cruising along, relaxing. Ambushed him. Every time. She just couldn't be stopped.

"Frank, I've been trying to reach you for days now! But with all that terrible noise! I just couldn't get through! Is everything, alright!"

Of course, everything was, alright. Up till right now.

"Look how far you've come, Frank! The girls care about you! They really do care! They just want to get to know you, Frank! Get to know the real Frank! Go with it, Frank! You're doing so well! Don't ruin everything now! Relax and enjoy the ride! You need to try harder, Frank! You really do!"

So, what ride was she talking about. Not the one in the car. That's for sure. Not anymore anyway. Anyway, he was going with it now. All of it. Didn't understand all of it. But what was there to do but just go with it. Or, maybe go to another café. But that was never going to happen. Because there was no other café, like the magic café.

There're going to have a lot of fun with you.

Yeah. The understanding was fully there now. About fun. So that comment was no bother anymore. Maybe that compulsive wasn't such a big smart arse after all. Maybe he was on Frank's side as well. Just wanting to get to know him. The real him. Maybe. But he was one of them spies for sure. And the spies were everywhere. But they were never going to win. Ever.

To be able to look upon the world and his own existence in a positive way. Was something Frank was never able to do before. For whatever number of reasons. But reasons weren't important now. There was only one thing that was important. The only thing that really mattered. And that was that Frank knew about happy. Yes, he was happy for the first time, that he could ever remember. But not from the old life. There was no happiness in the old life. None at all. No. Full of misery that one. No remembering was even necessary.

Yeah well, he was never happy in the old life. That's just the way it was. So, this is only the new life we're talking about here. And it was all because of a lady who was never there. And a bunch of girls in the magic café. They took a sympathetic liking to an old has been. Taught him many things. About living. Took him under their wing and nursed him back to psychological health. Well, not actually nursed back into health. But nursed into health. A place never experienced before. A place never known about. A place that never even existed.

But the knowing of being there was appreciated now. And the compelling feeling to thank all the girls in the magic café was always there as well. One by one. But when he walked up to the counter, nothing was ever said in the way of a thank you. Or anything like appreciation. But there was a big smile for all of them now and some conversation. So, that was a big improvement. And there was always a little burst of internal warmth, whenever he heard the words; it's good to see you, Frank. And so, what are you having today.

Well, you know, Frank always became a little overwhelmed and a little embarrassed. And yes, emotional when he was at the counter. He thought he was over all the emotional stuff. But that was before he decided to thank them all. That was another ballgame altogether. An advanced level of the same ballgame and he wasn't quite there yet. And he knew it.

So, he kind of forgot about thanking them. For everything. The realisation was only just hitting. About what the life was before discovering the magic café and what the life was now. He owed these girls so much. And the gratitude was there. But expressing that to them. Well, that's when the emotional attacks really started. The emotional attacks he'd suffered all through the old life. And now they were in the new life as well.

"Oh finally!"

"What! What finally! What have I done wrong now?"

He hadn't spoken to himself for a while now, you know. And he'd forgotten to put a disc in as well. So, it was his own stupid fault, that she was into him again.

"Sorry Frank! Nothing! You've done nothing wrong! It's just that it's taken so long! But I knew you'd get there in the end! I've always had great confidence in you, Frank! I was never going to give up on you!"

What the hell, did she expect anyway. He was doing the best he could. And if she thinks this is the end. Well, what a big surprise she's got coming. Anyway, she wasn't needed anymore anyway. Things were all under control in the new life now. So, she can go to hell. Find someone else to get stuck into.

Look how far you've come. Look how far you've come. Sick to death of hearing that all the time. She'd only ever been a pain in the arse, anyway. Better off without her. And she was sounding so desperate too, you know. Couldn't help but notice the desperation in her voice now. Not the calm in control lady he'd become so used to. There was something going on, alright. That's for sure.

There was still a bit of fight left in the old dog yet, you know. Yeah. In the old dog, maybe. But in the new life. There's a young pup, bounding around everywhere. Well, it thinks it's a young pup. And the only bounding around it does, is between its ears. But try telling it that. But Frank was still only in learning mode, you know. So, there were excuses available. And he was getting smarter all the time. Just very slowly. Then the volume went up to full blast.

Even going to the café in the first place was kind of not even Frank's decision anyway. After swimming, the hunger always took over. But the thought about the café, so close to the baths. Too expensive. No, never entered the serious thinking at all. And quite often, walking straight past the front entrance happened. On the way back to the car. There was plenty of cheap cafes around. So why go in there.

But there was some kind of attraction to the place. Hard to explain. But it was there. It was always there, every time he got anywhere near the place. And it got stronger and stronger. After fighting it off for several months, is when it happened. Frank, found himself at the counter. Not even remembering walking into the place. And here he was ordering lunch. There was a special on and it was vegetarian. So that was his first meal at the magic café.

There was a constant thought process happening now. Of wondering who these girls really were. Maybe this wasn't even a real café anyway. But lots of other people went there as well. So, it must be a real café. Maybe there're all in on it. All members of some secret organisation. No, that couldn't possibly be right could it. Couldn't all be in on it, could they? Couldn't all be spies. Or, maybe they could.

But there was always that something there, that couldn't be fully explained. And the lady never said anything about that. About the café. She said lots of other things. About the girls and how wonderful they all were and everything. But nothing about the actual café. That always drew him back. Like a moth to a flame. Yes, there was something about the magic café, alright. Just another problem that couldn't be solved.

Why was this one old, half dead, compulsive addict selected as the chosen one anyway. The one to have such gentle kindness sprinkled down upon him. The one to have feelings put into the worn-out old heart. Yeah, these café girls got stuck into him. Right from that very first visit. Killing him, with their caring kindness. Except for you know who.

And there was another constant thought. About them being aliens. Yeah, they must be aliens. From some distant galaxy. That could be it, you know. Disguising themselves as hard working, very friendly café workers. Yes, that had to be it. And Frank had to be one of them. Well, not a café girl.

Just a long-lost alien. That would explain why the lady who wasn't there, appeared in the hospital in the first place. To retrieve this way-wood fool. Return him to where he belonged. Or maybe just add him in. Make him an unwilling member of some secret alien race. That he was now willing to become a member of. Without even really knowing why. Yes, that would explain everything.

But then again, science fiction movies were a favourite thing to watch, you know. Anything that wasn't real. So, maybe that's where that idea came from. But there was always a headache on the way, if the thinking about anything went on for too long. Watching the television, may not be such a good idea after all. Or reading the newspapers. And maybe all those discs, that mysteriously appeared. That'd probably been listened to or watched too many times. Should be thrown out. With the rest of the garbage.

In her dying days. Frank got to know his mother. She told him stuff about her early life.

"Got home from school. There was a big black car parked at the front of the house!"

"This lady came up to us."

"Your mother's dead so you all have to come with us."

Why these thoughts were in there again, just didn't make any sense. But then the thinking, arrived at another conclusion. There was a lady in his mother's life as well. And things didn't turn out too well for her either. So, maybe this is the same lady. Like a family ghost. That just turned up and caused all kinds of confusion in the head. That was an explanation worth considering too, you know. Before the headaches started again. But the thinking kept going anyway.

They all ended up in some orphanage somewhere. But maybe it wasn't really an orphanage. Maybe it was a spaceship or something. Three of them were fostered out. But even the family researcher, didn't know too much about all that. Two brothers didn't realise they were in the same orphanage, until they accidentally bumped into each other one day.

But maybe that was no accident. And how come they recognised each other straight away, anyway. That wouldn't have happened. Not like that. There was something funny going on there.

Mum was always treated more like a slave. Doing house work and all the other dirty little jobs around the house.

One brother visited the family home after several years. Got in contact out of the blue one day. Dropped in for an emotional reunion and then just disappeared again. But he may not have even been there in the first place.

"Frank! Frank! You're doing it again!"

There must be something wrong with this disc. It's like there's two songs playing together.

"Frank! Frank! Stop it! Stop it! You're doing it again! Listen to me Frank! Frank! Frank!"

Oh, for fucks sake. There was no choice. Just had to listen.

"What! What am I doing again!"

Knew it was her, alright.

"Daydreaming, Frank! You're daydreaming! You need to stop that! There's no point trying to remember everything that happened all the time! There's nothing that can be done about all that now! What happened, happened! You can't change anything! You have a new life now! Relax and enjoy it! Don't keep going back over things, that you can't do anything about! And please, Frank! Stop using that terrible word!"

She was losing the plot now, alright. That's for sure. Maybe she could do with a new life herself. Anyway, there was another bible story starting up now. From one nightmare. Straight into another one.

Many compulsive gamblers in the early days of their recovery, through looking back over their past life. Burden themselves with guilt and remorse, about money they have lost. Opportunities they have missed. Or lack of progress at work.

Well, who'd ever cared about the lack of any progress at work. Fuck work anyway. Only people who work, are the people who have to work.

Our experience has shown that if we are to recover, these things must be left in the past and we must move on. Guilt and remorse, can cripple us. They are close to self-pity. We must strive to replace them with the acceptance of responsibility.

To sum up, our experience has shown us that if we care to embark on a new life, free from gambling and all the problems and misery that gambling generates, then we must close the book on the life we are leaving behind.

There was a kind of mental block thing happening here now, you know. There was a voice there, alright. And it was the lady. But it wasn't the lady now. Well, it was the lady first. But she's not there anymore. Gone. And thank God for that. But there was another voice in there. Just what wasn't needed right now. Two voices to deal with. Getting louder and louder. Well, one was. The other one could have been the controller. And now there was another one. But it was the music disc. So, everything was okay again.

Met another brother. And nephews and nieces. Learnt a little of what happened to everyone.

Mother was stunted emotionally. Never given chance to blossom.

Shirt lifters, mate. Fucking poofters.

This guy was even older than Frank. Another warped up old druggist and alcoholic. Fucking carpet chewers, mate. Girls with girls and boys with boys. The worlds going fucking crazy, with all this shit.

Then a voice started yelling so loud, it just had to be listened to. More than the other one. The music one. Or the other one. There was just no ignoring it any longer.

"Frank! Frank! You're doing it again! Stop it! Just stop it! The old life's gone now! Let it go, Frank! Just let it all go! And please, stop using that terrible word,

Frank! You're so much better than that now! You really are! Get your act together, Frank! Please, just get your act together!"

Yeah. Should have known. She's back again. Heard that, alright. She's not letting go of this one either. That's for sure. But this wasn't the old life where're talking about here. There were no carpet chewers and shirt lifters in the old life. Just poofters and lesbians. She should know that. But yeah. Suppose the thinking lost it there for a while. Getting a little carried away. Listening to music can do that, you know. Especially, when it's up full blast. But she was winning again, damn it.

"Why do you always have to be right anyway?"

But there was no point waiting for an answer either. She never answers any questions, you know. Well, sometimes she does. But most of the time she doesn't. And she was getting more spun out all the time now. She was losing it, alright. Maybe he was winning after all. And maybe that's why she was losing it. Yeah. That had to be it.

Anyway, it's always easy for her to say, forget about the old life. Just like that. If it was that easy, it would have already happened by now wouldn't it. She mustn't even have an old life. Otherwise, she'd understand about memories and how they won't go away. Especially the ones you don't want to remember. But it's worse trying to remember the ones you do want to remember. When you can't remember them. And what's even worse than that, is when they both get mixed up. And that causes another kind of confusion altogether. Another recurring nightmare to put up with. Well, something had to do done about this situation.

"I want my old life back! Just give me back my old life back! You had no right taking my life off me! I want it back! Give me back my old life!"

And this was yelled out so loud. Lucky he wasn't stopped at the traffic lights or anything.

"Oh Frank! Settle down! It's, not that bad! Really! It's not that bad! You're just going through a difficult adjustment period! That's all! Relax, Frank! Just relax! Everything will be just fine! You'll see! It'll all work out in the end! You must try a little harder, Frank! Try and be a little more resilient!"

She just doesn't understand anything does she. Should have never changed the disc. But the concentration had gone out the window.

Anyway, if they went walking around like that, why didn't anyone have the right to look at them and maybe start thinking. What the hell. Imagine what goes on behind closed doors. Just imagine what they get up to. What do these alternative monkeys talk about anyway.

But then again, they were created by the previous generation, weren't they? Wasn't their fault, their heads were all screwed up. Look at how monkeys treat each other anyway. The mum, dad and the kid's business. Better off with no kids at all. Problem solved. But some monkeys need to stick it and some need it stuck. It's as simple as that. They just can't help themselves. Or weren't you supposed to think about stuff like that. It the new life anyway. Yeah. Getting all worked up. That's for sure. This new life's not all it's cracked up to be, eh.

Yeah. Monkeys sticking it here and monkeys sticking it there. Monkeys just sticking it everywhere. What a fucking joke.

"Oh dear! This is dreadful! You're doing it again, Frank! Try just concentrating on yourself, Frank! Your own personal growth and development! And your adjustment to your new life. Don't worry about anyone else. And please! Stop talking about monkeys and what they get up to! And all that other nonsense! Just, do your own thing, Frank! And everything else will fall into place! Don't overthink it all, Frank! Trust me, Frank! I know what I'm talking about!"

"Yeah right! Sure, you do!"

Yeah well, maybe she does and maybe she doesn't. But she doesn't know anything about monkeys and what they get up to. That's for sure. Anyway, home had been reached. Without any unscheduled stops. Relaxation time on the veranda, with a nice strong coffee. But that didn't last very long. The relaxation that is.

"He's not improving at all! Getting worse if anything! You've done your best, dear! You truly have! But there is a limit to our patience!"

"Yes, we have given this one every chance! We should have already let him go! How you managed to talk us into persevering with him, is beyond my understanding! It truly is!"

"Yes, I agree! It's time to let this one go! Nothing more can be done with him! You've done your best, dear! We all know that!"

"No! No! Please! Just a little more time! That's all he needs! Just a little more time! He'll get there! I know he will! I know he can do it! Please, just a little more time!"

"Excuse me, but he's already had more time! More time than any of the others ever had!"

"Yes, that's right! This one's holding up the whole programme! There could have been at least three others on their way by now! Enough, is enough!"

"He's just a slow learner! That's all! He can do it! I know he can! Please! I don't want to fail! Three more weeks! Just three more weeks! That's all I ask! Just three more weeks!"

"Slow learner! He's a complete dunce! A waste of time! Intractable!"

"Well, he can drive one to the edge at times! There's no denying that! But we can't deny the progress that he's made! And he has made significant progress! We can't let him go now! We just can't!"

"Oh! Yes, we can dear! Yes, we can! And we must! This one jeopardises the future of the entire programme! He's wasted enough of your time and ours! Goodness me dear, look what he's done to you! You must let him go! You must! Before he drags you down with him!"

"No. I'll never let him go! I'll never give up on him! I promised him I wouldn't. He believes in me! And I believe in him! I know he can do it. I just know he can! He will get there in the end! He will!"

"Of dear! You've become personally attached! That's, the worst possible development! You should know better than that! To become personally attached! It's the first lesson we all learn! The most critical one! Never become personally attached to an intractable! I'm sorry dear! But you're just not cut out for this rehabilitation programme! And besides, he's end has already come!"

"Ok! That's enough! We can't talk around in circles forever! The decision needs to be made! One way or the other! It's dragged on far too long already! Three more weeks! Or cut him loose!"

"I say cut him loose!"

"I agree! Cut him loose! He's a dead loss!"

"No! No! Please!"

"That's enough, dear! The decision needs to be made now! And that's all there is to it!"

"Oh alright then! Another three weeks! I'll go along with that! What difference can it make now! Although, I do think he's a complete waste of time!"

"I'm looking at it, from a different perspective altogether! There's never been one quite like this before! Not to my knowledge! So, hopeless! So, ignorant! So stubborn! I could go on, but I won't! My point is! We may actually be able to learn something here! To add to our already comprehensive database! Regarding complete failures!"

"That's not fair! Just look at how damaged he was at the start! He's come so far! You must all realise that! We can't just abandon him!"

"Of course, we can dear! I think he's taught us all we need to know! You must let him go! It's always hard to let the first one go, dear! We all understand that! And I do sympathise with you! I really do! But you must let him go! You must! You have no choice!"

"No, you're wrong! I won't let him go! I just can't do it to him!"

"Ok! Ok! I, think we've covered everything we need to here! It appears I have the deciding vote! After listening very carefully to what's been said. In favour and against. And taking into consideration your personal attachment dear. Which I totally disagree with! I have made my decision. And this was not an easy decision."

"But I do understand and appreciate, the significance of our comprehensive database. And whatever information that can be added to the knowledge we have already accumulated, could prove very useful for future reference. Especially regarding such unfortunate, irretrievable individuals, as this one has proved to be. If another three weeks can prove productive in this regard, then I believe we have everything to gain and nothing to lose."

"Oh, thank you! Thank you so much!"

"Be careful, dear! He'll end up destroying you, if you're not careful!"

"Yes, be careful dear! Be very careful!"

"I will! I will! He'll make it! You'll see! He'll make it!"

Suddenly, some real heavy thinking started. A spillage of new information. Been building for a few years now. Well, far longer than a few years. A whole lifetime would be more like it. And what was already known about the new lifetime as well. But Frank couldn't take it anymore. Out they came. Don't hoard your thought's Frank. Let them out, Frank. Blah, blah, blah.

Yeah. Out they came. No stopping them. Especially, all the new stuff. Pouring out like a tap.

The hospital. The lady. The exercises. Swimming. Gym. No, to hell with the gym. The magic café. The café girls. And the young fella. Can't leave him out. The smiling faces. The questions. The little memory tests. From vegetarian to vegan. The breakdown in communication blockages. The emotional strengthening. All the subtle hints. The need for less programmed routines. Build-up of self-confidence. In talking to the girls. And the young fella. Belief in himself.

Yeah. Everything an old, reprogrammed reprobate required to evolve into a new individual was now in there. And functioning. Wasn't fully understood yet. But it was all in there. And the multitude of confused feelings were all good. Most of the time anyway. Yeah. Settling into the new rhythm of positive thinking. In the new life.

Probably left a few things out here, you know. But the new memory was never going to be perfect, was it? But the two main things were always there. No more hoarding thoughts. No more head full of secrets. Yes. The main two developmental alterations necessary to adapt and survive in the new life. Without going completely crazy. No. No more going crazy. And what a relief that was.

But the craziness would be missed, you know. Yeah. It would be missed. No doubt about that. The old life was full of all kinds of craziness. And all this craziness was still being remembered and missed. And that's why Frank wanted the old life back. And it's why he didn't want it back at all.

There were other benefits as well, you know. With the new life business. No more grog. No more pot. No more cigarettes. No more bouts of the deep, dark depression. No more visits to any of the black worlds. Well, there was always one with the door slightly open. That's for sure. But the one into the new life was completely open. Well almost. And there was a huge sign. And it said, come on in.

You're welcome. And when he walked in, there was mostly young people in there. And they were all smiling. And they all walked up and gave little cuddles. And whispered short comments into his ears. Like, Hello Frank and It's good to see you.

"That's it, Frank! Now you've getting it! A new world! Full of young people! Who understand where you've come from! And what you've been through! There're your family now, Frank! You belong somewhere! Yes Frank! You finally belong somewhere!"

Yeah. Well. They couldn't possibly know everything, could they? But they were all mind readers, you know. Already knew that. So, they probably did know everything there was to know. But why point out all the negatives. There's a new, positive mind-set happening here now. So why not just go with it.

"Yes, Frank! Yes! Just go with it! Follow your instincts, Frank! Follow your instincts! I knew you were going to make it, Frank! I always knew you were going to make it! Don't let yourself down now, Frank! Please don't let yourself down now! And please! Don't let me down either, Frank! Please don't let me down!"

There was that desperation again. And there was another word she used. So, on went the computer.

Resilient; Strong. Tough. Hardy. Able to withstand or recover quickly from difficult conditions. Babies are generally far more resilient, than new parents realise.

A strong, tough baby. Yeah. That sounds about right.

"Hello, I'm Frank and I'm a compulsive gambler!"

Yeah, all the compulsives introduced themselves, at the start of every meeting. And this time, the controller picked the first page to be read. Sometimes the same pages get read over and over, at just about every meeting and this was often one of them. Maybe the controller's favourite. And this bit was the favourite bit of the favourite page. Under the heading;

Why the Obsession Never leaves.

Try not to make any major decisions concerning your life, for the first two years of sobriety. Unless it is unavoidable. Remember, we are like babies. We need to grow strong, before making any major decisions. That could lead us to disaster and back to gambling.

Lots more reading gets done and then it's time for the break and then the sharing starts. This may already be in here somewhere. More than once. But short-term memory, is a big problem with the compulsives, you know. There's one paragraph in the GA bible, that explains it very well.

Short-Term Memory.

The short-term memory seems to be a characteristic of the compulsive gambler. How many times did we gamble all our money away, suffer the pain of defeat and the pain of reality, only to be lifted to the highest levels of sheer joy, when we laid our hands on more money or had the occasional win. Instantly, our past troubles were forgotten. "This time it will be different." It never is. It always ends with the same result. Misery and pain.

Yeah. Right. Here we go again.

"Hi, I'm Frank and I'm a compulsive gambler!"

"Hey, Frank!"

"Hi, Frank!"

"Hello, Frank!"

"I haven't played poker machines for another week!"

"Hey, that's great, Frank!"

"Well done, Frank!"

"Yeah. I'm just going with it now. Other people don't bother me anymore. And all the shit they come out with. I've come such a long way. So, I can't go and ruin it all now! I'm more resilient! I knew I was going to make it! Anyway, thanks for letting me share!"

All the usual clapping and good wishes were absorbed. Brought all the good feelings to the surface. Every time. There were several more shares and then the usual ending the meeting chants. And then some little conversations here and there. Between certain compulsives, who got along better with some of the other compulsives. Then some of the other compulsives got along with them. And some of the compulsives just said their goodbyes and took off and Frank was one of them.

Back on the veranda. No negative attacks, on the way back. No sudden urges. No pressure from any of the dark shadows. Music blasting away. So, no interruptions from the lady. Yeah. It'd been a good day, alright. And a good night's sleep, came easy enough.

What a great, warm sunny day. No wind. Not even a breeze. Very quiet. Birds flying around. The early morning exercise routine had been completed. Breakfast was over with. Relaxing on the favourite old, sagging, falling apart leather lounge chair. Sipping on another extra strong, extra hot coffee. But, just had to get up and find out.

Retrograde; backward. Backwards. Reverse.

Kind of figured it meant something like that. So, back out to think about it and the implications. The lady wouldn't have used that word, if she didn't have a good reason. Because she never said anything without a good reason.

There's no understanding how this next brainwave happened either. But it was there so, it was back inside to the computer. And the scrolling went down a little further this time.

Dragonfly; Dragon fly as a spiritual guide. The dragon fly enters our life when our joy diminishes or when we start taking things too seriously. They are our reminder to lighten up our thoughts and habits.

Because of their connection to water, dragonflies are tied to our emotional selves. They are the perfect guides to ask questions like;

What emotion is it that I need to explore?

Am I hiding something from myself or others?

Am I using this emotion as a smoke screen for something more important?

Holy shit. This got the lights flickering, alright. And there was some kind of emotional upheaval happening as well. But there was also a need to keep reading.

Call on the guidance of the dragonfly when you are struggling to adapt. The energy it brings will give you flexibility and a fresh perspective. So many of our problems contain an element of not being able to accept our emotions.

They end up overtaking us and stalling our growth. Dragonfly energy is perfect for digging in, embracing and understanding emotions.

If you are stuck in an emotional pattern or just stuck in a temporary rut, give-over to the dragonflies transformational power.

Holy shit. It was all starting to make sense now. All this spiritual garbage. That wasn't garbage. That would never have been understood or accepted in the old life. But it was starting to be now. The tall one, knew what she was doing all right. Should really thank her. Even if it was just to trick him in the first place. And it was a plastic one, that she stuck on the glass. But she was gone now. Just like a lot of the other café girls were gone. And that was always happening, you know. Getting to know the café girls and how they freely gave something special. After they were gone.

There're going to have a lot of fun with you.

But a real invasion of the brain took place, when slogging it out in the pool later that morning. There was no going back was there. No. Not anymore. Not with anything. All the bad habits. All the negative thoughts. All the bad memories. The disappointments. The failures. The emotional eruptions. All gone. Well should be. And will be. Yeah. It was now or never. Crunch time. The big turning-point.

A mountain had been climbed. The choice was a simple one. Drift into the peaceful, green valley on the other side. Or, lose the balance and tumble all the way back down and probable crack the head open, on a rock on the way. And landing with a great thud, at the bottom. Yeah. An easy choice for most people. The old Frank would have struggled terribly with a decision of such magnitude. Well, the mountain wouldn't have been climbed in the first place. Not even attempted. But this new Frank, came with new attitudes. About many things. Including the idea of a better life. A new life, which he now had. And no stuff ups were going to happen. That was the new plan anyway. Yeah. The, new life plan.

But the plan was kind of not completely full right now, was it? Especially without the poker machines in there. Which were still missed terribly. And the cravings were a constant companion. Then another heading from the bible appeared and dominated the thinking.

Filling the void.

The time we spent gambling, is now on our hands and we don't know what to do. Many of us were day gamblers for long hours, and some nights, and some weekends. Some others, only before or after work. To escape worries. But it got out of control and now we have to quit.

Suddenly, we realise how much time was spent on our gambling careers. Not just gambling itself. We spent time worrying about the next time. The next big win. We had so many sleepless nights, worrying about all the lies we told. While thinking about how and when, we were going to do it all again.

As you can see, gambling controlled almost all of our waking hours. Now that we know there is help and we are trying to abstain from gambling, one day at a time, what do we do with all this time? How do we fill the void? There are many ways and things we can do, to put a little balance in our lives. We do need to be careful, because we are compulsive people. Too much of one thing, can be more harmful than good. So, we strive for a balance. Step two of our recovery programme states— "Came to believe in a power greater than ourselves could restore us to a normal way of thinking and living."

Well, it's understandable that a headache was now on the way, after all that remembering. Especially the bit about the power, greater than ourselves. Still knew that was a lot of bullshit. Anyway, an extra four laps had been done. So, now the schedule was out of whack. By about fifteen minutes.

"Hi Frank! Bit late today! What's going on?"

This was the have a little chat girl. But then she moved aside and nice eyes moved in, to take the order. Hadn't seen her for ages.

"Oh hello! I haven't seen you for ages! Not for about two years!"

"And you remembered me!"

"Yeah! It must be the eyes! You've got really nice eyes, you know!"

Yeah. Really just said that. And nice eyes got all flustered. Not him. The emotional control had improved so much by now, you know.

"So, what have you been doing with yourself?"

"Oh, the usual stuff. Exercising! Swimming! Eating properly! Keeping busy! Thinking about lots of things! I really like coming here and talking to you guys! You girls here are the best!"

She was as red as a beetroot by now. The eyes were sparkling. The smile looked wider than her face. And she could hardly even talk. Frank was just standing there looking at her. And then the café girl smile readjusted to normal and she was back. So, down to business.

"So, is it your favourite meal today, Frank?"

"I've got a few favourite meals now! Which one are you talking about!"

That got her by surprise. Yeah. Two can play at their game. But she caught on straight away. There were smiles all around, behind the counter.

"How about the third one!"

"So, which one would that be?"

"Don't tell me you've forgotten, Frank!"

Now there were giggles all round, behind the counter. And the smile on Frank's face, just kept on expanding. It turned into a big smile off. A great moment, alright. Probably the best moment in the magic café, up to this point. That's for sure.

"No, I haven't forgotten! I was just seeing, if you had forgotten!"

And this little fun game would have continued, but there was a little cough coming from behind. And after turning and noticing the line up behind the little cough, the time had come to order and get moving. These café girls can get down to the serious business when they need to, you know.

"Ok, Frank! What will it be then!"

"I'll have a vegan burger and the coffee, thanks!"

"Sure, Frank! Shouldn't be too long! Good to see you again!"

"Yeah. Good to see you too!"

And that was that. Both the smiles were gone. Swiped the card and headed for the favourite table. Which had just become available. So, the luck was there this time. And as usual, the thinking went straight out the window. And straight back to gambling. And all the complications about how to stop playing them poker machines.

"Hi Frank! What are you looking at out there!"

Ok. Here we go again. But interruptions like this were of no concern anymore. Whenever things happen often enough, the getting used to it thing happens. And this was one of those things, that had been gotten used to. So, there was no problem. And he'd never even seen this girl before. Not that could be remembered anyway. Anyway, it was none of her damn business, was it?

"Oh, just the ships! There's, nine coal ships out there! I always count the coal ships!"

Honesty will come into your life, if you let it.

Well, there wasn't time for any honesty was there. She got him by surprise. There were coal ships out there, you know. They just weren't getting counted. Not this time anyway.

"That's interesting! What do you do with yourself after you leave here, Frank? Have you got any hobbies?"

Hobbies. What the fuck are hobbies anyway. Actually, it was a well-known thing what hobbies were. But instant reactions are instant reactions aren't they. There'd never been any time for hobbies. Hobbies were for dickheads, who had nothing better to do with themselves. In their spare time.

"I've never had much time for hobbies."

That was the only honest answer available. There was no way any hobbies were going to enter the new equation. Imagine sitting around building model aeroplanes, or looking through a stamp album. Must be joking.

"I like counting sailing boats and little fishing boats too, you know! When there're out there!"

A change of subject is always a good idea, you know. Especially when you wanted someone to disappear. Like now.

"Yes, there always is!"

And she took a quick look out the window. For about two seconds.

"But what about hobbies, Frank! Do you have any hobbies?"

No. No getting rid of her that easy. Had the bit between the teeth, alright. Going nowhere. Why can't she just piss off and leave him alone. Maybe just make up one. Should, do the trick.

Honesty will come into your life, if you let it.

Ok. Honesty. What a pain in the arse. Honesty, or a big lie. One or the other. Or, maybe just a little lie and kind of half honest. That might work.

"No, I don't have any hobbies. Nothing I do ever works out anyway. So, I just don't do anything!"

And that was the honest truth. Almost.

"Well, I better be getting back upstairs now, Frank! Nice talking to you!"

"Nice talking to you too!"

255

Yeah. Should have known. Another upstairs girl. Have to go up there one day. See how many of the girls who have disappeared are up there. Probably all of them. Frank had well and truly had enough of this upstairs downstairs business by now, you know. They were probably all up there laughing at him anyway.

There're going to have a lot of fun with you.

"Oh Frank! That's not the new life attitude at all! You can do better than that, surely! And besides, you love all the fun you're having with the girls now. Just admit it! Yes Frank, it's time you started admitting lots of things. Instead of just pretending!"

Yeah. Knew she was just having fun with him. Whoever she was. And he knew about pretending as well. Yeah. Maybe it was time to stop pretending. The understanding was there now, you know. About pretending. And there was understanding there as well, about the chances of winning. Getting less and less all the time. There was no doubt about that now. None at all.

"There you go, Frank! Enjoy!"

Nice eyes again. But she just stood there, after delivering lunch and coffee. Looking down, with the usual smile. And those nice eyes were looking even nicer. And she just kept them focused, right into his eyes. Until he blinked. Only once. But he blinked. Yeah, lost again. But the urge was building, you know. To give a bit back. Due for a win after all.

"Well, so what have you been doing with yourself anyway!"

"Oh, I've just had a break for a while, that's all! It's good to be back again! You're looking good, Frank!"

Bloody hell. She just had that one all loaded up. That's for sure. So, that was the end of the smart-arse comments. Niceness had taken over the new programme again. They had him covered from every direction now.

"So are you! And you really do have nice eyes, you know!"

Yeah. Getting braver all the time now. Was either that, or just sit there like a dummy and let her make a mashed potato out of him. Just before wandering off, she just happened to mention one more thing.

"I've got a new hobby now, Frank! I've started painting! I'm not very good yet! But I'm having lessons!"

Right. It's happened again hasn't it. And just the way she said it. And now her café girl smile was just killing him. So, the focus had no choice. Straight back out the window.

"Maybe you would enjoy painting, Frank! Why don't you give it a try! It's good to see you again, Frank! See you later!"

No time for any answer either, because she was already half way back to the counter, before any words were there. Here one minute, gone the next. They were good at doing that.

So, back to the poker machine nightmare. It was all under control now anyway and smart-arse comments like that were not helping at all. She could go and paint whatever she liked. And good luck to her.

Lunch wasn't really enjoyed this time. Hurried down and the decision was made, to get out of there without being seen. Had enough for one day. But it was half way out, when two of them suddenly appeared, from out the back.

Stick up for her friends, went straight for the cash register. And the other one, stood right beside her. Both with the usual smile, dominating their whole face. But the other one had never been seen before. Probably another one of those upstairs girls. And usually would have just been ignored. But significant progress had been made now. So, straight up to a foot in front of her. Got in her face, alright.

"Are you new here? Or another one of those, upstairs girl? What's your name, anyway!"

Yeah. Getting braver all the time.

"I've been here for ages, Frank! I'm usually in the function room. Or in the restaurant! Or in the bar area! Everyone just calls me Jesus!"

What. Jesus. She must be joking.

"So, if I come in here and see you, I can say hello Jesus and that'll be okay will it!"

They both just cracked up. Stick up for her friends, took a quick sideways glance at Jesus. Then continued counting the money in the till. Jesus was so flustered-up, she couldn't say another word. Standing there, like a smiling statue. Things were dead quiet, for only a few more seconds.

"My names not really Jesus! They just call me that sometimes!"

Then she burst out laughing. Couldn't stop herself. Finally calmed down enough to introduce herself. It was just an ordinary name, you know. So, no surprise. She just had to be called the Jesus girl after that. No thinking required. None at all.

She was seen around every now and then. One day, after missing out on all the favourite tables. Frank was just sitting outside, waiting patiently. Out comes

Jesus. All loaded up with meals. Kept going to the wrong tables. Going back inside and coming back out again. And sometimes, still went to the wrong tables. Walking around in a daze. Completely confused, alright. Mind not on the job. That's for sure.

No wonder they kept her upstairs. Out of the way. But she kept stopping right in front of Frank, after finally delivering all the meals to the right tables. Looked down at him for a few seconds. Usual café girl smile glued on. Didn't even look like saying anything. Then off she'd go. And this routine was repeated a few more times. What the hell was going on here?

There're going to have a lot of fun with you.

Of great fascination was how many meals these café girls could carry around at the same time, without dropping any. Even if they didn't know where they were going. Or what they were doing. Which didn't seem to happen very often. You have to give them credit for that. Except maybe the Jesus girl, who didn't seem to have a clue about anything. She could have been religious, you know. With a name like that.

Anyway, back in the car and off went the thinking again. About the current new life situation. With no interruptions either. Music was up full blast. Everything was going well, considering. Next minute, he's in a line up at traffic lights. Stopped right in front of an arts and crafts shop. There was a parking spot available and an instant decision was made. Before Frank knew it, he was looking at rows of tubes of paints. Paint brushes. Empty picture frames. Every size you could think of.

"Do need any help there, sir?"

The poor guy answered like a robot. "Well, I was thinking about a hobby of some sort."

Left the shop with everything a budding artist could possibly need.

So, half the pigeon loft became an art studio and before long there were paintings hanging all around the walls. Mainly of pigeons, country scenes and faces. They were all shockers. Tell that easy enough. Especially one of them. His favourite one. A picture that had been terrorising the brain for months had been transported onto canvas.

But it looked nothing like the original. That's for sure. There was a big smile every time it was looked at. The new defence against TMBGITW and it started working straight away. The description of this portrait is not important. Didn't look much like TMBGITW at all. That's for sure.

But the only thing that really mattered was that now it represented TMBGITW. Yeah, so that took care of her, once and for all. And what a relief that was. And his mother now faced little competition, when it came to dominating the newfound sensibilities of the long-lost son. And what a feeling of relaxation and self-satisfaction that created. Yeah. Peace at last.

"How did you know about the reno's, Frank?

Frank didn't really know about the reno's, you know. But he'd been going upstairs to the bar area for a few weeks. To check out all the upstairs girls. And the menu, of course. But there were never any upstairs girls up there. Not the ones he knew about anyway. Been getting told about the upstairs girls for about two years, you know.

There're going to have a lot of fun with you.

"There's reno's starting in two weeks. So, you'll need to go upstairs from now on. But the restaurant will only be open from 8am till 11am for breakfast. Then it's only available for lunch. And you will need to book a table first."

This was the young fella talking who, just happened to be the manager. And what a shock it was to be told that one day. Never would have guessed in a million years. All the girls were always joking around with him, you know. So, he must have been okay. And he got listened to as well.

But then something occurred to Frank. They must have all been managers in the magic café. Because they were always calling someone else the manager. And whoever the manager was, he was always calling someone else the manager.

There're going to have a lot of fun with you.

Anyway, Frank knew all about how the restaurant worked, because have a chat had already told him and even booked him in one day. And he'd been in the bar area a few times as well. There was only one vegan meal available in each area. So, Frank only ate up there two or three days a week.

"Who told you about the reno's Frank?"

"No one told me anything about the reno's!"

"So, how come you've started going upstairs?"

"Well, I'm not sure why. I just got this feeling one day about going upstairs. So, I started going upstairs. That's all. I love the vegan pizza on the menu up there. I've never had such a big pizza. Covered the whole plate. Just managed to eat it all!"

The young fella just smiled he's own personal variation of the café girl smile. Didn't believe him. Tell that easy enough. But didn't say anything. Turned around and took off out the back. There was no need to mention anything about checking up on the upstairs girls either.

"Hi Frank! So, what are you having today?"

"Well, I guess I'll have the first favourite meal one last time!"

"Okay, no worries! How did you know about the reno's, Frank?"

Right. Here we go again. The forgotten name girl was into him now. But at least she remembered what the first favourite meal was. But they weren't going to win this one. And staying in control was the only way to get on top of this developing situation. That's for sure.

"Reno's? What reno's? I don't know anything about any reno's!"

Now it was a café girls turn to get all confused. But Frank just stood there looking at her, like nothing unusual was going on. But the re-engineered emotional structure was having a great time. I can tell you that. Total control was happening, alright. Yeah. Total control. And what a great feeling of satisfaction that was.

"Hi Frank! Who told you about the reno's?"

"Hi Frank! Who told you about the reno's?"

"Hi Frank! Who told you about the reno's?"

Yeah. Every time he got within earshot, that's what he heard. From all of them. But the answer was always the same.

"No one told me about the reno's!"

Honesty will come into your life if you let it.

Thing is, no one did tell Frank about the reno's. But somehow, he just decided it was time to check out upstairs. The idea just popped into his head. Came out of nowhere. So, maybe he did know about the reno's.

There're going to have a lot of fun with you.

"Oh no, I'm starting to tell them how I think. What I'm thinking about. How my mind works and everything. What have they done to me anyway?"

Yeah. The no more pretending thing had already started.

Honesty will come into your life, if you let it.

Yeah. Frank's telling them how he thinks. What he's thinking about. How the mind works. Everything. Yeah, they were responsible for this new life creation. That was the main thought right now. Invading the entire emotional, biological infrastructure. But in a good way. And what a great feeling that was. The pleasure of it all just couldn't be denied.

Honesty will come into your life, if you let it.

Yeah. Honesty was such a great thing, you know. And what a relief it was to no longer carry the burden of dishonesty around. Like a heavy weight, around the neck. Chocking his brain to death.

And yeah, he was over TMBGITW now as well. Really over her. The new picture was really working. And his mother's warm, smiling face was always there now. Well, most of the time anyway.

"Come on now, Frank! You know better than to think like that! They both have warm, smiling faces! You know that!"

Yeah. He knew that, alright. She got him again. But now was a good a time as any, to try and get some truth out of the lady. About what really happened. Yeah. Getting braver all the time. And what a surprise it was when she actually came good with some answers.

"It was you all the time wasn't it?"

"No, not all the time, Frank. Although, I have been with you all the way. You know that don't you. I've always been there for you, Frank. All the way! Right from the very beginning!"

"Yes! Yes! I can see that now. I think I understand it all now!"

"That's wonderful, Frank! I knew you were going to make it! We all knew you were going to make it!"

"So, it was her wasn't it? She's the one who gave me a new life."

"Yes Frank! That's right!"

"So, it was her all along then?"

"Yes Frank, that's right! Well, not quite all the way! Just most of the way! I'm the one who found you! But she's the one who started the ball rolling! She saw something good in you!"

"I really stuffed up, didn't I."

"Well, yes! That's one way of putting it, Frank! But don't be too hard on yourself. Starting a new life was never going to be easy for you. We all understood that! But you're a big success now, Frank! You've made it! We all knew you would! There was never any doubt about that! None what so ever! It just took a little longer than expected, that's all!"

"I didn't know what I was doing most of the time! I didn't understand! It was all so confusing, you know!"

"Yes, it was very confusing for you, Frank! We understand that! We knew it would be! Starting a new life always is! And no, you didn't understand Frank! How could you! But that was then, and this is now! And knowing what you know

261

now, you'd do things differently. Isn't that right, Frank? This is your new life now! Not your old life!"

"Yes! That's right! This is my new life! And yes, I would do things differently!"

"Oh Frank! Yes! You're really starting to understand it all now. See, it's never too late! I'm so proud of you Frank! Where're all just so proud of you! We knew you could do it! We never gave up on you, Frank! Not for a minute!"

Then the thinking got very serious.

"I'm never going to see her again, am I?"

"It's very unlikely, Frank! She's moved on with her life and you need to move on with yours!"

"Right..."

"Sometimes, you meet certain people in your life for a reason, Frank!"

"Right."

"There you go Frank!"

It was the marshal girl, with the lunch and coffee. Just when things were getting fully understood, another interruption. Just what wasn't needed, right at that moment.

"Do you remember the last manager that was here?"

Oh, for Christ's sake. Here we go again. The mind-reading game again. How was he supposed to know what manager she was talking about, anyway.

"Uh, no! She might have been here before I started coming here!"

Might have forgotten. Might be in denial. Or maybe just straight out lied.

Honesty will come into your life, if you let it.

Yeah right. Fucking GA.

Maybe she knew and maybe she didn't. She probably did. And if she mentions anything about going on to bigger things, she'll get hers. That's for sure.

"Now, now, Frank! This is not the time for any retrograde thinking! Stay positive Frank! Stay positive!"

Yeah right. Stay positive.

"Are you sure you don't remember her? I'm sure she was still here, when you were coming here!"

"Uh! Well! Maybe she was! I'd have to think about it! Maybe it'll come to me!"

Honesty will come into your life, if you let it.

Bloody hell.

"Come on now, Frank! You can do it!"

"Oh, yes! That's right! She could have been! I had a bit of a personality clash with one of the girls here. Early on! Maybe, it was her! I kind of don't remember that much about it."

That shut her up. But she still had that café girl smile on her face as she turned and walked away. Then she stopped and came back. Oh, no. There was no time to get anymore answers ready either.

"So, what do you do with yourself? When you leave here, Frank!"

Eh. Well. That one came out of nowhere. What's it got to do with her, anyway.

"Oh, not much! Nothing I ever do works out anyway! So, I just don't do anything!"

That was the most honest answer available. And it's the one that came out. Because he suddenly remembered how they operated. There was no way he was going to mention anything about his newfound hobby. Because that's what she was waiting for. He just knew it. He was telling them too much already. But they didn't need to know everything, did they? Yeah. Getting smarter all the time.

So, the marshal girl just stands there. Head half turned. One eye looking down and with a kind of smile and a look of wonder on her face. Or, it could have been disbelief, you know. Then she was off again. Left Frank there, wondering whether she knew a little, a lot or everything. More like everything.

Yeah. There was some kind of conspiracy going on here. Again. There had to be. But the brain was in overload. Again. The lady had just drained it out. Again. That's why. And the marshal got him thinking about something he didn't want to be thinking about. It's just wasn't fair. Nothing was ever fair.

Trying to work it all out was just too much. And the girls, you know. All seemed to have bigger smiles on their faces these days. And the meals seemed, larger than usual. And the favourite table, always seemed available. There was something going on, alright. And this is when it really started to get serious. The real new life thinking. And this thinking, almost exploded the brain. Again.

Evaluation time. And it had nothing to do with the parade outside the window. Or the lady. Or GA. Or that damn compulsive. It was all about the girls in the magic café. And what they meant to him. What qualities they all had. How they all helped him, by just talking to him. And teasing him. And always interrupting the thinking. And annoying him. And teaching him about having fun. While they were filling him up with kindness. Making him feel special. Gradually adjusting the mental attitudes.

Especially about girls. And yes, girl power. That he'd never known anything about before. But these café girls were all full of girl power, you know. But in a good way. He knew that now. And he was realising who he really was. Yeah. He loved all of them. And he was actually thinking about telling them all as well. Again. And that was real progress. But it was also another reason, for possible brain explosion activity. No, it wouldn't be a good idea to tell them anything about loving them. Even if it was in a good way. Yeah. Getting smarter all the time.

I mean, this lonely old man, who could hardly even talk properly. Going through all kinds of withdrawals. Forgot what was going on. From one minute to the next. Stared at people, till they felt uncomfortable. And still couldn't make any kind of decision. Especially important ones.

Not to mention the secret battles with the addictions. They couldn't possibly know anything about all that, could they? There was no memory of saying anything about all that. Or maybe there was. But there was one thing he was sure about. He did love every one of them. But that was another secret addiction they couldn't possibly know anything about. Well, they probably did know. Yeah. They knew, alright. Of course, they did. They knew everything.

There're going to have a lot of fun with you.

The discovery of fun. Of genuine communication, with no underlying plots of trickery or deceit. He'd always understood what a sneaky, whingeing, manipulating lot females were. Especially the older ones. But the real truth was he didn't really know too much at all. There was a head full of new thinking developing now. But they could have all still been spies too, you know. That idea was always lurking around in there as well.

Honesty will come into your life, if you let it.

Yeah. New realisations were nothing unusual now. Like how simply shagging some girl and loving her were two completely different things. And knowing that when he was in the café, everything they did was all about him. About him and only him. Bringing him out. The real Frank. The one hiding in there. The one that didn't even know he was in there at all. Come out. Come out. Wherever you are. Yeah. There were big internal changes happening, alright.

There're going to have a lot of fun with you.

Helping him adapt to the new life and the new world. Training him in other words. Preparing him. Assisting in the gradual development of the new thought processes. That were absolutely necessary, for a successful transition. Replacing the miserable old life attitudes. With the new life, positive attitudes. And surely if they were all a part of the spy network, they wouldn't be doing any of that would they.

"Oh Frank! You've truly got it now! You're getting so close! So close! I just knew you were going to make it! I always knew you were going to make it! I never gave up on you Frank! Ever! Not for a minute!"

And you know what. Frank was getting it. He truly was. Trying so hard now. To truly understand, what it meant to wipe out a previous existence and start all over again. To be given this second chance. To be given a new life, without having to die first. Well maybe dying did happen. Almost. A few times. And now, he was in his mid-sixties for Christ's sake. And starting all over again. I mean, who would ever have thought that was possible.

But you know, he still wasn't completely convinced. There was still that nagging doubt. About whether he'd just dreamed the whole thing up. Or maybe he'd accidentally dropped a few LSD tabs and forgotten all about it. Maybe overdosed. Maybe he was actually dead and didn't even know it. Maybe he'd come back soon and the whole trip would be over. Maybe everything was already over.

How did they all know so much about him anyway. They all knew exactly what to say and do. To penetrate the thick skull. That had never happened before. But he'd been invaded, alright. More than a few times. And defeated. Every time. But there was no real feeling of defeat at all.

"Defeat is how it all starts, Frank! Then victory!"

Ok. Well, he'll need to think about that one for a while.

And now, a big drift off was developing. There was no stopping it either. Such a strong force. A surprise attack, from inside the emotional structure. Too powerful to resist.

Whoa. What the… How is this all happening. That was years ago, when that happened. This can't be happening. It's already happened. It can't be happening again. But it was happening again. And this is what was happening.

Yes. The day had finally come. Eternal peace at last. The only peace she would ever really know. And you wouldn't believe it. Frank got up there and read out the eulogy. And that was such a difficult thing to do, you know. What an emotional wreck. Right from the very first word. Stopping occasionally and catching the breath only happened, when the words got stuck. The end only happened, because the words ran out. And so had the tears. And so had Frank. He was gone.

But you see. Frank was never really there anyway. Well, physically he was there. At the funeral. He was actually the only one there. And he was up there reading out the eulogy. But the mind was in reflection mode, at the same time. When the reading stopped, is when he came back. And so did everyone else.

The following, is much of what was said. When there was no one there. Our mother, did share some intimate knowledge with us, from time to time. Especially in her later years. Some of which, some of us knew about. Some of which, a few of us knew about. And some of which, none of us knew about.

She was six years old. When her and an older brother and sister, arrived home from school that day. There was a big black car parked in front of the house.

"Your mother's dead! So, you have to come with us!"

They were driven away and placed in an orphanage. Immediately becoming wards of the state.

"I was too frightened to say boo to a matchstick"

So, creating her own world, surrounded by a wall of silence. Was no big surprise. And it didn't take long.

"I loved to sing! I wanted to be a singer! They told me to be quiet! I wasn't allowed to sing anymore! I wasn't allowed to do anything!"

Yes. Whatever dreams she had were soon crushed. The bond she shared with her mother had already been crushed.

Eventually, they were fostered out to aunt and uncle. It was so good of them to take all three. But the older brother became a little uncontrollable. So, he went back to the orphanage. The closeness she shared with her sister became even stronger.

She'd lost everything else familiar to her. Just like that. Except for her one older sister. They were all each other had.

Many bouts of illness were suffered, during her childhood years. Resulting in mastoids in her ears and partial deafness.

"My childhood was very lonely and painful! With little affection!"

Whatever happened to her older sister was not known for many years. Nothing was ever mentioned about that. One day, she just seemed to disappear. Nothing was ever explained.

"But I didn't think about my life too much. I didn't know any better. I lived in it. Grew up in it. That was the way it was. When I saw my own children, with their homes and families. With their interaction with each other and the affection shown to one another. I realised only then, what I had missed out on."

Being raised to become a housewife was normal for a "welfare" child. As was leaving school at fourteen years of age. But because of her illnesses, it was decided to leave her in school, till she was sixteen.

Then the "welfare," found her a job. In a factory. Packing flour. But by then, she wanted to be a stenographer. But that required further training and would cost money. So, that was not an option. Not for her anyway. She passed the Intermediate Certificate with honours and found herself a job as a tailoress. And what an achievement that was.

Our mother as a young woman was very attractive and articulate. But, also shy and somewhat withdrawn. And that sad, far-away look stayed with her. Right till the end. She had this way of pretending everything was fine. But of course, it wasn't. She never complained. Never put anyone down. She never had a bad word to say about anyone.

She was always there, for all her children. Feeding, clothing, packing school lunches and all the domestic chores that are required by a dedicated housewife and mother. Her strength and determination, to raise all her children was only to be admired and appreciated. And I'm sure, a few of us here, wished we did better in that regard. And I have to admit, to being one of them.

She wasn't so good with the verbal communication. That was always a real struggle. Only in her later years, did she become determined, to discover the individual that she truly was. A person in her own right. She began to express her personal opinions. Became assertive and more or less demanded, that we all listen to what she had to say. Instead of mostly just ignoring her. Like some of us always did. And I have to admit to being one of them. I probably ignored her, more than anyone else.

Yes, she was going to talk and we were going to listen. Whether we liked it or not. This was a complete reversal, of what we had always known. And it took a while to get used to. Especially for the girls. Because when the girls got together, they all wanted to do all the talking. All at once. Sorry girls. But you know it's true.

Our mother was out of her shell. So, look out. Getting to know our mother and who she really was made us laugh a lot. And made most of us cry a lot. And made most of us wonder a lot. And made most of us feel so lucky as well. To have such a wonderful mother. Who'd been through so much. But still became the kind, gentle soul she was. Although, some of us may not have realised just how lucky we were. And I must admit, to being one of them. Probably the worst one.

Our mother, never smoked a cigarette. Never touched a drop of alcohol. And didn't even know what drugs were. Till a younger brother found my stash of smokes and pot, hidden under the house. There was no lecture. Didn't say what a very bad boy you are, or anything. She just looked at me. Slowly moved her head from side to side, with a slight tightening of the mouth. And with a look in her sad eyes. That said, I'm very disappointed in you. But she never said a word. Not one word. Maybe she already knew that I was the black sheep of the family. And no words were going to change that.

As dedicated as our mother was. There was never any emotional attachment. Never any little cuddles. No effort to show affection. No confidential little talks between mother and child. Not that I can remember anyway. Talks that would have been helpful, for a growing boy. Or girl, for that matter. Yes, she always struggled with that kind of stuff. But nobody's perfect. She gave us all, what she had the ability to give us. Everything she had in her. And you can't do any better than that. No one can give, what they haven't got to give.

Fair to say, we all got to know our mother better, during her final years in the nursing home.

Rest in peace now mum.

Frank was so drained out, by the time he finished talking, you know. Had to disappear for a while. Get the head back together. Dry the face up.

There was much more said at the funeral. By one sister, who read her own eulogy. And by some other people, who got to know their mother as well. But what's been said here, is enough to remember.

The lady was bound to have something to say, you know. That was for certain. But at least she waited for a few hours. After Frank had returned home. Sitting on the veranda. Eyes closed. But not asleep. Onto the third cup of coffee already. Mind still racing. The odd tear leaking out.

If it'd been the old life, there would have been empty beer cans everywhere by now. And the remaining roaches, of a few fat joints.

Yeah. Wouldn't be long now. I'm so proud of you, Frank. We're all so proud of you, Frank. Blah. Blah. Blah. Yeah, could feel it coming.

"Oh, Frank! What you said was just so wonderful! You really have excelled yourself this time! You really have! Your mother would be so proud of you! She'd almost given up on you! And we all appreciate, how hard that must have been. To get up there like that! And say all those wonderful things. And mean every word! Only someone of strong character could do that Frank! And you did it! And yes! I am so proud of you, Frank! We are all just so proud of you!"

Yeah, he knew she'd turn up, alright. Right on schedule. When he was just sitting there, quietly. Nice and relaxed. Well, he wasn't relaxed this time. That's for sure. Strung right out, more like it. And he would never admit it, you know. But he wasn't only expecting the lady to visit. He was actually looking forward to it. He'd have been so disappointed, if she hadn't been there.

So, here he is. Still sitting on the veranda. With a huge smile on the face. Feeling just so proud of himself. Never been in a better place in the whole of the two lives. And he knew it. Yes. Everything was falling into place right now. Well, almost everything.

Then the thinking started up again. The funeral scene was in focus. Yes, he was there. But wait a minute. That was in the old life. So, how could he be there and on the veranda at the same time. When he didn't even have a veranda. Because he was living somewhere else when the funeral happened. So, the lady couldn't possibly know about that.

She'd only been hanging around, since the new life started. Well not hanging around. It shouldn't be said like that. More like hovering. But the appreciation was there now. Her kind, gentle, sweet voice and her reassuring words, always did the trick. That just had to be admitted. But never to the lady. No. Never.

But it didn't explain how she could have been there. I mean, the funeral was around thirteen years ago. Unless there were two of them. Yeah. That would explain everything. No, there couldn't possibly be two of them. If there was another one, then they'd have both been talking at the same time. Wouldn't have been able to help themselves. And the confusion would have caused, complete madness. And there wasn't complete madness there again. But there could have been, you know. Always a possibility. Anyway, it doesn't matter. All that mattered now was getting some sleep.

But there was no getting any sleep. All that coffee had the eyeballs popping. Mind still racing. Blood pressure would have been up again. Body getting restless. Thought of two ladies in the head. And that little bitch, who's picture would be back around and dominating again. Sooner or later. You could bet on that.

No. No. No. That's not right. Can't keep calling her that. How could he still call her that, after what she did. Out of the goodness of her heart. Part of which she gave to him. Only he was too unaware to know what to do with it. Didn't even know he had it. Until it was much too late.

Oh no. He knew straight away. The other picture was turning around again. All the pressure, you know. So, the water gets guzzled down. The exercise footwear goes on and off and running. Nowhere in particular. Just running. Maybe for an hour. Came back, completely stuffed. Crashed onto the bed. Sleep at last.

"You were right all along, dear! He really is going to make it! We'd all given up on him! But you didn't give up! Not for a minute! You've done so well with him! You really have! Congratulations! This success will no doubt, make the next one so much easier to guide through the rehabilitation process!"

"Yes, dear! Congratulations are in order! We always did have great confidence in you! We really did! We all knew you were going to get him there! We never gave up on you! Not for a minute!"

"Yes Frank! You're getting so close now! So close! Welcome to your new life, Frank! I'm so glad you've made it! Where're all so glad you've made it!"

What. That couldn't possibly be her again. Or them. No, it couldn't be. And, no it wasn't. It wasn't anyone. No, it wasn't anyone. But they were the last words in the thinking. As the sleep took over and shut the whole day down. Finally.

But it didn't shut down completely, because a dream started percolating and gradually building up into maybe a mini nightmare. And it was that damn picture again, that caused it.

"Yeah, she was a real classic, that one! Got stuck right into me! What a— "

"Don't go talking about her like that! She's gone on to bigger things now! There're, a great lot of girls here! I won't sit here and listen to anything said against them! So, just be careful what you say!"

Whoa. Wasn't expecting that at all. And then this bloke had a sip of his coffee and looked off in the opposite direction. This short conversation happened well into proceedings you know. Just after she disappeared for good. The favourite table was unavailable. Frank made the mistake of sitting outside, near a complete stranger and suddenly opening up. He wasn't to know that this stranger knew all about the magic café and the girls who worked there. Especially one of them. The main one. At that time anyway.

"Yes, they are aren't they! She was the most beautiful girl I've ever seen!"

That came out without even thinking. Then the stranger got up and walked away. Frank was left there staring at the ocean. Feeling like he'd never felt before. Halfway to feeling guilty about something he didn't understand and why he was feeling the way he was.

Several months later, this same stranger was seen sitting at an aluminium table above the ocean baths. The urge was there and the words were there as well. They needed to be said and they were said.

"Hey, how you going?"

The stranger looked up with a smile on his face. And for some reason, it reminded Frank about the café girls. It was exactly the same smile, that's why. The eyes were warm and friendly. There was no surprise when Frank appeared and there was a calmness about him as well, which was more than a little disarming. But nothing could stop what had to be said.

"Do you remember when you told me about the girls in the café? What a great bunch of girls they were! Well, you were right! There're, the best! It just took me a while to work it out!"

There was no answer. But the smile got bigger. The eyes intensified a little and the gentle warmth was still there as well. There was an unspoken message received. And it was unmistakeable. He'd felt it before. Many times. Everything was fine. Relax. Nothing to worry about.

This stranger then slowly turned his head away. No more words were necessary. So, Frank continued on his way with a big smile on his face and the warm feelings that always came with it, got even warmer. He was in a good place, alright. The stranger was never seen again.

"Hello, I'm Frank and I'm a compulsive gambler."

"Hi Frank!"

"Hi Frank!"

"Hello Frank!"

"I haven't played poker machines for another week!"

"Oh, well done, Frank! Well done!"

"Good on ya, mate!"

"Yes, thanks everyone! I'm so proud of myself! I'm really getting it now! I'm a much stronger character! I've really excelled myself. I'm so close. I think

I'm going to make it. Sometimes you meet certain people for a reason, you know."

"That's right Frank! We're all here for each other! That's what GA is all about! Helping each other. Supporting each other. You need to be here, Frank! We all need to be here!"

The controller just couldn't help it sometimes. Always on about the GA thing, you know. Well after all, that is what it's all about. With the gambling side of things. The poker machines. Yeah. If it wasn't for the controller and GA and all the other compulsives, the Frank that was here now, wouldn't be here at all. Not in GA anyway. But in some pub or club somewhere pushing the button, and wasting all the money. Knew that, alright.

"Yes, I know that. And I wouldn't have been able to get where I am now, if it wasn't for you guys. I owe everything to GA and to everyone who comes here. You guys are great!"

"You have to move on with your life, you know. If you stuff up, it's usually because you don't understand. Knowing what I know now, I'd do things differently. I've learnt from my mistakes. I knew I had big problems, but I never gave up on myself. Not for a minute. I've even got a hobby now, you know! I've started painting. I'm not very good yet. But maybe I'll start having lessons! Anyway, thanks again. And thanks for letting me share!"

Got a rip-roaring applause for that share. Best one ever. And what was said was all the truth as well. It's just that the real reason, for the big improvements in this sucker's life was more to do with the lady who wasn't there. The most beautiful girl in the world. Still calling her that again now, you know. And the magic café girls, who were all respected and loved so much. But would never know anything about it. But more than likely, already knew all about it. Yeah. They knew, alright.

"Yes, well done, Frank!"

"Good on ya, Frank!"

'Yeah, well done Picasso!"

There was an even bigger applause, when that one came out.

Several other compulsives who needed to share, shared. The controller then took control and ended the meeting in the usual way.

All together now.

To the God of our own understanding.

God grant me the serenity to accept the things I cannot change, the courage to change the things I can, and the wisdom to know the difference.

Frank had learnt to accept this God bullshit by now. Because the understanding was there. Letting go of the old stubbornness that restricted all forms of progress was the only way to move forward and thrive in his new life. He knew it wasn't a real God that gave him the strength and determination, you know. But if that's what the other compulsives needed to believe well, that was their decision. And good luck to them.

All together now.

Thanks for sharing. Thanks for caring. Keep coming back, the meetings make it.

Yeah. He'd learnt to accept the hand holding bit as well.

End of meeting. So, he's out of there.

Yeah, the magic café girls were the real reason. With all their influence. Their caring. Their sharing. Their fun way of communicating. And all in a good way. While pretending to know nothing about what was happening. Or take any credit for all the positive changes. That was worked out after a while.

But nothing was ever said by the girls or by Frank. And that was very interesting. And it was a lot more fun that way as well. And fun was what it was always all about. And learning. Yeah. Learning about fun and becoming who he really was at the same time. But stretched out over about three year's altogether.

But yeah, they probably did know. And so would the lady. But maybe not TMBGITW, who would never be seen again. And thank God for that. There was always too much torment going on, whenever she was around anyway. And torment wasn't supposed to be a part of the new life. And she was the worst torment, that had ever been known. But she was well and truly forgotten about by now. Even her picture wasn't there anymore. She was gone, alright. End of story.

Honesty will come into your life, if you let it.

Year right. Yeah. Some things were just never gotten over, were they? Have to admit that one day.

"Hi Frank! It's so good to see you! Bit late today! Been for your swim?"

"Yeah, hi! Bit late today. Yes, been for a swim. Didn't do as much today! Took it easy, for a change!"

"That's ok! It's good to take it easy sometimes. Haven't been playing up, have you?"

"What! Who me! Play up! I never play up! Not anymore anyway. I'm too old to play up!"

That put a little smile on her face. This was the have a little chat girl. Not that a little chat was needed right now. But she was such a nice girl and how could he not talk to her. And he stuck to the truth this time, you know. Exactly. No exaggeration. No half-truths. No fibbing. Just the straight-out truth. And what a good feeling that was.

Honesty will come into your life, if you let it.

Yeah right.

There're going to have a lot of fun with you.

Yeah right.

Maybe she knew and maybe she didn't. But it didn't matter. Because that smile was there. The magic café girl smile. Just loved that smile. And he loved all the smilers too. But that was an internal dilemma thing happening. A personal dilemma. But love had come into the worn-out old heart as well now, you know. That wasn't so worn out anymore. And that was a good thing. And a good feeling to have going on in there. But no one else could ever know about that. And that word was finally looked up, you know. The word, love. And there were lots of meanings. They went on forever. But this one caught the attention.

Love; a strong feeling of affection and concern toward another person, as that arising from kinship or close friendship. A strong feeling of sexual attraction.

So, that meant you had to get close to them. If you liked the look of them and found them sexually attractive. Make friends. Show affection towards them. And then shag them. The girls, that is. No shirt lifting going on here. That's for sure. But the idea of shagging so many girls, at his age. No, that was never going to happen. Kill him for sure. Yeah. Getting smarter all the time.

"Frank! Frank! You need to do better than this! You really do!"

Har. Har. Har. Got her this time. Only joking. Having a bit of fun, you know. Yeah. Knew she'd come in on that one. Sucked her right in.

"Oh Frank! Dear oh dear! What am I going to do with you! Right when I think you've got it, you go and disappoint me again! Please don't disappoint me anymore, Frank! Please don't!"

Well, maybe it was the lady who needed to learn about fun. She obviously had no sense of humour either. The café girls could teach her a thing or two. That's for sure.

Although, tricking the lady was one thing. But admitting the full understanding of what love was. Another thing all together. But yes. The full understanding was getting there. About love and a whole lot of other stuff. Was all about growth and development. Frank's growth and development. The whole time. Growth and development. Yeah, right from the start. And having fun along the way.

And the fun started, right from that very first step, into the magic café. And right into the clutches of the magic café girls. Yeah, right into their caring clutches. And who would have ever thought something like that was possible. Not this old bonehead. That's for sure. Knew the luck had changed as well. Don't you worry about that. Not at first, of course. Bit slow. Always took a while for things to sink in, you know.

The new girls coming and going, didn't bother him anymore either. Or the upstairs girls. Sudden changes were no problem anymore. They were never even up there in the first place, you know. Went up there one day out of curiosity. Not one downstairs girl in sight anywhere.

"I just went upstairs for a look around! There's no one up there!"

"Oh, they must all be on holidays! It's a quiet time now!"

Yeah right. Well, there were a few up there. But none of the ones that he'd ever seen before.

On the way to the table, he spotted the car girl. Sitting with some other girl, with a baby in between them. In a baby highchair provided by the café. This was just before the reno's started, by the way.

"Oh hi! Haven't seen you for a while! What have you been up to?"

There was no problem opening up with the conversation now, you know. Not with anyone.

"Oh, I've been around! Just taking a break for a while!"

And this friendly chit chat could have gone on forever. But Frank was more in control these days and could start and end conversations with any of the café girls. Because they had taught him how, that's why.

"Oh well, it's good to see you! Have a good lunch!"

This girl had repeated her name several times. But Frank, for some reason could never quite get it. So, before he left on this occasion, he got her to spell it out. And after he sat down, took out his piece of paper and wrote it down. After repeating it several times, realised it sounded like car. So, that's how she became the car girl.

And after that little problem was solved, some uncontrollable looking out the window dominated the concentration. Yeah. G-strings, shirt lifters and carpet chewers everywhere. And all the other weird and wonderful looking monkeys, walking along. The thinking started going ballistic, alright.

Yeah. Here was Frank checking out all the monkeys again, when the worst thought that could possibly enter the thinking, entered the thinking. After surviving all the traumas and torture of the old life and experiencing all the new found traumas and torture of adapting to the new life, all he could ever really hope to become was a monkey. Just another dumb arse monkey. Well, all the monkeys weren't dumb arses, you know. He knew that, alright. But he couldn't think of anything else to call them. That's just where the thinking was anyway.

"Frank! Frank! Just stop it! Stop it! Just stop it!"

"What! What have I done now?"

"All this talk you're going on with! All this ridiculous talk!"

"What talk! What are you talking about anyway!"

She could get right off the track sometimes, you know.

"You know exactly what I'm talking about, Frank! This nonsense, has to stop! Have a good think about what you're saying! You're so much better than this now, Frank! So much better! But, you're still such a rascal, aren't you Frank! Still such a rascal! Let the new Frank emerge! We all know he's in there! Now, just get back on track! And let the new Frank emerge!"

Still a rascal, eh. Get back on track, eh. Well, could have been a lot worse. Anyway, it wasn't the lady who said anything about a track in the first place, was it?

"Ok. Ok. I'll have a think about it."

"Yes Frank! Please do! And Frank, you need to get that monkey business right out of your head! You really do! You're much more that a monkey now, Frank! You really are! You need to believe that Frank! You really do! I know you can get there, Frank! We all know you can get there!"

She's probably right, you know. As usual. Can still get a bit carried away at times. Yeah. Off the track again. Off the new life track. But he didn't want to be off the new life track. So, getting back on track was what needed to happen. No more mucking around. Frank didn't really want to be a monkey either, you know. Not really. But he was. He knew that. The lady doesn't know what she's on about.

Yeah. They were just normal monkeys walking along. Out and about. Exercising together. Talking together. Laughing together. Out dogging. Oops. Walking their dogs. Monkeys, walking their dogs. That's pretty funny, eh. Some were jogging. Shirtless. Sweat pouring out of them. Posers. Some girls, jogging or powerwalking. In their skin tight gear. Posers. All posers.

No. No. No. Not posers. Just other monkeys out and about, enjoying themselves. There began a real pounding between the ears now, you know. It suddenly happened again. The realisation that the thinking, didn't want to keep thinking, the way it was thinking. So, the thinking had to rethink, how it was thinking. And from that moment on, that's what started happening. Didn't want the lady getting stuck into him again. That's for sure. Maybe everybody wasn't a monkey after all.

The metamorphosis was in completion mode now. And somehow, during the process the grub managed to transform into a beautiful butterfly. Just as the controller predicted. Well, maybe not so much beautiful. But a butterfly all the same. And more beautiful that any grub. That's for sure.

A beautiful butterfly. And, who would have ever thought that was possible. And being a beautiful butterfly was much better than just being a dumb arse monkey. But Frank had already accepted the idea of being a dumb arse monkey. Until just recently that is. So, now the idea of being a beautiful butterfly was fully accepted. And what a good feeling that was.

That controller must be some kind of a fortune teller, or something. Or a genius. Or maybe even a genie. Or maybe had just been around long enough to know. Knew where the solid ground was and knew how to get there and stay there. Yeah. The controller was in control, alright. Just not completely. Or maybe just didn't know anything about dumb arse monkeys.

Getting stuck in the GA programme wasn't all good you know. With the controller always pointing out what you were doing wrong and what to do about it, and what not to do about it. Yeah. Stick to the GA programme or your life is completely not worth living. Yeah. The controller could be a real know it all pain in the arse at times. That's for sure. But in a good way. And all the other compulsives laughing at him all the time. That wasn't easy to put up with either, you know. But that wasn't a good way to be looking at things.

And the controller watched the whole thing too, you know. The old life, to the new life. The gradual transformation. So, the lady wasn't the only one who knew Frank. Better than Frank knew Frank. Or the café girls, who knew everything there was to know. Without even having to say anything. Because they just knew and Frank knew they just knew. And TMBGITW. Who knows what her game really was.

There're going to have a lot of fun with you.

But there was no way the controller was ever going to know all about all the Franks. That was something only Frank could know about or understand. And only Frank could keep them all under control. And there was no way the controller could ever find out about the lady. That's for sure. But you know, those other Franks. They didn't seem to be around much anymore. And that was another thing to contemplate. But there was no room for them in the new life anyway.

But there was no way of ever getting rid of super Frank. Although, there was a new super Frank now. The new life super Frank. The sober, pot free, level headed, responsible, semi articulate, smiling, fun loving and loving super Frank. And who would ever have thought that was possible. Not Frank. That's for sure.

Not that a great fight hadn't been put up, either. By all of them. Especially super Frank, who eventually came out on top. And thank Christ for that. The other Franks all just seemed to disappear. Defeated. One by one. After all, this was a very stubborn grub where're talking about here. Didn't want to change a thing.

And the lady got him by surprise in the first place. Been unconscious for three days. And she suddenly turns up and starts talking about a new life. Like that's what was going to happen. And that was that. But that's exactly what did happen. A new life. It wasn't fair. But he was just loving it now. And that was the main thing.

And that's when the battle between the Franks really began, you know. And the battle with the lady followed soon after. Well, that battle probable started well before the battle between the Franks. And TMBGITW had to go and get herself in there didn't she? And complicate things up even more.

And the rest of the girls in the magic café started working on the Franks as well. And then that smart arse compulsive, just had to go and say, what he didn't have to go and say, didn't he? So, what chance did the poor bastards have. None. That's what. None at all.

But the leftover super Frank was just so glad all this really happened, you know. And that it wasn't just some kind of extended LSD trip, that went horribly wrong. Otherwise, the progression from the old life, to the new life would never have happened in the first place. And it did happen. There was no doubt about that now. Yeah. And it didn't take the lady to point it out either. Yes. Getting smarter all the time.

And it could have been the imagination taking over the thinking again, you know. But the café girls seemed to be smiling at him more and more. The people walking past all looked happier. The other customers all seemed to be smiling and chatting away between mouthfuls. Yes, everyone was smiling. So, what else could possibly happen, apart from Frank smiling too. And that's what happened. The smiling activity was really catching on, alright. Yes, this new life was really taking off.

There're going to have a lot of fun with you.

Even the shirt lifters and the carpet chewers looked happier. Oops, sorry about that. Members of the gay community. The alternatives. Yeah, that sounds much better. Usually smiling as well. And then a thought did occur. These alternatives, always seemed happier than the straights. If it can be put that way. I mean, how could the previous miserable looking generation, create this seemingly happier next generation. And what a contemplation that was.

Well, maybe it even started with the lady who wasn't there. But she was there. And she's been there ever since. So, she was probably there from the beginning. Well, if she'd always been there, then she had to be there from the beginning didn't she? But it's only now that really counts.

Not the beginning. Well, the beginning is always important, of course. Especially getting off to a good start. That's what the thinking was now anyway. And the new life got off to a much better start than the old life. That's for sure. Yes, getting smarter all the time.

Yeah. Frank had finally made it. Well and truly made it. No more doubts. No more dark shadows. No more negative thoughts. Not all the time anyway. Just so proud of himself, you know. Didn't think he was ever going to get there, but he did. Fancy that. The biggest achievement in the whole two lives.

"Yes Frank! You've well and truly made it now! And yes, you should be so proud of yourself! So very proud! It's been a very challenging journey for you! I knew it would be! We all knew it would be, Frank! But we knew you'd make it! We knew you could do it, Frank! We all had great confidence in you! Otherwise, I wouldn't have bothered! None of us would have bothered! But that's why you were chosen in the first place, Frank! We all knew you could do it! So, make the most of your second chance, Frank! We all know you will!"

There was an unbearable silence now. The lady was gone. And there was this feeling that she wouldn't be coming back, ever again.

"Wait! Don't go! I don't want you to go! Come back! I still need you! Come back! Please! Come back!"

"Let him go dear! It's time to let him go!"

"Yes, let him go dear! Or we'll have to let him go for you!"

"Yes dear! You must let him go now! There's nothing more you can do!"

"Yes, you've done all you can with this one! And although he has suffered the occasional relapse, it's time to set him free! Free from yourself and free from us as well! It's up to him now! We can't help him anymore!"

"Yes, I fully agree! There are no more chances available for this one! We can't support him any longer! He's been propped up long enough! Too long as a matter of fact! We've learnt all we can from him!"

"His profile will no doubt prove invaluable for future reference. If we should ever select another one, with such a depleted character and feelings of deeply entrenched, self-worthlessness! Of course, you have done an admirable job with him dear! But yes, we must cut him loose! It's time we all moved on to bigger things! Is anyone in disagreement? No! Ok then! Case closed!"

"There is a wonderful hospital just a short distance south of here. How about you try your luck there, dear!"

"Yes! Thank you! That sounds like a good idea! But I'm not quite finished with this one yet! There's, a few last things I need to say!"

Final farewells are never easy, you know.

"Frank! Frank! Stop it! Stop all your silly talk! Your new life is in your hands now! You must take control! Follow your instincts now, Frank! That's all you need to do! I have done everything I can for you! We have done everything we can for you! It's all up to you now! The new Frank must emerge! You don't need me anymore. You don't need any of us anymore! You, don't need anything else now, Frank! Just yourself! And stay strong, Frank! Stay strong!"

"Stick to the plan, Frank! Stick to the new plan and everything will be fine! You'll see! I need to go now, Frank! It's time to move on! For me! For all of us! And for you too! Goodbye Frank! And good luck!"

"No! No! Don't go! Please don't go!" I still need you! Don't leave me! I'll be all alone! What am I supposed to do now! Don't go! You have to tell me what to do next!"

But she was gone. Yes. Gone for good this time.

What the problem was, it was the same one that it always had been. Making decisions. The time had come, to start making his own decisions. Big life changing decisions. And that was unknown territory in the new life.

The pleading could have gone on forever, you know. But it was hopeless. And once this realisation was recognised and accepted. Once and for all. And the all-alone feeling was truly identified. And nothing else was there, except empty space. No dark shadows. Well, there were a few grey shadows left hanging around. But there was certainly, only one Frank. The newly created super Frank. The one and only super Frank. Sitting there, with nothing else and no one else but himself. And that was not a good feeling to be having. Not right then anyway.

So, the first major decision was made. But, not before some very heavy thinking. Either the new Frank emerges, without any life support. Or the new super Frank becomes the old super Frank and retreats back into the remaining grey shadows. And rebuilds them to their former blackened glory. Yeah. What a tough decision.

And the consequences both super Franks would need to face were well and truly known now. That's for sure. But he had come such a long way and was far more resilient. So, that was something worth considering, before the final decision was made. And when the final decision was made, it was the best decision that could have been made. Considering all the available information. And the new super Frank, finally did emerge. And it was his decision and he made it all by himself. And what a good feeling that was.

"Who told you about the reno's, Frank?"

"How did you know about the reno's, Frank?"

"Yes, who told you about the reno's, Frank?"

Yeah. They were still all into him about the reno's.

But Frank had no idea about how he knew about the reno's. He just knew. One day, he just got this feeling. Yeah. The idea just popped into the thinking. About going upstairs and checking things out. Get to know all the upstairs girls, who were never even up there. But the ones that were up there, got stuck into him straight away.

"Nice haircut, Frank! It suits you!"

"Yes, you look good, Frank! So, a vegan pizza and a zero Heineken!"

"Uh yeah! That's right!"

"Hey, nice haircut, Frank!"

And this last comment was just from some customer on the way out, you know. And with that same smile as well. It's was like everyone in the whole café knew what was going on. There were all in on it. They just had to be.

Yeah. They knew his name. They knew he'd just had a haircut. And they knew what he was having for lunch as well. Something should have been said in self-defence, you know. But it was a well-known fact by now. To just not bother. Because the café girl smile would have just got wider and warmer and their eyes would have sparkled up even more. And he would have been left standing there, feeling all warm and fuzzy. And he just loved it when that happened. So, maybe that's why he stopped saying anything. But he always said something anyway.

"Gee you girls are on the ball!"

No comment. Just the usual smile.

There're going to have a lot of fun with you.

"We accidentally put someone else in your spot, Frank! Hope you don't mind!"

Well, he didn't really mind at all. But this time he did say something. But he should have thought about it first.

"Well, can't you just kick them out!"

That took the smile off her face. For a few seconds anyway. But she caught on very quick. And this one was like the tall one, you know. Kind of aloof. Liked being in control. Set him straight, alright. But in a good way.

"No, I can't do that Frank! There're regulars as well. That's their favourite spot too. And they did get here first! We just forgot about you, that's all."

Then the usual smile just busted out, all over her face. He didn't like being forgotten about either. But what could he do but smile straight back. They both understood the game. The new life smiling, fun game.

"How did that go Frank!"

"Apart from where I had to sit, just fine!"

Yeah. Another big smile both ways. This was another upstairs girl. She'd led Frank to his spot and taken his order a few times.

I'm glad you enjoyed it! Nice haircut by the way! It suits you! The new Frank is here!"

"Nice haircut, Frank!"

"Nice haircut, Frank!"

"Nice haircut, Frank!

Yeah. They were coming from everywhere again.

And here's Frank lapping up all this new attention, you know. Glowing like an effervescent balloon. A new level had been reached, alright. And what a great feeling that was. A feeling of elation and self-satisfaction. But the same realisation was there only much stronger. About all the café girls and how they'd transformed this old reprobate, into something well on the way to being human. A human monkey. But not a dumb arse monkey. That's for sure.

Of course, there was still the on-off again battle against the machines, you know. One of the main psychological implants from the early GA days, still pulsated. From time to time. Still filed away up the back. Brought out like a weapon. Whenever the obsession rose its ugly head, trying to take over the new life and destroy it. Just like it destroyed the old one. But not this time. This time it will be different.

Yes, the controller was always drumming this one into all the compulsives.

One thing we have to face up to, is the fact that we are compulsive gamblers. Not we were compulsive gamblers. Not even ex compulsive gamblers. Today I am a compulsive gambler. Tomorrow, I will still be a compulsive gambler. And I will die a compulsive gambler. The only decision to make, is whether I will die free from an active life of gambling, or not.

Yeah, that one was always there. Because it always had to be there. But not everyone's perfect, eh. Anyway. What the lady doesn't know, won't hurt her, will it. And she's gone for good now anyway. And there were still the Acapulco Gold seeds there. And the girls in the magic café, didn't need to know what was going on all the time either. A few joints here and there wouldn't hurt, you know. And if there was a need to sneak off, for a carton. Well, who's business was that. And if a big bust happened, well so what. Give GA a miss. Who's to ever know.

"Oh Frank! Your still such a rascal aren't you. You need to stick to the plan, Frank. Stick to the plan and everything will be ok. You'll see! You'll see! You'll see! Just stick to the plan, Frank! Blah! Blah! Blah! But I've forgotten what the plan was! I need you to remind me about the plan! If you came back just once more and reminded me about the plan, I'll be ok! Just come back one more time!"

"You've probably forgotten about the plan yourself! That's why you won't come back! You've forgotten about the plan! You're just as bad as I am! You're hopeless! That's what you are! Just bloody hopeless! Anyway, I don't need you anymore! I didn't even need you in the first place!"

Trying to trick the lady into coming back was never going to work, you know. And Frank kind of knew it wouldn't work. But he was desperate and it was worth a try.

But yeah. That's what she would have said again, alright. And a big mouth full after that, as well. But there was no fooling the lady was there. No, she was way too smart. Right from the start. Had it all figured, the whole way. Worth a try but. Just to get her back. Didn't work.

But there were still the magic café girls. The ones that were still there that is. Many had finished their university degrees. Found jobs. Never to be seen again. They were all missed too. Every one of them.

There was a favourite one, you know. And she was beautiful, of course. Not just to look at either. But beautiful on the inside. Could feel her beauty, going all through the body. She was there from the start as well. And she was still there. But there had always been a wariness about her. She seemed aloof. So, it was a stand-off situation with this one. For a long time. There was always an awkward politeness. But never any real conversation.

Until one day. There was another awakening. The confidence had been building for a while now and the self-consciousness had almost disappeared. So, this one girl got signalled out, for special attention. That meant she got the eyeball treatment. Started to get spoken to. Like there wasn't the barrier there. That had always been there.

Frank walked straight up to her. They looked at each other and then, the weird eye thing happened again didn't it. Like what he knew would happen. Just like it had before, a few times. But not with this girl. Yeah. The other way around this time. And what a good feeling that was. And she had the most beautiful eyes, you know. They were a blue green colour. But went a dark emerald green colour, when they were looked into properly. With determination. Then they came back to the blue green colour. Yeah, getting braver all the time. And she didn't frighten him anymore either. Not one bit.

The weird eye thing, did have him fooled for quite a while, you know. And the wonder of that warm feeling that went all the way through the body. Just like a few times before, with a few of the other girls. But this was a different kind of weird feeling altogether. Yeah, there must have been heaps of these weird feelings, you know. Depending on which girl was involved.

But the café girl smile was always the same. That warm, penetrating smile. This girl's cheeks, went dark crimson and she had a mouth full of sparkling white teeth, that had never been seen before. And she went all sheepish as well.

So, that had to mean something. Surely. It was love, alright. On one side anyway. But whether she finds that out or not, is anyone's guess. Well not really. He'll never be saying anything. That's for sure.

Anyway, she already had a boyfriend. Made a point of letting that slip out one day. And thank goodness for that. Because there was always a growing feeling there, you know. Of loving her. In a good way, of course. But just imagine what would have happened, if he cornered her one day in the middle of the café. Grabbed hold of her. Drew her close and whispered sweet things into her ear. But the previous attempt at that sort of impulsive behaviour, still troubled the thinking. So, it didn't happen. And thank Christ for that. Yeah. Getting smarter all the time.

This girl, has already been mentioned several times already, you know. But there's no way she can ever be identified as the most favourite café girl. That just wouldn't be right. No. Not right at all. Yeah, getting smarter all the time.

So, back on the veranda, pumped full of coffee. In full contemplation mode. About the new life situation and all the adjusted thinking necessary, for full adaptation. Yeah, there was a head full of new information that wasn't so new anymore. And wasn't causing all the early confusion, when the psychological alterations started involuntarily reshaping the already fragile emotional structure. Yeah. They'd been coming from everywhere, alright. Had Frank spinning out all over the place. In all kinds of trouble. But not anymore. Yeah. Getting smarter all the time.

The lady was well and truly out of the picture now. TMBGITW was out of the brain and so was the picture. The old one anyway. Or at least pushed into what was left of the dark shadows. His mother was still in there somewhere. She turned up every now and then, with some good advice and lots of encouragement. Her picture was the dominate one now. And she was always smiling as well. But it was nothing like the café girl smile. No. No smile could ever be compared to the café girl smile. But at least his mother was smiling. Making up for all those lost years, maybe.

The café girls will always be in there, of course. And now that special smile had invaded Frank's face as well. Could feel it there. And it was like a constant companion. And he knew exactly what it looked like. Especially, when looking in a mirror. Yeah. Looking in a mirror was no problem now. Happened every chance he got. Liked what he was looking at, alright.

That smart arse compulsive understood what was happening. Even before it all started happening. Well, it's not really fair calling him that anymore is it. What he said was in a good way. That was fully understood by now. And besides, his smile was a very familiar one. And so was the smile on the face of that fuckwit, who wasn't really a fuckwit. But he never got told he was a fuckwit in the first place. So, he wouldn't know anything about that thinking. And what a good feeling that was.

Even the deviates, hanging around the pool had that smile on their face. It wasn't noticed at first, of course. Because they were all just devious little, dumb arse, pool monkeys. But it's amazing how deviates, can suddenly appear to be anything but deviates. But some of them would have still been deviates. There could be nothing worse than a devious little, dumb arse, smiling pool monkey. That's for sure. And lots of the other monkeys wandering around had that same smile spread across their face as well.

Yeah, that smile was like a virus. But in a good way. And now, Frank had caught the same virus. And for the very first time, started to feel less like an alien and more like one of the normal smiling monkeys. Or not so normal smiling monkeys. But they were all smiling monkeys, alright. Now that he really did feel like one of them. For the first time in the whole new life. And what a good feeling that was. To finally fit in. And that was the main thing. To actually fit in.

Yeah. To finally make it and know that he'd finally made it. And the old addictions weren't going to escape and destroy the new life either. They'd been driven out. Defeated. Or at least locked up anyway. And he did it all by himself.

Yeah. The resilience was there now, stronger than ever. And super Frank was going to win. No matter what happened now, he was going to win.

There was no stopping him. No fooling him anymore. Not by the lady anyway, because she was long gone. And not by the café girls, because by now, he knew all their tricks. But he still loved them all anyway. In a good way. And certainly not by TMBGITW. She'd been well and truly taken care of. And not by anyone else either. And who needs GA anymore. That place was only for out-of-control compulsives. And that know-it-all controller, didn't know everything either. And that was a good thing to know.

Yeah. Being in complete control was the best feeling ever. Frank did get a lot of help, you know. He knew that and admitted it, alright. But he thanked everyone. And how long are you supposed to feel indebted to other people for anyway. What, are you supposed to keep thanking them forever? They don't own you or anything.

Frank had already forgotten about the short-term memory problem, you know. But that didn't matter, because it wasn't even thought about. You can't do anything about what's already happened. He understood that now.

Anyway, he was the smartest monkey he knew now. That's all that really mattered. Didn't need anything from anyone anymore. And what a great feeling that was. To not need anyone anymore. It's all up to him now. Who do they think they are anyway.

Frank would be forever grateful, of course. Well, what else could he be but grateful.

But this was Frank's new life now. Not anyone else's. And he didn't have to put up with all those other monkeys and all the trouble they caused. That's for sure. He was on his way to bigger things. And now that he fully understood the overall situation, they were never going to win, were they?

"Oh Frank!"

Did you just hear something?